essential
MEDITERRANEAN

essential
MEDITERRANEAN

MURDOCH BOOKS

Published in 2011 by Murdoch Books Pty Limited

Murdoch Books Australia
Pier 8/9
23 Hickson Road
Millers Point NSW 2000
Phone: +61 (0) 2 8220 2000
Fax: +61 (0) 2 8220 2558
www.murdochbooks.com.au

Murdoch Books UK Limited
Erico House, 6th Floor
93–99 Upper Richmond Road
Putney, London SW15 2TG
Phone: +44 (0) 20 8785 5995
Fax: +44 (0) 20 8785 5985
www.murdochbooks.co.uk

Publisher: Kylie Walker
Project Editor: Melody Lord
Food Editor: Anneka Manning
Editor: Anna Scobie
Concept Design: Vivien Sung
Designer: Susanne Geppert

Photographers: Jared Fowler, Julie Renouf
Stylist: Cherise Koch
Food preparation: Alan Wilson

National Library of Australia Cataloguing-in-Publication Data

Title: Essential Mediterranean
ISBN: 978-1-74266-090-5 (pbk.).
Series: New essential.
Notes: Includes index.
Subjects: Cooking, Mediterranean.
Dewey Number: 641.591822

A catalogue record for this book is available from the British Library.

Printed by 1010 Printing International Limited, China

IMPORTANT: Those who might be at risk from the effects of salmonella poisoning (the elderly, pregnant women, young children and those suffering from immune deficiency diseases) should consult their doctor with any concerns about eating raw eggs.

CONVERSION GUIDE: Cooking times may vary depending on the oven you are using. For fan-forced ovens, as a general rule, set the oven temperature to 20°C (35°F) lower than indicated in the recipe. We have used 20 ml (4 teaspoon) tablespoon measures. If you are using a 15 ml (3 teaspoon) tablespoon, add an extra teaspoon for each tablespoon specified. We have used 60 g (Grade 3) eggs in all recipes.

flavours from the edge of the sea

In this book we take you on a culinary journey along the shores of the sparkling blue Mediterranean. Food ideas from Greece, Turkey, Italy, France, Spain, North Africa and the Middle East are all explored. Examples of the diverse tastes of each country or region are the delicacies enjoyed as part of the meze in Greece, antipasto in Italy and tapas in Spain. Wonderful recipes from all the countries and regions reflect the cooking styles, eating habits and customs of the people of the Mediterranean. Many of the spices, herbs, vegetables and other ingredients are common throughout these beautiful places that sit on the rim of the sea. However, the rich history and interesting origins of those who live there has led to a difference in the way these ingredients are utilised. Along our journey, this remarkable approach to cooking is brought out in the recipes we explore with you.

contents

special features

zarzuela de pescado (page 185)

mediterranean cuisine

The Mediterranean region is linked not only by the sea and a temperate climate, but also the long and tumultuous history of conquests and occupations. The Phoenicians, Egyptians, Greeks, Carthaginians, Persians and Romans all wove a part in the fabric of the Mediterranean, leaving behind visible remnants of trade routes and great civilisations. For centuries, the Mediterranean Sea was a very active trade route and this resulted in a rich history of cultural exchange. It is not surprising that food ideas crossed national boundaries and were adapted to suit people with different needs.

This book reflects this history because many recipes seem remarkably similar. Dishes such as stuffed capsicums (peppers), baked eggplants (aubergines), fish stews and filo pastries all appear in many versions, scattered throughout the book as we travel along the Mediterranean. On the other hand, many recipes, such as Beef Provençal (page 142), the Greek Moussaka (page 38) and Tunisian brik (page 211) lead us unmistakably to the country of origin. Many of these 'national' dishes appear with numerous variations throughout their homelands but still retain their cultural identity.

The Mediterranean region is rich in resources and varied in landscape and the geographical and culinary focus in this book stretches from Spain down to Morocco and Algeria, then follows the shores of the Mediterranean to cover Tunisia, Libya, Egypt, Israel, Lebanon, Syria and Turkey in the east and Greece, Italy and southern France in the north.

The Arabs had a great impact upon the food of the Mediterranean. Travelling along the trade routes, they brought with them fragrant rose and orange flower waters, pomegranates, citrus fruits, pine nuts, walnuts, eggplants and zucchini (courgettes). They also brought spices such as saffron, cumin, cloves, nutmeg and cinnamon.

what is mediterranean cuisine?

There is no one Mediterranean cuisine. Because of the history of the region, it remains one of the most colourful and vibrant collections of cuisines in the world. However, you could almost define the Mediterranean landscape by the cultivation of olive trees and the use of olive oil. Other quintessential ingredients are vegetables such as zucchini, tomatoes, eggplants, capsicums and garlic, as well as fruits, pulses and grains, pasta, fresh herbs, spices and nuts.

The cuisine's heavy reliance upon seafood is a natural one, while the supply of red meat is sometimes more problematic due to the often inhospitable hilly terrain further inland, which makes farming of livestock difficult. A glass of wine is an integral part of the meal for many Mediterranean countries. Generally, the flavours of the Mediterranean are strong and robust and natural flavours are not drowned or masked by butter or creamy, rich sauces.

The Mediterranean diet has received a lot of attention over the past decade from dietitians and nutritionists. At present, there is much research into the theory that the incorporation of olive oil and abundant seafood and fresh fruit and vegetables into the diet, combined with minimal consumption of red meat and animal fats in the form of butter, cream and lard, may be associated with a low incidence of coronary heart disease, obesity, diabetes and cancer.

In this book you will find a selection of classic Mediterranean recipes. We have not included recipes from the north of Italy which embrace influences from the colder countries, sometimes making them unrecognisable as having the same heritage. If you ask an Italian about Italian food, you would find that no one cuisine exists. Instead, you would learn of regional cuisines linked closely to the history of the people and the land. So rather than Italian cooking, locals talk of Venetian, Florentine, Neapolitan or Sicilian cooking, to name a few. The chapter on France focuses on Provence, a region isolated not only historically but also climatically from the rest of France. Provence enjoys more hours of sunlight than any other region in France, and the fact that it is warmed by the sun and lapped by the Mediterranean draws it closer to its southern cousins. Nearly all the recipes in this book are derived from resourceful peasant cuisines with powerful basic ingredients such as saffron, garlic and anchovies, to enhance the flavour of fresh vegetables and simple cuts of meat.

tips for success

■ Use top-quality ingredients, preferably when they are in season. Tomatoes are a prime example so, wherever possible, use fresh tomatoes that have been ripened on the vine. Otherwise, use good-quality tinned tomatoes such as Italian roma (plum), which are regarded as superior because they are processed when they are at their peak.

■ Use fresh herbs where possible. Choose those with erect stalks and leaves that are not dark or limp. To store fresh herbs such as parsley, basil and coriander, rinse them briefly in cold water, then shake dry and wrap in damp paper towels. Store them in a sealed plastic bag in the crisper section of the refrigerator.

■ Some recipes call for dried herbs. Try to buy dried wild herbs, usually still on the branches, from speciality delicatessens, as they have much more flavour and are truly evocative of the wild Mediterranean hills.

■ Ground spices differ in flavour if you toast and grind them yourself. Toast and grind a small amount and put them in an airtight container. If you have to rely on pre-ground spices, remember that they lose their flavour and scent with age.

■ To plan a meal using this book, you can put together an all-Spanish feast or a totally Moroccan meal, but you can also combine dishes from different countries. A feast of small dishes, from Greek Dolmades (page 18) to Turkish Hummus (page 54) and Italian Stuffed sardines (page 78), all served with bread, would not look at all unusual. Indeed, the beauty of these small dishes is that they are so versatile. Plan the meal using seasonal, quality produce and garnish in the traditional Mediterranean way with roughly chopped herbs, toasted almonds or pine nuts, olives or perhaps a simple drizzle of extra virgin olive oil. You may even like to serve wines from the same regions as the food.

Our star rating:
When we test recipes, we rate them for ease of preparation. The following cookery ratings are used in this book:

✸   A single star indicates a recipe that is simple and generally quick to make, perfect for beginners.

✸✸   Two stars indicate the need for a little more care or a little more time.

✸✸✸ Three stars indicate special dishes that need more investment in time, care and patience, but the results are worth it. Even beginners can make these dishes as long as the recipe is followed carefully.

mediterranean pantry

anchovies
A small fish from the herring family found mainly in southern European waters. Although anchovies can be eaten fresh, they are rarely found fresh outside Mediterranean fishing ports as they are delicate and need to be eaten or processed quickly. More commonly, anchovies are cured and packed in oil, salt or brine and are readily available in tins or jars.

arborio rice
A short-grained plump rice imported from Italy. Used in both sweet and savoury dishes, arborio rice is particularly suitable for making risotto because the grains absorb a lot of liquid and become creamy but still retain their firmness.

artichoke hearts
The fleshy centres or 'hearts' of the thistly artichoke head. Available whole or quartered, tinned or in jars, chargrilled or plain, in olive oil or brine.

bocconcini
Small mozzarella balls are known as bocconcini or baby mozzarella. A smooth, mild, unripened cheese originally made from buffalo's milk but now usually made from cow's milk, bocconcini should be refrigerated covered in the whey in which it is sold. It will last for three weeks but should be discarded if it shows signs of yellowing. Drained and sliced, bocconcini is used in salads, as pizza or bruschetta toppings, or in pasta dishes.

borlotti beans
Slightly kidney-shaped, this large bean is a beautifully marked, pale pinkish brown with burgundy specks. Popular in Italy, borlotti beans have a nutty flavour and are used in soups, stews and salads. When in season they are available fresh, otherwise dried or tinned can be used.

burghul
Also known as bulgur or cracked wheat, burghul is wheat that has been hulled, boiled or steamed, then dried and cracked. It is a staple in the Middle East and requires little or no cooking, just soaking. Sold coarsely or finely ground.

calasparra rice
This white medium-grained Spanish rice is traditionally used to make paella. If it is not available, arborio, carnaroli or vialone nano varieties can be used instead.

cannellini beans
These white, kidney-shaped beans are also known as Italian haricot beans or white kidney beans. Mildly flavoured and slightly fluffy in texture when cooked, they are good all-purpose beans for use in soups, casseroles, stews and salads. Available dried or tinned.

capers

The pickled buds of a shrub that grows wild in many parts of the Mediterranean. Capers have a sharp, sour taste and are sold in seasoned vinegar or packed in salt that needs to be rinsed away before use.

cedro

This is the candied peel of the citron, a large, thick-skinned citrus fruit that dates back to ancient times. Cedro is available in some speciality food stores.

chickpeas

Chickpeas were first grown in the Levant and ancient Egypt. There are two kinds of chickpea, the large white garbanzo and the smaller brown dessi. Some of the most popular Middle Eastern dishes, including hummus, have chickpeas as their basis. They can be boiled, roasted, ground, mashed and milled and are available either dried or tinned.

chorizo

A Spanish sausage, with many regional varieties, that is based on pork, paprika and garlic. Chorizo is sliced, char-grilled and served as tapas and is also cooked in paellas, stews and soups.

couscous

This cereal is processed from semolina and is basically tiny grains of pasta. Instant couscous is ready in less than 5 minutes. It is generally used as a high-carbohydrate accompaniment to meat and vegetable dishes.

feta cheese

A soft, white cheese ripened in brine. Originally made from the milk of sheep or goats, but often now made with the more economical cow's milk. Feta cheese tastes sharp and salty and can be eaten as an appetiser, cooked or marinated. It is an ingredient in traditional Greek salad.

filo pastry

Filo or phyllo is a paper-thin pastry made from flour and water. It is used widely in eastern Mediterranean countries for the making of both sweet and savoury dishes. The paper-thin layers are lightly greased and are either stacked to make things such as baklava, or otherwise one or two layers are rolled up to enclose a filling as for cheese triangles.

frisée

Part of the chicory family, frisée is also known as curly endive or endive. Frisée is a winter salad green and has a mild, bitter flavour. It is well matched with robust flavours such as bacon, walnuts or mustard.

haloumi

A salty Middle Eastern cheese that is traditionally made from sheep's milk. The curd is cooked, then matured in brine, often with herbs or spices. It is most often grilled or fried and used in salads or on bread.

kefalotyri cheese

A very hard, scalded and cured sheep or goat's milk cheese with a mild flavour. Its use depends on its age. When it's young it is a table cheese, at six months old it is used in cooking, and when more mature it makes an excellent grating cheese. Parmesan or pecorino can be substituted.

marsala

A fortified wine from Marsala in Sicily that comes in varying degrees of dryness and sweetness. Dry Marsalas are used in savoury dishes and drunk as an aperitif. Sweet ones are suitable for putting in dessert dishes such as zabaglione and are also served with desserts.

molokhia

The deep-green leaves of this plant are used as a vegetable in many Mediterranean countries. In Egypt it is used to make one of the national dishes, a soup of the same name. The leaves give the soup a gelatinous texture. Molokhia is available from speciality food stores and comes fresh, dried or frozen.

mozzarella

A smooth, fresh white cheese with a mild, slightly sweet flavour. Traditionally made from buffalo's milk, it is now also made with cow's milk. Used as a table cheese and in cooking, it melts well and is good on pizzas. Shapes vary from pear to block.

nigella seeds

Also called black onion seeds, these seeds have a nutty, peppery flavour. They are used in the Middle East and India as a seasoning for vegetables, legumes and breads. Often confused with black cumin.

okra

Also known as ladies' fingers because of its shape, this green, slightly curved, ridged pod is popular in the eastern Mediterranean. It has a lot of small seeds and has a very glutinous texture that can be lessened considerably by soaking in lemon juice mixed in salted water before cooking. Okra is a natural thickening agent, so is useful in casseroles. Available fresh or tinned.

orange flower water

Sometimes called orange blossom water, this is an essence made by distilling the flowers of the bitter Seville orange. The oil rises to the top and is used in perfumery while the watery part is used extensively in eastern Mediterranean countries to flavour pastries, puddings, syrups and drinks.

pancetta
This is the belly of the pig that has been cured in salt and spices. There are many regional variations, some matured longer than others, or with different aromatics. It is usually sold rolled into a sausage shape and cut into very thin slices and is popular in many pasta dishes.

parmesan
A hard cow's milk cheese that is widely used in Italian cooking, either grated and added to dishes or shaved to use as a garnish. Always buy parmesan in a chunk and grate it as you need it, rather than using ready-grated. Parmigiano Reggiano, from Parma in northern Italy, is the most superior parmesan.

pecorino
One of Italy's most popular cheeses, with virtually every region producing its own variety, pecorino is made from sheep's milk, always using the same method. Ageing and preservation methods vary.

polenta
Also known as cornmeal, these ground, dried corn kernels are a staple in northern Italy. Polenta is most often made into a porridge and flavoured by mixing in butter and parmesan. After it is cooked, it can also be spread into a thin layer in a dish, then allowed to set before frying or grilling and being served with vegetables or with toppings as an appetiser.

pomegranate molasses
Also sold as pomegranate syrup or concentrate, this is the boiled-down juice of a sour variety of pomegranate used in Syria and Lebanon. The molasses has an unusual sweet-and-sour flavour and is used in sauces and dressings.

porcini mushrooms
Used in Italian and French cooking, these have a brown cap and thick white stem. Also known as cep mushrooms, they come fresh or dried. Soak dried ones in warm water, then rinse. The strained soaking water can be used. Dried porcini have a strong flavour and should be used sparingly. Good in risottos and omelettes.

preserved lemons
These are lemons pickled in salt and spices. They need to be rinsed before use and the pulp removed and discarded. Preserved lemons are used mainly in North African cuisine to flavour couscous and traditional tagine dishes.

prosciutto
An Italian ham that has been cured by salting, then air-drying. Aged for up to 10 months, it is then sliced thinly and doesn't require cooking. Prosciutto di Parma is the classic Italian ham traditionally served as an antipasto and also used extensively, diced or shredded, in cooking.

provolone

A golden-yellow Italian cheese with a glossy rind, provolone is often moulded into a pear shape before being hung to mature. While it is young, provolone is mild and delicate and often used as a table cheese. As it matures, the flavour becomes sharper and it can be used for grating. Provolone is often smoked.

puy lentils

These tiny, dark-green lentils are considered a delicacy in France and are relatively expensive. Unlike most other lentils, they keep their shape and have a firm texture after cooking. They are used mostly for making salads and side dishes.

ras-el-hanout

A North African spice blend comprising up to 27 ingredients including ground cumin, cinnamon, cardamom, ginger, turmeric, nutmeg, cloves, rosebuds, peppercorns and oregano. Traditionally, it also contains aphrodisiacs such as the Spanish fly beetle.

rocket

This salad green, also known as arugula or rugula, is native to the Mediterranean. The peppery flavour increases as the leaves grow. Often served on cooked pizzas, or in a mixed green salad.

rosewater

A distilled essence, extracted from roses, used in the eastern Mediterranean to flavour sweets such as Turkish delight and other sweet dishes, as well as drinks.

saffron

The thread-like stigma of a violet crocus, this is the most expensive spice because of the hard work involved in extracting it from the flowers. Luckily, only a small amount is needed to impart the distinctive flavour and colour to a dish. The colour and flavour varies according to the origin and quality. Saffron is sold as threads or in powdered form but the latter is often adulterated with dyes.

salt cod

Cod fillets that have been salted and dried. Salt cod, or bacalao, needs to be soaked for at least two days before use. Available from speciality food stores.

semolina

This is the product obtained from the first milling of durum wheat. Semolina can be coarse, medium or fine and is used for making pasta, gnocchi, puddings or cakes.

silverbeet

Also known as Swiss chard, silverbeet is often confused with English spinach. The main difference is that the large, crinkly leaves have more texture than spinach and are suited to longer cooking because they don't collapse the way spinach does. Both the leaves and stems can be eaten but need to be blanched before being braised, gratinéed or used as pie fillings.

sumac

A reddish berry with a sour, fruity flavour that is ground to a powder. Used mainly in Syria and Lebanon to add flavour and colour to meat, fish and vegetable dishes.

sun-dried tomatoes

Available either dry and loosely packed, or in jars in oil. The dry variety need to be rehydrated before use: cover with boiling water and leave for about 10 minutes. If buying sun-dried tomatoes in oil, choose those in olive oil as you can use the oil for cooking to add extra flavour to your dish.

tahini

A paste made from ground sesame seeds, tahini adds a strong nutty flavour and is popular in the eastern Mediterranean.

tarama

Salted and dried grey mullet roe used to make the popular Greek dip taramosalata. Cod roe is more readily available, so it is often used as a substitute for grey mullet roe when making taramosalata.

tomato passata

This is a bottled tomato sauce commonly used in Italian cooking and many Mediterranean recipes. The sauce is made with fresh, ripe tomatoes that are peeled, seeded and slowly cooked down with basil, onion and garlic. The thickened sauce is then passed through a sieve before being bottled.

vine leaves

Young leaves from the grape vine, blanched then preserved in brine. Available in packets, jars and tins.

za'atar

Popular in Turkey and North Africa, this spice blend is a mixture of toasted sesame seeds, dried thyme, sumac and salt. The proportions vary from region to region. It is used as a seasoning for meats and vegetables and is also mixed with oil to dip bread into, or sprinkled on pide (Turkish/flat bread), Lebanese or pitta bread that has been brushed with olive oil and then lightly toasted.

greece

Dreaming of lazing in a taverna, with the sparkling waters of the Mediterranean and brilliant blue skies as a captivating backdrop, sets the mood for a Greek cooking adventure. Greek people approach healthy, hearty eating with a similar vitality to that which pervades all aspects of their lives. Traditionally, in many parts of Greece, the sea was one of the main sources of food, but these days lamb and beef, as well as fresh herbs, fruit and vegetables all play a vital role in the cuisine. Kalamata olives, dolmades and taramosalata are quintessentially Greek and can be part of a meze spread to whet the appetite. We have given just a sampling of Greek dishes so you can adapt them as cooks in Greece would do.

dolmades
(stuffed vine leaves)

✳ ✳ ✳

Preparation time: **55 minutes**
Cooking time: **50 minutes**
Makes **24**

200 g (7 oz) packet vine leaves
   in brine
250 g (9 oz/1 cup) medium-grain white rice
1 small onion, finely chopped
1 tablespoon olive oil
60 g (2¼ oz) pine nuts, toasted
2 tablespoons currants
2 tablespoons chopped dill
1 tablespoon finely chopped mint
1 tablespoon finely chopped flat-leaf
   (Italian) parsley
80 ml (2½ fl oz/⅓ cup) olive oil, extra
2 tablespoons lemon juice
500 ml (17 fl oz/2 cups) chicken stock

1 Soak the vine leaves in cold water for 15 minutes, then remove and pat dry. Cut off any stalks. Reserve some leaves to line the saucepan and discard any that have holes or look poor. Meanwhile, soak the rice in boiling water for 10 minutes to soften, then drain.

2 Place the rice, onion, olive oil, pine nuts, currants, herbs and salt and pepper, to taste, in a large bowl and mix well.

3 Lay some leaves vein-side-down on a flat surface. Place 1 tablespoon of filling in the centre of each, fold the stalk end over the filling, then the left and right sides into the centre, and finally roll firmly towards the tip. The dolmades should resemble a small cigar. Repeat with the remaining filling and leaves.

4 Use the reserved vine leaves to line the base of a large, heavy-based saucepan. Drizzle with 1 tablespoon of the extra olive oil. Add the dolmades, packing them tightly in one layer, then pour the remaining oil and lemon juice over them.

5 Pour the stock over the dolmades and cover with an inverted plate to stop the dolmades moving around while cooking. Bring to the boil, then reduce the heat

Fold the sides of the vine leaf into the middle and roll up towards the tip.

Pack the dolmades tightly into the pan and pour on the oil and lemon juice.

When the dolmades are cooked, remove from the pan using a slotted spoon.

and simmer, covered, for 45 minutes. Remove the dolmades using a slotted spoon. Serve warm or cold, with lemon wedges, if desired.

NOTE: Unused vine leaves can be stored in brine in an airtight container in the fridge for up to a week.

skordalia (garlic sauce)

Preparation time: 15 minutes
Cooking time: 15 minutes
Makes 2 cups

500 g (1 lb 2 oz) floury potatoes
   (such as King Edward),
   cut into 2 cm (¾ inch) cubes
5 garlic cloves, crushed
ground white pepper, to taste
185 ml (6 fl oz/¾ cup) olive oil
2 tablespoons white vinegar

1   Bring a large saucepan of water to the boil, add the potato and cook for 10 minutes, or until very soft. Drain thoroughly and mash until quite smooth.
2   Stir the garlic, 1 teaspoon salt and a pinch of white pepper into the potato, then gradually pour in the olive oil, mixing well with a wooden spoon. Stir in the vinegar and season, to taste. Serve warm or cold with bread or crackers as a dip, or with grilled meat, fish or chicken.

garlic

One of the smallest members of the onion family, garlic is also the most pungent. Indispensable, its essence imparts a crucial depth to many dishes such as skordalia. As well as its unique flavour, garlic has the advantage of being rich in vitamins and minerals.

As a general rule, the finer that garlic is crushed, the more of its pungent oil is released, hence the popularity of garlic presses. When choosing garlic, look for hard, large, round bulbs and always check underneath for any signs of unwanted mould.

tzatziki

tzatziki

Preparation time: 10 minutes
Cooking time: nil
Serves 6–8

2 Lebanese (short) cucumbers
   (about 300 g/10½ oz)
400 g (14 oz) Greek-style yoghurt
4 garlic cloves, crushed

3 tablespoons finely chopped mint
1 tablespoon lemon juice
chopped mint, extra, to serve

1   Cut the cucumbers in half lengthways, scoop out the seeds with a teaspoon and discard. Leave the skin on and coarsely grate the cucumber into a small colander, then sprinkle with salt and set the colander over a large bowl or the sink for 15 minutes to drain off any bitter juices.

2   Meanwhile, combine the yoghurt, garlic, mint and lemon juice in a bowl.
3   Rinse the cucumber thoroughly under cold water and then, taking small handfuls, squeeze out any excess moisture. Stir the cucumber into the yoghurt mixture and season with salt and pepper. Scatter with the extra mint before serving, or cover and refrigerate until needed. Serve as a dip with bread or as a sauce for seafood or meats.

keftedes (meatballs)

Preparation time: **15 minutes**
  + 1 hour refrigeration
Cooking time: **20 minutes**
Serves **4**

1 egg, lightly beaten
40 g (1½ oz/½ cup) fresh breadcrumbs
1 brown onion, finely chopped
2 tablespoons chopped flat-leaf
   (Italian) parsley
3 tablespoons chopped mint
500 g (1 lb 2 oz) minced (ground) beef
   or lamb
2 tablespoons lemon juice
plain (all-purpose) flour, for coating
vegetable oil, for shallow-frying
lemon wedges, to serve

1 In a large bowl, mix together the egg,
breadcrumbs, onion, herbs, beef and
lemon juice until well combined. Season
well, then with wet hands, shape the
mixture into large walnut-sized balls
and flatten slightly. Place on a tray, cover
and refrigerate for 1 hour.
2 Roll the balls in flour, shaking off
any excess. In a large frying pan, heat
the oil until very hot. Fry the meatballs,
in batches if necessary to avoid
overcrowding the pan, for 3–4 minutes
on each side, or until crisp and brown.
Drain on crumpled paper towels and
serve with lemon wedges.

quail in vine leaves

Preparation time: **15 minutes**
Cooking time: **25 minutes**
Serves **4**

12 black grapes
1 tablespoon olive oil
1 garlic clove, crushed
4 large quails
8 fresh or preserved vine leaves
4 prosciutto slices
black grapes, extra, to garnish

1 Preheat the oven to 180°C (350°F/
Gas 4). Cut each grape in half and toss
them with the oil and garlic. Place six
grape halves in the cavity of each quail.
2 If you are using fresh vine leaves,
blanch them for 1 minute in boiling water,
then remove the central stalk. If using
preserved vine leaves, wash them under
running water to remove any excess
preserving liquid.
3 Wrap each quail in a prosciutto slice
and place each on top of a vine leaf. Place
another vine leaf over the top of each
quail and wrap into parcels, tying with
kitchen string to secure. Roast on a lined
baking tray for 20–25 minutes, depending
on the size of the quail. Serve garnished
with the extra black grapes.

NOTE: Vine leaves are available from
speciality food stores.

quail in vine leaves

Mix the gruyére, egg and pepper into the feta.

Fold the pastry over the filling to form a triangle and then continue folding.

tiropitakia (cheese triangles)

✹ ✹

Preparation time: 35 minutes
Cooking time: 20 minutes
Makes 30

250 g (9 oz) Greek feta cheese
180 g (6¼ oz) gruyère cheese, grated
2 eggs, lightly beaten
ground white pepper, to taste
15 sheets filo pastry
125 ml (4 fl oz/½ cup) olive oil
125 g (4½ oz) butter, melted

1 Preheat the oven to 180°C (350°F/ Gas 4). Place the feta in a bowl and mash with a fork. Add the gruyère, egg and white pepper and mix.
2 Cut each filo sheet in half widthways. Keep the unused pastry covered with a damp tea towel (dish towel) to prevent it drying out. Lay a piece of filo lengthways on a work surface. Brush with combined oil and butter, then fold into thirds lengthways. Brush with oil and butter.
3 Place 1 tablespoon of the cheese mixture on the corner of the pastry strip. Fold this corner over the filling to the edge of the pastry to form a triangle. Continue to fold until the filling is

enclosed and the end of the pastry is reached. Repeat this process with the remaining pastry and filling.
4 Place the triangles on a lightly greased baking tray and brush them with the oil and butter mixture. Bake for 20 minutes, or until crisp.

NOTE: You can adapt these pastries to suit your personal taste. Try using ricotta instead of gruyère and adding finely chopped herbs. Flat-leaf (Italian) parsley, mint or thyme are all suitable.

lahano dolmathes (cabbage rolls)

✻ ✻ ✻

Preparation time: 30 minutes
Cooking time: 1 hour 35 minutes
Makes 12 large rolls

1 tablespoon olive oil
1 onion, finely chopped
large pinch of ground allspice
1 teaspoon ground cumin
large pinch of freshly
    grated nutmeg

2 bay leaves
1 large cabbage head
500 g (1 lb 2 oz) minced (ground) lamb
220 g (7¾ oz/1 cup) short-grain
    white rice
4 garlic cloves, crushed
50 g (1¾ oz/⅓ cup) pine nuts, toasted
2 tablespoons chopped mint
2 tablespoons chopped flat-leaf (Italian)
    parsley
1 tablespoon currants, chopped
250 ml (9 fl oz/1 cup) olive oil, extra
80 ml (2½ fl oz/⅓ cup) lemon juice
extra virgin olive oil, to drizzle
lemon wedges, to serve

1 Heat the oil in a saucepan, add the onion and cook over medium heat for 10 minutes, or until golden. Add the allspice, cumin and nutmeg and cook for 2 minutes, or until aromatic. Remove from the pan.

2 Bring a very large saucepan of water to the boil and add the bay leaves. Cut the tough outer leaves and about 5 cm (2 inches) of the core from the cabbage, then carefully add the cabbage to the boiling water. Cook for 5 minutes, then carefully loosen a whole leaf with tongs and remove. Continue to cook and remove the leaves until you reach the core. Drain, reserving the cooking liquid and set aside to cool.

3 Take 12 leaves of equal size and cut a small 'V' from the core end of each to remove the thickest part. Trim the firm central veins so the leaf is as flat as possible. Use three-quarters of the remaining leaves to line the base of a very large saucepan.

4 Combine the lamb, onion mixture, rice, garlic, pine nuts, mint, parsley and currants in a bowl and season well. Take a cabbage leaf and, with the core end closest to you, form 2 tablespoons of the mixture into an oval and place in the centre of the leaf. Roll up, tucking in the sides. Repeat with the remaining leaves and filling. Place tightly, in a single layer, in the lined saucepan, seam side down.

5 Combine 625 ml (21½ fl oz/2½ cups) of the reserved cooking liquid with the extra olive oil, lemon juice and 1 teaspoon salt and pour over the rolls (the liquid should just come to the top of the rolls). Lay the remaining cabbage leaves over the top. Cover and bring to the boil over high heat, then reduce the heat and simmer for 1¼ hours, or until the lamb and rice are cooked. Carefully remove from the pan with a slotted spoon, then drizzle with the extra virgin olive oil. Serve with the lemon wedges.

pickled cauliflower

Preparation time: 10 minutes
Cooking time: 10 minutes
Serves 4–6

500 ml (17 fl oz/2 cups) white wine vinegar
1 tablespoon yellow mustard seeds
½ teaspoon cumin seeds
3 bay leaves
185 g (6½ oz/¾ cup) caster (superfine) sugar
400 g (14 oz) cauliflower, cut into florets

1   Put the vinegar, mustard seeds, cumin seeds, bay leaves and sugar into a saucepan. Stir over medium heat until the sugar has dissolved. Bring to the boil, then reduce the heat and add the cauliflower. Simmer for 4 minutes, or until just tender, but still firm. Remove from the heat and leave the cauliflower to cool in the liquid. Can be served chilled or at room temperature.

NOTE: To store the cauliflower, wash a glass jar with a lid in hot soapy water, then rinse thoroughly in hot water. Place the jar in a 120°C (235°F/Gas ½) oven to dry for about 20 minutes, or until ready to use it. Don't dry with a tea towel (dish towel). Put the hot liquid and cauliflower in the jar and seal while still hot. Will keep, unopened, for up to 3 months.

beetroot with skordalia

Preparation time: 25 minutes
Cooking time: 55 minutes
Serves 6–8

1 kg (2 lb 4 oz) medium-sized beetroot, including leaves
60 ml (2 fl oz/¼ cup) extra virgin olive oil
1 tablespoon red wine vinegar
½ quantity of skordalia (page 19), to serve

pickled vegetables

The ancient art of pickling is particularly important in countries such as Greece, where seasonal availability and high temperatures make preserved foods an integral part of the diet. Born of necessity, pickles are also prized for their crisp texture and diversity, as most commonly available Mediterranean vegetables can easily be pickled. They are invariably served as part of a meze selection or as an accompaniment to main meals.

beetroot with skordalia

1   Cut the stalks from the beetroot bulbs, leaving a short piece attached. Trim any tough tops from the leaves, then cut the stalks into halves or thirds and wash well.
2   Brush the bulbs to remove any dirt. Cook the beetroot in boiling salted water for 30–45 minutes, depending on their size, until tender when pierced with a sharp knife. Remove with a slotted spoon and cool slightly.
3   Return the water to the boil, add the leaves and stalks, and more water if necessary, and then boil for 8 minutes, or until the stalks are tender. Drain and squeeze the excess water from the leaves using your hands.
4   Put on rubber gloves and peel the skin from the beetroot bulbs. Cut each bulb in half and then into thick slices. Arrange the beetroot leaves, stalks and sliced bulbs on a serving plate. Combine the oil and vinegar and season, to taste. Drizzle over the beetroot leaves, stalks and bulbs, and serve the skordalia on the side.

offal

Although in Greece offal dishes are often associated with religious festivals such as Easter, they were historically regarded as poor people's food and formed the basis of many traditional meals. Offal such as liver and brains are suited to poaching, sautéing, grilling and frying, although care must be taken not to overcook liver as it toughens easily.

liver with oregano

✹ ✹

Preparation time: 15 minutes
Cooking time: 10 minutes
Serves 6–8

500 g (1 lb 2 oz) lamb's liver
30 g (1 oz/¼ cup) plain (all-purpose) flour
½ teaspoon paprika
2 tablespoons olive oil
2 tablespoons lemon juice
1 teaspoon dried or chopped
   fresh oregano

1 Trim off any fatty deposits from the liver. Pat the liver dry with paper towels, cut into 2 cm (¾ inch) slices and cut the larger slices in half or into thirds.
2 In a shallow dish, combine the flour, paprika and ½ teaspoon each of salt and cracked black pepper. Heat the oil in a frying pan over medium heat. Toss a third of the liver in the flour, shake off the excess and fry for 1 minute on each side, or until browned, but still pink inside. Drain on crumpled paper towels and place on a warm plate. Cover with foil to keep warm. Repeat with the remaining liver.
3 Remove the pan from the heat and stir in the lemon juice — it should bubble in the hot pan. When the bubbles subside, pour the pan juices over the liver and sprinkle with oregano. Serve hot.

miala tiganita (fried brains)

✹

Preparation time: 20 minutes
   + 30 minutes soaking time
Cooking time: 20 minutes
Serves 6

6 lamb's brains
1 tablespoon lemon juice
¼ teaspoon whole white or
   black peppercorns
plain (all-purpose) flour, seasoned,
   for coating
olive oil, for frying
chopped flat-leaf (Italian) parsley,
   to garnish
lemon wedges, to serve

1 Soak the brains in cold, salted water for 30 minutes. Drain, then peel off the membrane and discard all the bloody parts. Place the rest in a saucepan. Cover with cold water and add the lemon juice, peppercorns and 1 teaspoon salt. Bring to a gentle simmer, cover and cook for 15 minutes, or until tender. Do not allow the liquid to boil.
2 Drain the brains and pat dry with paper towels. Cut into 1 cm (½ inch) slices and coat with the flour. Pour the oil into a heavy-based frying pan to a depth of 1 cm (½ inch), heat the oil and fry the brains until they are golden brown. Drain on paper towels, then season, to taste. Sprinkle with parsley and serve with lemon wedges.

liver with oregano

plain yoghurt

Pour 1 litre (35 fl oz/4 cups) of milk into a saucepan, bring slowly to the boil over low heat and simmer for 5 minutes, stirring frequently. Remove from the heat and set aside to cool until lukewarm. Gently stir 60 g (2¼ oz/¼ cup) of plain yoghurt into the milk, then pour into a large bowl. Cover the bowl with plastic wrap and wrap the bowl in a thick cloth or towel. This keeps the heat in, thus helping the culture in the yoghurt to ferment the milk. Leave in a warm place for up to 12 hours, until the yoghurt has thickened. Don't leave the yoghurt to stand any longer because it will progressively become more acidic. Refrigerate for at least 4 hours before using. Makes 1 litre. To make another batch of yoghurt, you can use 60 g (2¼ oz/¼ cup) of your home-made yoghurt as a starter.

kalamaria toursi (pickled squid)

✸ ✸

Preparation time: 30 minutes
  + 1 week pickling time
Cooking time: 10 minutes
Serves 4

1 kg (2 lb 4 oz) small squid
4 fresh bay leaves
4 oregano sprigs
10 whole black peppercorns
2 teaspoons coriander seeds
1 small red chilli, halved and seeded
625 ml (21½ fl oz/2½ cups) white wine
   vinegar
2–3 tablespoons olive oil
lemon wedges, to serve
chopped flat-leaf (Italian) parsley,
   to serve, optional

1 To clean the squid, gently pull the tentacles away from the tube (the intestines should come away at the same time). Remove the intestines from the tentacles by cutting under the eyes, then remove the beak if it remains in the centre of the tentacles by using your fingers to push up the centre. Pull away the quill (the transparent cartilage) from inside the body and remove. Remove and discard any white membrane. Under cold running water, pull away the skin from the tube (the wings can be used). Cut into 8 mm (⅜ inch) rings.

2 Put 2 litres (70 fl oz/8 cups) water and 1 bay leaf in a large saucepan. Bring to the boil and add the squid rings and 1 teaspoon salt. Reduce the heat and simmer for 5 minutes. Drain and dry well. Pack into a sterilised 500 ml (17 fl oz/ 2 cup) jar with a sealing lid (see Note). Add the oregano, peppercorns, coriander

seeds, chilli and remaining bay leaves. Add the vinegar, then enough olive oil to cover by 2 cm (¾ inch). Seal and refrigerate for 1 week before opening. To serve, remove from the marinade if desired and garnish with lemon wedges and parsley, if using.

NOTE: To sterilise jars, wash the jar and lid in hot soapy water, rinse well in hot water and then dry in a 120°C (235°F/ Gas ½) oven for 20 minutes. Do not dry with a tea towel (dish towel).

salata horiatiki (greek salad)

Preparation time: 20 minutes
Cooking time: nil
Serves 4

1 telegraph (long) cucumber, peeled
2 green capsicums (peppers)
4 vine-ripened tomatoes, cut into wedges
1 red onion, thinly sliced
16 kalamata olives
250 g (9 oz) Greek feta cheese, cubed
24 flat-leaf (Italian) parsley leaves
12 mint leaves
125 ml (4 fl oz/½ cup) good-quality olive oil
2 tablespoons lemon juice
1 garlic clove, crushed

1 Cut the cucumber in half lengthways, discard the seeds and cut into bite-sized pieces. Cut each capsicum in half lengthways, remove the membrane and seeds and cut the flesh into 1 cm (½ inch) wide strips. Gently mix the cucumber, capsicum, tomato, onion, olives, feta, parsley and mint in a large salad bowl.
2 Place the oil, lemon juice and garlic in a screw-top jar, season and shake well. Pour over the salad and serve.

greek salad

What is widely known as Greek salad is but one of the numerous salads served in Greece. Its Greek name, *salata horiatiki*, translates as Greek country or village salad. It is a rustic salad with tomato, cucumber, feta cheese, olives and capsicums (peppers) as its staple ingredients, although cos (romaine) lettuce, anchovy fillets, flat-leaf (Italian) parsley, capers and oregano are not unusual additions.

eggplant salad

eggplant salad

Preparation time: 20 minutes
    + 30 minutes standing time
Cooking time: 1 hour 35 minutes
Serves 6

1 kg (2 lb 4 oz) large eggplants (aubergines)
125 ml (4 fl oz/½ cup) olive oil
1 onion, finely chopped
½ teaspoon ground cinnamon
4 garlic cloves, crushed
800 g (1 lb 12 oz) tin chopped tomatoes
2 tablespoons chopped coriander (cilantro) leaves
3 tablespoons chopped flat-leaf (Italian) parsley

1 tablespoon lemon juice
2 tablespoons chopped mint
150 g (5½ oz) Greek-style yoghurt
25 g (1 oz) pine nuts, toasted

1 Cut the eggplants into 2 cm (¾ inch) cubes. Put in a colander, sprinkle generously with salt and stand over a bowl. Leave for 30 minutes, then rinse under cold water and pat dry using a tea towel (dish towel).
2 Heat 2 tablespoons of the oil in a large frying pan and fry batches of eggplant until golden, adding more oil if necessary. Drain on paper towels. Heat another 2 tablespoons of the oil in the pan and fry the onion for 1 minute. Add the cinnamon and half the garlic, cook for 1 minute, then add the tomatoes. Add the eggplant and simmer, uncovered, for 1 hour, or until the mixture is quite dry. Add half of each of the coriander and parsley. Stir and leave to cool.
3 Mix the remaining 2 tablespoons of oil with the lemon juice and add the remaining garlic and the mint. Stir into the yoghurt. Toss the pine nuts through the salad and garnish with the remaining fresh herbs. Serve at room temperature with the garlic yoghurt dressing.

haloumi with salad and garlic bread

Preparation time: **20 minutes**
Cooking time: **10 minutes**
Serves **4**

4 firm tomatoes
1 Lebanese (short) cucumber
140 g (5 oz/4 cups) rocket (arugula)
80 g (2¾ oz/½ cup) kalamata olives
1 loaf unsliced crusty white bread
100 ml (3½ fl oz) olive oil
1 large garlic clove, halved
400 g (14 oz) haloumi cheese
1 tablespoon lemon juice
1 tablespoon chopped oregano

1 Preheat the oven to 180°C (350°F/ Gas 4). Heat the grill (broiler) to high.

2 Cut the tomatoes and cucumber into bite-sized chunks and place in a serving dish with the rocket and olives. Mix well.
3 Slice the bread into eight 1.5 cm (⅝ inch) slices, drizzle 1½ tablespoons of the olive oil over the bread and season. Grill until lightly golden, then rub each slice thoroughly with a cut side of the garlic clove. Wrap loosely in foil and keep warm in the oven.
4 Cut the haloumi into eight slices. Heat 2 teaspoons of the oil in a shallow frying pan and fry the haloumi slices for 1–2 minutes each side, or until crisp and golden brown.
5 Whisk together the lemon juice, oregano and remaining olive oil to make a dressing. Season to taste. Pour half the dressing over the salad and toss well. Arrange the haloumi on top and drizzle with the remaining dressing. Serve immediately with the warm garlic bread.

kalamata olives

Hailing from Kalamata in the southern Peloponnese, these almond-shaped olives are considered to be Greece's best, due to their fruity, rich flavour and firm flesh. Packed in either olive oil or wine vinegar to accentuate their robust taste, they are often found on a meze plate, and in salads, sauces and breads.

kakavia (fisherman's soup)

☀

Preparation time: 20 minutes
Cooking time: 20 minutes
Serves 6

2 onions, thinly sliced
400 g (14 oz) tin chopped tomatoes
750 g (1 lb 10 oz) potatoes, cut into 5 mm
    (¼ inch) slices
1 teaspoon chopped oregano
150 ml (5 fl oz) olive oil
2 litres (70 fl oz/8 cups) fish stock
500 g (1 lb 2 oz) raw prawns (shrimp), peeled

1.5 kg (3 lb 5 oz) skinless, firm white fish
    fillets (such as cod, jewfish or snapper),
    cut into chunks
125 ml (4 fl oz/½ cup) lemon juice
chopped flat-leaf (Italian) parsley,
    to garnish

1 Layer the onion, tomatoes and potato in a large heavy-based saucepan, seasoning each layer with salt, pepper and oregano.
2 Add the oil and stock and bring to the boil. Reduce the heat and simmer for 10 minutes, or until the potato is tender.
3 Add the prawns and fish and cook for 5 minutes, or until the seafood is cooked. Add the lemon juice, spoon into bowls and top with the parsley.

kakavia

kakavia

Although bouillabaise is the most famous of a large number of Mediterranean fish stew or soup dishes, there are many others, including the Greek version, kakavia. It is named after the kakavi, which is a three-legged cooking pot taken by ancient Ionians on their fishing expeditions. This version was always filled with the smallest fish from the catch, olive oil, onions and saffron. Today, it is still made with whatever small fish are available but tomatoes, rather than saffron, are used to give the dish colour.

cannellini bean soup

☀ ☀

Preparation time: 20 minutes
    + overnight soaking
Cooking time: 1 hour 15 minutes
Serves 8

500 g (1 lb 2 oz) dried cannellini beans
2 tablespoons olive oil
2 onions, chopped
2 garlic cloves, crushed
450 g (1 lb) ripe tomatoes, peeled and
    chopped
3 tablespoons tomato passata
    (puréed tomatoes)
2 large carrots (400 g/14 oz), diced
2 celery stalks (200 g/7 oz), trimmed
    and diced
1.75 litres (61 fl oz/7 cups) vegetable or
    chicken stock
2 bay leaves
2 tablespoons lemon juice
30 g (1 oz/½ cup) chopped flat-leaf (Italian)
    parsley

1 Place the beans in a bowl, cover with cold water and leave to soak overnight.
2 Drain the beans and rinse under cold water. Heat the oil in a very large saucepan. Add the onion and cook gently for 10 minutes, stirring occasionally. Stir in the garlic and cook for 1 minute.
3 Add the cannellini beans, tomato, passata, carrot, celery and stock. Stir and add the bay leaves. Bring to the boil, then reduce the heat to low–medium and simmer, covered, for 45–60 minutes, or until the beans are tender.
4 Stir in the lemon juice and season with salt and pepper, to taste. Stir in some of the parsley and use the rest as a garnish.

NOTE: This soup makes a perfect entertaining option. It can be made a day ahead as the flavour improves with time. Reheat over low heat and if it's too thick, add a little water.

avgolemono soup with chicken

✳ ✳

Preparation time: **20 minutes**
Cooking time: **35 minutes**
Serves **4**

1 onion, halved
2 whole cloves
1 carrot, cut into chunks
1 bay leaf
500 g (1 lb 2 oz) boneless, skinless chicken
    breast
70 g (2½ oz/⅓ cup) short-grain white rice
3 eggs, separated
60 ml (2 fl oz/¼ cup) lemon juice
2 tablespoons chopped flat-leaf (Italian)
    parsley
4 thin lemon slices, to garnish

1 Stud the onion with the cloves and place in a large saucepan with 1.5 litres (52 fl oz/6 cups) water. Add the carrot, bay leaf and chicken and season. Slowly bring to the boil, then reduce the heat and simmer for 10 minutes, or until the chicken is cooked.

2 Strain the stock into a clean saucepan, reserving the chicken and discarding the vegetables. Add the rice to the stock, bring to the boil, then reduce the heat and simmer for 15 minutes, or until the rice is tender. Meanwhile, shred the chicken.

3 Whisk the egg whites in a clean, dry bowl until stiff peaks form, then beat in the yolks. Slowly beat in the lemon juice. Gently stir in about 170 ml (5½ fl oz/ ⅔ cup) of the hot (not boiling) stock and beat thoroughly. Add the egg mixture to the stock and heat gently, but do not let it boil, otherwise the eggs might scramble. Add the chicken and season to taste.

4 Set aside for 2–3 minutes to allow the flavours to develop. To serve, spoon into bowls, sprinkle with the parsley and garnish with the lemon slices.

saltsa avgolemono (egg and lemon sauce)

Bring 375 ml (13 fl oz/1½ cups) chicken stock to the boil in a small saucepan. Mix 1 tablespoon cornflour (cornstarch) with enough cold water to make a paste. Add to the stock and stir until the mixture thickens. Simmer for 2–3 minutes, then remove from the heat and cool slightly. Separate 3 eggs and beat the whites in a large bowl until stiff peaks form. Add the yolks and beat until light and fluffy. Mix in 2–3 tablespoons lemon juice. Gradually pour in the thickened stock, beating constantly. Return the sauce to the pan and cook over low heat, stirring constantly for 1–2 minutes. Season, to taste, remove from the heat and stir for 1 minute. Pour immediately over the dish it is to dress. Serve with Dolmades (page 18), poached fish or steamed vegetables. Serves 4.

chickpeas

Legumes play a vital role in the famed health-enhancing Mediterranean diet. Chickpeas were first grown in the Levant and ancient Egypt and have become an important food in many countries. They are the basis of many very popular Mediterranean dishes. Dried chickpeas should be soaked in cold water before they are cooked. This reduces the cooking time.

fried chickpeas

Preparation time: 10 minutes
+ overnight soaking time
Cooking time: 15 minutes
Serves 6

275 g (9¾ oz/1¼ cups) dried chickpeas
vegetable oil, for deep-frying
½ teaspoon paprika
¼ teaspoon cayenne pepper

1 Soak the chickpeas overnight in plenty of cold water. Drain well and pat dry with paper towels.
2 Fill a deep saucepan one-third full of oil and heat to 180°C (350°F), or until a cube of bread dropped into the oil browns in 15 seconds. Deep-fry half the chickpeas for 3 minutes. Partially cover the saucepan, as some of the chickpeas may pop, and don't leave the oil unattended. Remove with a slotted spoon, drain on crumpled paper towels and repeat with the remaining chickpeas.

3 Deep-fry the chickpeas again, in two batches, for 3 minutes each batch, or until browned. Drain well again on crumpled paper towels. Combine the paprika and cayenne pepper with a little salt and sprinkle the mixture evenly over the hot chickpeas. Allow the chickpeas to cool before serving.

fava (split pea purée)

Preparation time: 10 minutes
Cooking time: 1 hour 20 minutes
Serves 4–6

60 ml (2 fl oz/¼ cup) olive oil
1 onion, finely chopped
330 g (11½ oz/1½ cups) dried yellow
split peas, rinsed
1–2 tablespoons lemon juice
2 tablespoons baby capers, rinsed,
to garnish
60 g (2¼ oz) feta cheese, crumbled,
to garnish
2 tablespoons extra virgin olive oil,
to serve
1 lemon, cut into small wedges,
to serve
crusty bread, to serve

1 Heat the oil in a large heavy-based saucepan over medium heat and cook the onion for 5 minutes, or until softened.
2 Add the split peas and 1.25 litres (44 fl oz/5 cups) water to the saucepan and bring to the boil. Reduce the heat, cover and simmer for 45–50 minutes, or until the peas are very tender and falling apart. Stir frequently during cooking to prevent the split peas catching on the base of the saucepan. Uncover and cook for a further 15–20 minutes, or until the mixture has reduced and thickened. Season with salt and pepper, to taste, and stir in the lemon juice.
3 Serve the fava warm or at room temperature, garnished with capers and crumbled feta. Drizzle the extra virgin olive oil over the top and serve with lemon wedges and crusty bread.

fried chickpeas

Fresh mussels must be thoroughly scrubbed with a stiff brush to remove any grit or weed.

After scrubbing, pull out the hairy beards. Discard any broken or open mussels, or those that don't close when tapped on the work surface.

mussels saganaki

Preparation time: 45 minutes
Cooking time: 25 minutes
Serves 6

750 g (1 lb 10 oz) black mussels
420 g (15 oz) ripe tomatoes
125 ml (4 fl oz/½ cup) dry white wine
3 thyme sprigs
1 bay leaf
1 tablespoon olive oil
1 large onion, finely chopped
1 garlic clove, finely chopped
2 tablespoons tomato paste
   (concentrated purée)
½ teaspoon sugar
1 tablespoon red wine vinegar
70 g (2½ oz) feta cheese, crumbled
1 teaspoon thyme

1 Scrub the mussels with a stiff brush and pull out the hairy beards. Discard any broken mussels, or open ones that don't close when tapped. Rinse well.
2 To peel the tomatoes, score a cross in the base of each tomato. Put the tomatoes in a heatproof bowl and cover with boiling water. Leave for 30 seconds, then transfer to cold water and peel the skin away from the cross. Cut the tomatoes in half and finely chop the flesh.
3 Put the wine, thyme sprigs and bay leaf in a large saucepan and bring to the boil. Add the mussels and cook for 4–5 minutes, or until just opened. Strain the liquid into a heatproof bowl and reserve. Discard any unopened mussels. Remove the top half-shell from each mussel and discard.
4 Heat the olive oil in a large saucepan, add the onion and stir over medium heat for 3 minutes. Add the garlic and cook for

1 minute, or until it begins to turn golden. Pour in the reserved mussel liquid, increase the heat and bring to the boil, then boil for 2 minutes, or until almost dry. Add the tomato, tomato paste and sugar, then reduce the heat and simmer for 5 minutes. Add the vinegar and simmer for another 5 minutes.
5 Add the mussels to the pan and cook for 1 minute, or until heated through. Spoon into a warm serving dish. Top with the crumbled feta and thyme. Serve hot.

NOTE: Saganaki refers to the utensil used to cook the food in. It is a frying pan with two handles, used for cooking a range of meze as it can be transferred from stovetop to table. Any pan of a suitable size can be used.

meze

Derived from the word meaning 'half', meze refers to individual dishes as well as the style of eating. These little dishes are eaten before a meal or as a meal in their own right, and are perfect for communal eating.

origins of meze

In the region's non-Muslim communities, the habit of eating a variety of small dishes originated from the custom of not drinking alcohol without having food to nibble on. Even in bars and restaurants, wine, beer, raki, ouzo and arak are accompanied by a few dishes such as slices of melon, feta cheese, olives and bread. Visitors to Greece are pleasantly surprised, when ordering ouzo in a bar, to receive a complementary mezethakia plate with feta, olives and sliced tomato. In Greece there is a specific grade of taverna called mezepoulio, which only serve mezethakia. The close connection between eating and drinking is also demonstrated in Turkey where a meze table is commonly referred to as a raki table.

In communities where alcohol is not consumed, meze platters are served with coffee or syrups. It is not uncommon for Jewish families to share a meze table after the Sabbath or festival morning services.

Meze are integral to the Levantine lifestyle and many social gatherings are conducted around a meze table. Once they were only eaten in wealthy households or restaurants and for special occasions such as religious holidays and weddings. However, today they are a common feature of everyday household hospitality. Many modern kitchens contain the fundamentals of a meze selection including cheeses, sausages, olives, home-made pickles and dips, fresh tomatoes and cucumbers in readiness for unexpected guests. The homes of keen cooks often contain freezers filled with bread doughs and filled filo pastries that can be heated as required.

Meze dishes are an ideal showcase for the Mediterranean region's quintessential flavours such as olives, olive oil, eggplant (aubergine), garlic, cheese, chickpeas, yoghurt, nuts, tomatoes and seafood. Many of the most popular meze dishes have crossed over from street food, with falafel, hummus, meatballs and baba ghanoush being some of the more well-known examples.

The mixture of textures, tastes and aromas are limitless so it is important to consider a contrast of colours and flavours when choosing a meze selection. It is also common to combine cooked and uncooked dishes. Some dishes are served hot and others at room temperature. The dishes range from salads, dips, breads, nuts, pastries, stuffed vine leaves, marinated or pickled seafood and suitable condiments.

what constitutes meze?

Essentially, any regional dish that can be served in small portions can be part of a meze table. Many meze dishes double as accompaniments to main dishes, making the crossover between courses of a meal more fluid and flexible. Many restaurants compete with the number of meze dishes offered, with some serving upwards of 70 dishes to lure customers.

Although intended as appetisers, the ritual of nibbling meze can stretch over several hours, especially at parties where the range of dishes is so inviting.

While meze can be as simple as a bowl of mixed fresh herbs accompanied by nuts, more elaborate dishes often feature. Dishes such as Keftedes (page 20) and the Turkish speciality Cerkes tavugu (page 64) are fiddly to make but more filling.

Although the choices for meze are seemingly endless, it may be necessary to limit the number of dishes, especially when serving before a meal, as they are supposed to whet the appetite, not satisfy it. Depending on the number of dishes, meze can, however, constitute a whole meal or can be eaten with drinks at any time of the day.

stifatho

2 Add the meat all at once to the pan and stir over high heat for 10 minutes, or until the meat is well browned and almost all the liquid has been absorbed.

3 Add the garlic, wine, spices, bay leaf, vinegar, tomato paste, ¼ teaspoon cracked black pepper, some salt and 375 ml (13 fl oz/1½ cups) water to the pan and bring to the boil. Reduce the heat, cover and simmer for a further 1 hour, stirring occasionally, or until the meat is almost tender.

4 Return the onions to the saucepan, add the currants and stir gently. Simmer, covered, for 15 minutes or until the meat is very tender. Discard the cinnamon. Serve with rice, bread or potatoes.

NOTE: For a richer flavour, use 375 ml (13 fl oz/1½ cups) beef or veal stock instead of water in this recipe, or 250 ml (9 fl oz/1 cup) each of wine and water.

sofrito (veal cooked with vinegar)

Preparation time: **10 minutes**
Cooking time: **1 hour 50 minutes**
Serves 6–8

60 g (2¼ oz/½ cup) plain (all-purpose) flour
large pinch of cayenne pepper
1 kg (2 lb 4 oz) veal steaks
60 ml (2 fl oz/¼ cup) olive oil
1 bay leaf
5 garlic cloves, crushed
170 ml (5½ fl oz/⅔ cup) red wine vinegar
625 ml (21½ fl oz/2½ cups) beef stock
chopped flat-leaf (Italian) parsley, to serve

1 Combine the flour with the cayenne and season well with salt and pepper. Lightly coat the veal with the seasoned flour, shaking off any excess.

2 Heat the oil in a large, deep frying pan over high heat and cook the veal a few pieces at a time for 1 minute on each side, or until lightly browned. Remove from the pan and set aside.

stifatho (spiced beef and onions)

Preparation time: **15 minutes**
Cooking time: **1 hour 35 minutes**
Serves 4

1 kg (2 lb 4 oz) chuck steak
60 ml (2 fl oz/¼ cup) olive oil
750 g (1 lb 10 oz) baby onions
3 garlic cloves, halved lengthways
125 ml (4 fl oz/½ cup) red wine

1 cinnamon stick
4 whole cloves
1 bay leaf
1 tablespoon red wine vinegar
2 tablespoons tomato paste (concentrated purée)
2 tablespoons currants

1 Trim the meat of excess fat and sinew, then cut into bite-sized cubes. Heat the oil over medium heat in a large, heavy-based saucepan. Add the onions and cook for 5 minutes, or until golden. Remove from the pan and drain on paper towels.

3 Add the bay leaf, garlic, vinegar and stock to the frying pan and bring to the boil, scraping up any residue from the base of the pan. Reduce the heat to low and return the veal and any juices to the pan. Cover with a lid or foil and cook, stirring gently occasionally, for 1½ hours, or until the veal is very tender and the sauce has thickened. If the sauce is too thin, carefully transfer the veal to a serving platter, cover loosely with foil to keep warm, and boil the sauce until it is the consistency of a smooth gravy. Sprinkle with parsley before serving.

chicken pie with feta

✳ ✳

Preparation time: 30 minutes
Cooking time: 1 hour 20 minutes
Serves 6

500 ml (17 fl oz/2 cups) chicken stock
1 kg (2 lb 4 oz) boneless, skinless chicken
    breast, cut into bite-sized pieces
60 g (2¼ oz) butter
2 spring onions (scallions), finely chopped
60 g (2¼ oz/½ cup) plain (all-purpose) flour
125 ml (4 fl oz/½ cup) milk
8 sheets filo pastry
60 g (2¼ oz) butter, extra, melted
200 g (7 oz) feta, crumbled
1 tablespoon chopped dill
1 tablespoon snipped chives
¼ teaspoon freshly grated nutmeg
1 egg, lightly beaten

1 Pour the stock into a saucepan and bring to the boil over high heat. Reduce the heat to low, add the chicken and poach gently for 10–15 minutes, or until the chicken is cooked through. Drain, reserving the stock. Add enough water to the stock in order to bring the quantity up to 500 ml (17 fl oz/2 cups). Preheat the oven to 180°C (350°F/Gas 4).
2 Melt the butter in a saucepan over low heat, add the spring onion and cook, stirring, for 5 minutes. Add the flour and stir for 30 seconds. Remove the pan from the heat and gradually add the

chicken stock and milk, stirring after each addition. Return to the heat and gently bring to the boil, stirring. Simmer for 3 minutes, or until the sauce thickens. Remove from the heat.
3 Line an 18 x 25 cm (7 x 10 inch) ovenproof dish with four sheets of filo pastry, brushing one side of each sheet with melted butter as you go and placing them buttered side down. The filo will overlap the edges of the dish. Cover the unused filo with a damp tea towel (dish towel) to prevent it drying out.
4 Stir the chicken, feta, dill, chives, nutmeg and egg into the sauce. Season with salt and pepper, to taste. Pile the

mixture on top of the filo pastry in the dish. Fold the overlapping filo over the filling and cover the top of the pie with the remaining four sheets of filo, brushing each sheet with melted butter as you go. Scrunch the edges of the filo so they fit in the dish. Brush the top with butter. Bake for 45–50 minutes, or until the pastry is golden brown and crisp.

NOTE: You can use puff pastry instead of filo pastry. If you do so, bake in a 220°C (425°F/Gas 7) oven for 15 minutes, then reduce the temperature to 180°C (350°F/Gas 4) and cook for another 30 minutes, or until the pastry is puffed and golden.

braised artichokes with broad beans

✹ ✹

Preparation time: **25** minutes
Cooking time: **35** minutes
Serves **4**

1 lemon, halved
6 large globe artichokes
4 spring onions (scallions)
80 ml (2½ fl oz/⅓ cup) extra
   virgin olive oil
300 g (10½ oz) shelled broad
   (fava) beans
3 tablespoons chopped dill

1 Squeeze the lemon into a large bowl of water and put the lemon shells in the water to make acidulated water. Using a small sharp knife, remove the hairy choke from each artichoke and peel away the prickly outer leaves. Trim the bases.
2 Cut each artichoke into quarters and put them in the acidulated water to prevent them browning while you prepare the rest. Thinly slice the spring onions.
3 In a large heavy-based, non-aluminium saucepan, heat the oil and cook the spring onion for 1–2 minutes, or until just softened. Add the drained artichokes, broad beans and dill and add just enough water to cover the vegetables. Cover and simmer for 30 minutes, or until tender. Drain and season, to taste. Serve warm, or at room temperature.

butterbean casserole

butterbean casserole

✹ ✹

Preparation time: **20** minutes
   + overnight soaking time
Cooking time: **2 hours 5** minutes
Serves **6–8**

185 g (6½ oz/1 cup) dried butterbeans
   (lima beans)
1 large onion
1 small carrot
1 small celery stalk
60 ml (2 fl oz/¼ cup) olive oil
1 garlic clove, chopped
400 g (14 oz) tin chopped tomatoes
1 tablespoon tomato paste
   (concentrated purée)
2 teaspoons chopped dill
extra virgin olive oil, to serve

1 Cover the beans with plenty of cold water and soak overnight. Drain well.
2 Bring a large saucepan of water to the boil, add the beans and return to the boil, then reduce the heat to medium and cook, partially covered, for 45–60 minutes, or until the beans are tender but not mushy. Drain well.

Cut small slits in the lamb and insert the garlic slivers.

Sprinkle the potatoes with oregano and seasoning.

3 Preheat the oven to 180°C (350°F/ Gas 4). Slice the onion and chop the carrot and celery. Heat the olive oil in a 2.5 litre (87 fl oz/10 cup) flameproof casserole dish over medium heat. Add the onion, garlic, carrot and celery, and cook for 5 minutes, or until the onion is translucent. Add the tomatoes, tomato paste and 125 ml (4 fl oz/½ cup) water. Bring to the boil, then reduce the heat and simmer for 3 minutes. Add the butterbeans and dill to the casserole dish, then season to taste.

4 Return to the boil, then cover and bake in the oven for 50 minutes, or until the sauce is thick and the butterbeans are soft. Serve hot or at room temperature, drizzled with extra virgin olive oil.

roast lamb with lemon and potatoes

❋

Preparation time: **20 minutes**
Cooking time: **3 hours**
Serves **6**

2.5–3 kg (5 lb 8 oz–6 lb 12 oz) leg of lamb
2 garlic cloves
125 ml (4 fl oz/½ cup) lemon juice
3 tablespoons dried oregano
1 brown onion, sliced
2 celery stalks, sliced
40 g (1½ oz) butter, softened
1 kg (2 lb 4 oz) potatoes, quartered

1 Preheat the oven to 180°C (350°F/ Gas 4). Cut small slits in the lamb and cut the garlic into slivers. Insert the garlic into the slits. Rub the entire surface with half the lemon juice, sprinkle with salt, pepper and half the oregano. Place in a baking dish and bake for 1 hour.

2 Drain the fat from the dish and add the onion, celery and 250 ml (9 fl oz/ 1 cup) hot water. Spread the butter over the lamb, reduce the temperature to 160°C (315°F/Gas 2–3) and cook for a further 1 hour. Turn the lamb during cooking to brown evenly.

3 Add the potatoes to the dish, sprinkle with the remaining oregano and lemon juice and some salt and pepper. Bake for another hour, adding more water if required and turning the potatoes halfway through cooking. Cut the lamb into chunks. Skim any excess fat from the dish and serve the cooking juices with the potatoes and lamb.

moussaka

✷ ✷

Preparation time: 20 minutes
  + 30 minutes standing time
Cooking time: 2 hours
Serves 6

2 large tomatoes
1.5 kg (3 lb 5 oz) eggplants (aubergines),
  cut into 5 mm (¼ inch) slices
125 ml (4 fl oz/½ cup) olive oil
2 onions, finely chopped
2 large garlic cloves, crushed
½ teaspoon ground allspice
1 teaspoon ground cinnamon
750 g (1 lb 10 oz) minced (ground) lamb
2 tablespoons tomato paste (concentrated
  purée)
125 ml (4 fl oz/½ cup) dry white wine
3 tablespoons chopped flat-leaf (Italian)
  parsley

CHEESE SAUCE
60 g (2¼ oz) butter
60 g (2¼ oz/½ cup) plain (all-purpose) flour
625 ml (21½ fl oz/2½ cups) milk
pinch of freshly grated nutmeg
35 g (1¼ oz/⅓ cup) freshly grated kefalotyri
  or parmesan cheese
2 eggs, lightly beaten

1   Score a cross in the base of each tomato. Put in a heatproof bowl and cover with boiling water. Leave for 30 seconds, then transfer to cold water and peel the skin away from the cross. Cut each tomato in half, scoop out the seeds and finely chop the flesh. Lay the eggplant on a tray, sprinkle with salt and leave for 30 minutes. Rinse and pat dry.
2   Heat 2 tablespoons of the oil in a frying pan and cook the eggplant in batches for 1–2 minutes each side, until golden and soft. Add a little more oil when needed. Heat 1 tablespoon of the olive oil in a large saucepan, add the onion and cook over medium heat for 5 minutes. Add the garlic, allspice and cinnamon and cook for 30 seconds. Add the lamb and cook for 5 minutes, or until browned, breaking up any lumps with the back of a spoon.

Add the tomato, tomato paste and wine, and simmer over low heat for 30 minutes, or until the liquid has evaporated. Stir in the chopped parsley and season to taste. Preheat the oven to 180°C (350°F/Gas 4).
3   To make the cheese sauce, melt the butter in a saucepan over low heat. Stir in the flour and cook for 1 minute, or until pale and foaming. Remove the saucepan from the heat and gradually stir in the milk and nutmeg. Return the saucepan to the heat and stir constantly until the sauce boils and thickens. Reduce the heat and simmer for 2 minutes. Stir in 1 tablespoon of the cheese until well combined.
4   Line the base of a 3 litre (105 fl oz/ 12 cup) ovenproof dish, which measures

25 x 30 cm (10 x 12 inches), with a third of the eggplant. Spoon half the meat sauce over it and cover with another layer of eggplant. Spoon the remaining meat sauce over the top and cover with the remaining eggplant. Stir the egg into the cheese sauce. Spread the sauce over the top of the eggplant and then sprinkle with the remaining cheese. Bake the moussaka for 1 hour. Leave to stand for 10 minutes before slicing to serve.

NOTE: You can substitute an equal quantity of sliced, pan-fried zucchini (courgettes) or potatoes, or a combination of both these vegetables for the eggplant if you desire.

stuffed capsicums

Preparation time: 25 minutes
Cooking time: 1 hour 15 minutes
Serves 6

175 g (6 oz) long-grain white rice
310 ml (10¾ fl oz/1¼ cups) chicken stock
6 medium-sized capsicums (peppers)
60 g (2¼ oz) pine nuts
80 ml (2½ fl oz/⅓ cup) olive oil
1 large onion, chopped
125 g (4½ oz/½ cup) tomato passata
    (puréed tomatoes)
60 g (2¼ oz) currants
2½ tablespoons chopped flat-leaf (Italian)
    parsley
2½ tablespoons chopped mint leaves
½ teaspoon ground cinnamon

1 Put the rice and stock in a saucepan and bring to the boil over medium heat. Reduce the heat to low–medium, cover tightly and cook for 15 minutes, or until the rice is tender. Remove from the heat and set aside, covered.

2 Bring a large saucepan of water to the boil. Cut off the tops of the capsicums, reserving the lids. Remove the seeds and membrane from the capsicums and discard. Blanch the capsicums in the boiling water (not the lids) for 2 minutes, then drain and leave upturned to dry on paper towels.

3 Preheat the oven to 180°C (350°F/Gas 4). Toast the pine nuts in a small frying pan over low heat until golden brown, then remove from the pan and set aside. Increase the heat to medium and heat 2 tablespoons of the oil. Add the onion and cook for 10 minutes or until soft, stirring occasionally.

4 Add the passata, currants, parsley, mint, cinnamon, cooked rice and toasted pine nuts to the pan. Stir for 2 minutes, then season with salt and pepper, to taste.

5 Stand the capsicums in a baking dish in which they fit snugly. Divide the rice mixture among the capsicum cavities. Replace the lids.

6 Pour 100 ml (3½ fl oz) boiling water into the dish and drizzle the remaining oil over the top of the capsicums. Bake for 40 minutes, or until the capsicums are just tender when tested with the point of a small knife. Serve warm or cold.

NOTE: You can use capsicums that are all the same colour, or a mix of different colours as we have done.

stuffed vegetables

Yemista, or stuffed vegetables, are an important feature of Greek gastronomy, and are popular in tavernas across Greece. Vegetarian versions are stuffed with rice, herbs, currants or raisins, and nuts. The addition of finely minced meat to this mixture is an example of Greek improvisation in making a small amount of meat go a long way, using it just as a flavouring.

kotopoulo me syko (chicken with figs)

Preparation time: 20 minutes
Cooking time: 1 hour 10 minutes
Serves 4

1.5 kg (3 lb 5 oz) chicken, cut into 8 pieces,
    giblets reserved, excess fat trimmed
1 tablespoon olive oil
12 dried figs, soaked in hot water for
    2 hours, drained
10 garlic cloves, unpeeled
1 large onion, thinly sliced
½ teaspoon ground coriander
½ teaspoon ground cinnamon
½ teaspoon ground cumin
pinch of cayenne pepper
2 bay leaves
375 ml (13 fl oz/1½ cups) ruby port
1 teaspoon finely grated lemon zest
2 tablespoons lemon juice

1 Preheat the oven to 180°C (350°F/ Gas 4). Lightly season the chicken. Heat the olive oil in a large heavy-based frying pan over high heat and cook the chicken in batches, skin side down, for 5 minutes, or until the skin is golden.
2 Remove from the pan and place in a single layer, skin side down, in a large baking dish with the giblets. Place the figs between the chicken pieces. Scatter the garlic and onion over the top, carefully pressing them into any gaps. Sprinkle the spices over, tuck in the bay leaves, then pour in the port. Cover and bake for 25 minutes, then turn the chicken, uncover and bake for 20 minutes, or until the chicken is just tender. Stir in the lemon zest and juice and bake for another 15 minutes, or until very tender.

kotopoulo me syko

arni yahni (lamb stew)

Preparation time: 25 minutes
Cooking time: 2 hours 15 minutes
Serves 4

3 tablespoons olive oil
1 kg (2 lb 4 oz) boneless lamb shoulder,
    cut into 2 cm (¾ inch) cubes
1 onion, chopped
2 garlic cloves, crushed
2 celery stalks, chopped
1 large carrot, chopped
4 ripe tomatoes, peeled, seeded and
    chopped
2 tablespoons tomato paste
    (concentrated purée)
1 teaspoon sugar
185 ml (6 fl oz/¾ cup) red wine
2 bay leaves
3 whole cloves
¼ teaspoon ground cinnamon

sweet and sour dishes

While most often associated with Chinese food, the tradition of sweet and sour dishes also has roots in the classical cooking of the Mediterranean, where the blending of opposite flavours and textures reflected mythological beliefs in achieving equilibrium among opposing forces. For example, meat has been cooked with fruit for centuries. Originally, fruit was used to tenderise tougher cuts of meat, but in Kotopoulo me syko (chicken with figs), the flavour of the figs blends beautifully with the spices and lemon.

250 g (9 oz) baby onions
350 g (12 oz) zucchini (courgettes),
    thickly sliced
chopped flat-leaf (Italian) parsley,
    to serve

1 Heat 1 tablespoon of the oil in a large saucepan, then brown the meat on all sides, in batches, adding more oil when necessary. Set aside.
2 Heat another tablespoon of oil, add the onion and cook for 4 minutes or until soft. Add the garlic, celery and carrot and cook for 1 minute before adding the tomato, tomato paste, sugar, wine, bay leaves, cloves, cinnamon and 375 ml (13 fl oz/1½ cups) water. Return the meat to the pan. Cover and bring to the boil, then reduce the heat and simmer for 1½ hours.
3 Meanwhile, in a separate frying pan, heat the remaining olive oil and cook the baby onions until they are golden brown and tender. Add the onions to the stew, along with the sliced zucchini, and cook for another 30 minutes or until tender. Sprinkle with the parsley and serve immediately.

souvlake (skewered lamb)

✳ ✳

Preparation time: 20 minutes + 30 minutes
    standing + overnight marinating time
Cooking time: 10 minutes
Serves 4

1 kg (2 lb 4 oz) boned leg of lamb,
    excess fat trimmed and cut into
    2 cm (¾ inch) cubes
60 ml (2 fl oz/¼ cup) olive oil
2 teaspoons finely grated lemon zest
80 ml (2½ fl oz/⅓ cup) lemon juice
125 ml (4 fl oz/½ cup) dry white wine
2 teaspoons dried oregano
2 large garlic cloves, finely chopped
2 bay leaves
250 g (9 oz/1 cup) Greek-style yoghurt
2 garlic cloves, extra, crushed

lamb

The popularity of lamb in Greece is linked to the country's hilly, often barren landscape. This terrain is not naturally suitable for cattle so, instead, sheep and goats are usually reared, both for their meat and milk. As meat was historically scarce and expensive, it is a food traditionally associated with religious feast days and other special occasions. During Easter, the most important religious festival for Orthodox Greeks, it is customary to spit-roast an entire lamb, including its entrails. As with all their meat, Greeks generally prefer lamb to be well done, so that it falls off the bone, but the recipes we have given can be cooked to your liking.

1 If using wooden skewers, soak them in water for about 30 minutes to prevent them from burning during cooking. Put the lamb in a non-metallic bowl with 2 tablespoons of the oil, the lemon zest and juice, wine, oregano, garlic, bay leaves and some cracked black pepper. Toss, then cover and refrigerate overnight.

2 Put the yoghurt and extra garlic in a bowl, mix well and leave for 30 minutes.
3 Drain the lamb. Thread onto eight skewers and cook on a barbecue or chargrill plate, brushing with the remaining oil, for 7–8 minutes, or until done to your liking. Serve with the yoghurt, some bread and a salad.

spanokopita (silverbeet and cheese filo pie)

✳ ✳

Preparation time: **25 minutes**
Cooking time: **1 hour**
Serves **4–6**

1.5 kg (3 lb 5 oz) silverbeet (Swiss chard)
1 white onion
10 spring onions (scallions)
60 ml (2 fl oz/¼ cup) olive oil
1½ tablespoons chopped dill
200 g (7 oz) feta cheese, crumbled
125 g (4½ oz/½ cup) cottage cheese
35 g (1¼ oz/⅓ cup) finely grated kefalotyri
   cheese (see Note)
¼ teaspoon freshly grated nutmeg
4 eggs, lightly beaten
10 sheets filo pastry
80 g (2¾ oz) butter, melted, to brush

1 Rinse and drain the silverbeet thoroughly. Discard the stems and shred the leaves. Finely chop the onion. Chop the spring onions, including some green.
2 Heat the oil in a large frying pan, add the onion and cook, stirring, over medium heat for 5 minutes, or until softened. Add the spring onion and silverbeet and cook, covered, over medium heat for 5 minutes. Add the dill and cook, uncovered, for 3–4 minutes, or until most of the liquid has evaporated. Remove from the heat and cool to room temperature.
3 Preheat the oven to 180°C (350°F/Gas 4) and lightly grease a 20 x 25 cm (8 x 10 inch), 2.5 litre (87 fl oz/10 cup) ovenproof dish. Put the cheeses in a large bowl. Stir in the silverbeet mixture and add the nutmeg. Gradually add the egg and combine well. Season to taste.
4 Line the base and sides of the dish with a sheet of filo pastry — keep the rest covered with a damp tea towel (dish towel) to prevent them drying out. Brush with some of the melted butter and cover with another sheet of pastry. Butter the sheet and repeat in this way, using five sheets of pastry. Spoon the filling into the dish and level the surface. Fold the exposed pastry up and over to cover the top of the filling. Cover with a sheet of pastry, brush with butter and continue until all the remaining sheets are used. Roughly trim the pastry with scissors, then tuck the excess inside the dish.
5 Brush the top with butter. Using a sharp knife, score the surface into squares. Sprinkle a few drops of cold water on top to prevent the pastry from curling. Bake for 45 minutes, or until puffed and golden. Rest at room temperature for 10 minutes before serving.

NOTE: If kefalotyri is not available, use pecorino or parmesan instead.

rice pilaff

In a heavy-based saucepan, melt 60 g (2¼ oz) butter over low heat. Add 1 finely chopped brown onion and cook, stirring frequently, for 5 minutes, or until softened. Add 400 g (14 oz/2 cups) long-grain white rice and stir well to coat. Add 1 litre (35 fl oz/4 cups) hot chicken or vegetable stock and bring to the boil, stirring frequently, then reduce the heat to low, cover tightly and cook for 10 minutes. Remove from the heat and set aside for 10 minutes. Fluff the rice with a fork and serve immediately. Pilaff can be pressed into individual oiled moulds and then turned out onto a serving dish. Serves 6–8.

oktapodi krasato (octopus in red wine stew)

✸ ✸

Preparation time: 30 minutes
Cooking time: 1 hour 10 minutes
Serves 4–6

1 kg (2 lb 4 oz) baby octopus
2 tablespoons olive oil
1 large onion, chopped
3 garlic cloves, crushed
1 bay leaf
750 ml (26 fl oz/3 cups) red wine
60 ml (2 fl oz/¼ cup) red wine
 vinegar
400 g (14 oz) tin chopped tomatoes
1 tablespoon tomato paste (concentrated
 purée)
1 tablespoon finely chopped oregano
¼ teaspoon ground cinnamon
small pinch of ground cloves
1 teaspoon sugar
2 tablespoons chopped flat-leaf (Italian)
 parsley

1 To prepare each octopus, using a small sharp knife, cut between the head and tentacles, just below the eyes. Grasp the body and push the beak out and up through the centre of the tentacles with your fingers. Cut the eyes from the head by slicing a small round off with a small sharp knife. Discard the eye section. Carefully slit through one side of the head and remove any guts from inside. Thoroughly rinse all the octopus under running water.
2 Heat the oil in a large saucepan, add the onion and cook, stirring often, over high heat for 5 minutes, or until it is starting to brown. Add the garlic and bay leaf and cook, stirring, for another minute. Add the octopus and stir to thoroughly coat in the onion mixture.
3 Add the wine, vinegar, tomatoes, tomato paste, oregano, cinnamon, cloves and sugar. Bring to the boil, then reduce the heat to low and simmer for 1 hour, or until the octopus is tender and the sauce

has thickened slightly. Stir in the parsley and season, to taste.

NOTE: The cooking time for octopus varies according to the size. Generally, smaller octopus are not as tough as larger ones and will take less time to cook.

kalamaria tiganita (fried squid)

✸ ✸

Preparation time: 20 minutes
Cooking time: 15 minutes
Serves 4

1 kg (2 lb 4 oz) small squid
vegetable oil, for deep-frying
plain (all-purpose) flour, well-seasoned,
 for coating
lemon wedges, to serve

1 To clean the squid, gently pull the tentacles away from the tube (the intestines should come away at the same time). Remove the intestines from the tentacles by cutting under the eyes, then remove the beak if it remains in the centre of the tentacles by using your fingers to push up the centre. Pull away the quill (the transparent cartilage) from inside the body and remove. Remove and discard any white membrane. Under cold running water, pull away the skin from the tube (the wings can be used). Slice the bodies into 5 mm (¼ inch) rings. Pat dry the rings, wings and tentacles.
2 Heat the oil in a deep, heavy-based saucepan to 180°C (350°F), or until a cube of bread dropped into the oil turns golden brown in 15 seconds. Toss the squid in the seasoned flour and shake off any excess. Fry the squid in batches, for 2–3 minutes each batch, or until golden. Serve with the lemon wedges.

oktapodi krasato

44

briami (potato and zucchini casserole)

Preparation time: 20 minutes
Cooking time: 1 hour 45 minutes
Serves 4–6

1 kg (2 lb 4 oz) ripe tomatoes
1 large red capsicum (pepper)
400 g (14 oz) small roasting potatoes,
    unpeeled
2 onions
400 g (14 oz) zucchini (courgettes)
60 ml (2 fl oz/¼ cup) olive oil
2 garlic cloves, crushed
1 teaspoon dried oregano
2 tablespoons chopped flat-leaf (Italian)
    parsley
2 tablespoons chopped dill
½ teaspoon ground cinnamon

1 Preheat the oven to 180°C (350°F/
Gas 4). Score a cross in the base of each
tomato. Put in a heatproof bowl and
cover with boiling water. Leave for
30 seconds, then transfer to cold water
and peel away the skin from the cross.
Cut the tomatoes in half, scoop out the
seeds and roughly chop the flesh. Cut the
capsicum in half, remove the seeds and
membrane and cut the flesh into 3cm
(1¼ inch) squares. Cut the potatoes into
1 cm (½ inch) slices. Slice the onions and
thickly slice the zucchini.
2 Heat 2 tablespoons of the oil in a
heavy-based frying pan over medium
heat. Add the onion and cook, stirring
frequently, for 10 minutes. Add the garlic
and cook for 2 minutes. Put all the other
ingredients, except the remaining oil, in
a large bowl and season generously. Add
the onion and garlic and toss together.
Transfer to a large ovenproof dish and
drizzle with the remaining oil.
3 Cover and bake for 1–1½ hours, or
until the vegetables are tender, stirring
every 30 minutes. Insert the point of a
small knife into the potatoes. If the knife
comes out easily, the potato is cooked.

vegetables in the greek diet

Greeks enjoy more vegetables
in their diet than most other
Europeans and eat them raw,
pickled or cooked in endless
ways. Restaurant menus
in Greece will usually list
numerous vegetable dishes
as courses in their own right,
not just as accompaniments to
meat. In tavernas across Greece
it is still possible for patrons to
enter the kitchen and peer into
the cooking pots and baking
trays so they can choose the
vegetable dishes that most
take their fancy.

stuffed tomatoes

Like much Greek food, stuffed tomatoes can be eaten either hot or cold. In fact, eating food piping hot as soon as it has been cooked is more of a modern habit in Greece, as historically most homes, except those of the wealthiest, did not have their own ovens. Instead, foods were cooked at the local bakery then eaten at room temperature later in the day.

tomates yemistes (rice-stuffed tomatoes)

❋ ❋

Preparation time: 40 minutes
Cooking time: 55 minutes
Makes 8

8 tomatoes
110 g (3¾ oz/½ cup) short-grain white rice
2 tablespoons olive oil
1 red onion, chopped
1 garlic clove, crushed
1 teaspoon dried oregano
40 g (1½ oz/¼ cup) pine nuts
35 g (1¼ oz/¼ cup) currants
30 g (1 oz/½ cup) chopped basil
2 tablespoons chopped flat-leaf (Italian) parsley
1 tablespoon chopped dill
olive oil, extra, to brush

1 Preheat the oven to 160°C (315°F/ Gas 2–3). Lightly grease a large ovenproof dish. Slice the top off each tomato and reserve. Spoon the flesh into a strainer over a bowl. Strain the juice into the bowl, finely dice the flesh and place in a separate bowl. Drain the tomato shells upside down on a wire rack. Boil the rice in lightly salted water for 10–12 minutes, or until just tender. Drain and cool.

2 Heat the oil in a saucepan. Fry the onion, garlic and oregano for 8 minutes, or until the onion is soft. Add the pine nuts and currants and cook for 5 minutes, stirring often. Remove from the heat and stir in the herbs. Season. Add the onion mixture and reserved tomato flesh to the rice and mix well. Fill up the tomato shells with the rice mixture. Spoon 1 tablespoon of reserved tomato juice over each tomato and replace the tops. Lightly brush the tomatoes with the extra oil and place in the ovenproof dish. Bake for 30 minutes, or until heated through.

kourabiethes (almond shortbreads)

✳ ✳

Preparation time: **20 minutes**
Cooking time: **20 minutes**
Makes **about 40**

250 g (9 oz) unsalted butter, softened
125 g (4½ oz/1 cup) icing (confectioners')
   sugar, plus extra, for dusting
1½ teaspoons natural vanilla extract
½ teaspoon finely grated orange zest
1 egg yolk
1½ tablespoons brandy
310 g (11 oz/2½ cups) plain (all-purpose)
   flour
1 teaspoon baking powder
30 g (1 oz/⅓ cup) ground almonds
40 g (1½ oz/⅓ cup) slivered almonds
2 tablespoons orange flower water

1 Preheat the oven to 160°C (315°F/
Gas 2–3). Line two baking trays with
baking paper. Beat the butter, icing sugar,
vanilla and orange zest in a bowl using
electric beaters until light and creamy.
Gradually add the egg yolk and brandy
and beat until combined.
2 Sift the flour and baking powder
into a large bowl, stir in the ground and
chopped slivered almonds, then stir into
the butter mixture. Form walnut-sized
pieces into crescent shapes and place
on the trays, leaving a little room for
spreading. Bake for 20 minutes, or until
just lightly coloured. Cool for 5 minutes,
then brush with the orange flower water.
Roll in the extra icing sugar to coat and
set aside on wire racks to cool. When
cool, dust more icing sugar heavily over
the top of the kourabiethes.

kourabiethes

Kourabiethes are a Christmas
speciality in Greece. Mounds
of the biscuits are found in
homes and the windows of
pastry stores at this time, then
by New Year all that remains is
a pile of sugar dust. While this
recipe has many versions, the
constants are that it is always
made with unsalted butter and
has a low proportion of sugar
in the dough so that it retains
its characteristic dense texture.
The biscuits are dusted liberally
with icing (confectioners')
sugar after baking.

kataifi me amigthala (shredded pastries with almonds)

Preparation time: 45 minutes
   + 2 hours standing time
Cooking time: 50 minutes
Makes 40 pieces

500 g (1 lb 2 oz) kataifi pastry (see Note)
250 g (9 oz) unsalted butter, melted
130 g (4½ oz/1 cup) ground pistachio nuts
230 g (8 oz/2 cups) ground almonds
625 g (1 lb 6 oz/2½ cups) caster (superfine) sugar
1 teaspoon ground cinnamon
¼ teaspoon ground cloves
1 tablespoon brandy
1 egg white
1 teaspoon lemon juice
5 cm (2 inch) strip lemon zest
4 cloves
1 cinnamon stick
1 tablespoon honey

1 Allow the kataifi pastry to come to room temperature, still in its packaging. This will take about 2 hours and makes the pastry easier to work with.

2 Preheat the oven to 170°C (325°/ Gas 3). Brush a 20 x 30 cm (8 x 12 inch) baking dish or tray with melted butter.

3 Place the nuts in a bowl with 125 g (4½ oz) of the caster sugar, the ground cinnamon, cloves and brandy. Lightly beat the egg white with a fork and add to the mixture. Stir to make a paste. Divide the mixture into 8 portions and form each into a sausage shape about 18 cm (7 inches) long.

4 Take a small handful of the pastry strands and spread them out fairly compactly, with the strands running lengthways towards you. The pastry should measure 18 x 25 cm (7 x 10 inches). Brush the pastry with melted butter. Place one of the 'nut' sausages along the end of the pastry nearest to you and roll up into a neat sausage shape. Repeat with the other pastry portions.

5 Place the rolls close together in the dish and brush with melted butter. Bake for 50 minutes, or until golden brown.

6 While the pastries are cooking, place the remaining sugar in a small saucepan with 500 ml (17 fl oz/2 cups) water and stir over low heat until dissolved. Add the lemon juice, zest, cloves and cinnamon and boil together for 10 minutes. Stir in the honey, then set aside until cooled. Remove the cinnamon stick and cloves.

7 When the pastries come out of the oven, pour the cooled syrup over the top.

Leave them to cool completely before cutting each roll into five pieces.

NOTE: Kataifi, a shredded pastry that is pronounced kah-tah-ee-fee, is available from Greek delicatessens and other speciality food stores. It is very important that the syrup is cooled and the kataifi is hot when pouring the syrup over, otherwise the liquid will not be absorbed as well or as evenly. These pastries will keep for up to a week if you cover them. Don't refrigerate them.

galaktoboureko (custard pie)

✳ ✳

Preparation time: **40 minutes**
Cooking time: **1 hour**
Serves **6–8**

1 vanilla bean, halved lengthways
750 ml (26 fl oz/3 cups) milk
110 g (3¾ oz) caster (superfine) sugar
110 g (3¾ oz) semolina
1 tablespoon finely grated lemon zest
1 cinnamon stick
40 g (1½ oz) unsalted butter, cubed

4 large eggs, lightly beaten
12 sheets filo pastry
60 g (2¼ oz) unsalted butter,
    extra, melted

SYRUP
80 g (2¾ oz) caster (superfine) sugar
½ teaspoon ground cinnamon
1 tablespoon lemon juice
5 cm (2 inch) strip lemon zest

1 Scrape the vanilla bean seeds into a saucepan. Add the bean, milk, sugar, semolina, lemon zest and cinnamon stick and gently bring to the boil, stirring constantly. Reduce the heat to low and simmer for 2 minutes so the mixture thickens. Remove from the heat. Stir in the butter. Cool for 10 minutes, then remove the cinnamon stick and vanilla bean and gradually mix in the egg. Preheat the oven to 180°C (350°F/Gas 4).

2 Cover the filo with a damp tea towel (dish towel). Remove a sheet, brush one side with melted butter and place, buttered side down, in a 20 x 30 cm (8 x 12 inch) baking tin. The filo will overlap the edges. Repeat with five more sheets, buttering each as you go.

3 Pour the custard over the filo and cover with the remaining pastry, brushing each sheet with butter as you go. Brush

Gradually mix the beaten egg into the mixture.

Use a small sharp knife to trim the pastry.

the top with butter. Using a small sharp knife, trim the pastry to the edges of the tin. Bake for 40–45 minutes, or until the custard has puffed up and set and the pastry is golden brown. Leave to cool.

4 Mix all the syrup ingredients with 80 ml (2½ fl oz/⅓ cup) water in a saucepan. Slowly bring to the boil, then reduce the heat to low and simmer for 10 minutes. The syrup will thicken. Remove from the heat and cool for 10 minutes. Remove the lemon zest.

5 If the filo has risen above the edges of the tin, flatten the top layer with your hand, then pour the syrup over the pie. This will prevent the syrup running over the sides of the tin. Allow to cool again before serving.

melomakarona (honey biscuits)

❄ ❄

Preparation time: **20 minutes**
Cooking time: **40 minutes**
Makes **20**

210 g (7½ oz/1⅔ cups) plain
    (all-purpose) flour
1 teaspoon baking powder
1 tablespoon finely grated orange zest
1 teaspoon ground cinnamon
60 g (2¼ oz/½ cup) walnuts,
    finely chopped
60 g (2¼ oz) unsalted butter, softened
55 g (2 oz/¼ cup) caster (superfine) sugar
60 ml (2 fl oz/¼ cup) olive oil
60 ml (2 fl oz/¼ cup) orange juice

SYRUP
75 g (2¾ oz) caster (superfine) sugar
2 tablespoons honey
1 teaspoon ground cinnamon
2 tablespoons orange juice

1 Preheat the oven to 180°C (350°F/ Gas 4). Line a baking tray with baking paper. Sift the flour and baking powder into a bowl. Mix in the orange zest,

cinnamon and half the walnuts. Cream the butter and sugar in another bowl using electric beaters until pale and fluffy. Mix the oil and orange juice and add, a little at a time, to the butter and sugar mixture, whisking constantly.

2 Mix the flour mixture into the butter mixture, in two batches, then bring the dough together with your hands. Shape tablespoons of dough into balls and place on the tray. Flatten slightly and bake for 20–25 minutes, until golden. Allow the biscuits to cool on the tray.

3 To make the syrup, mix all the ingredients with 60 ml (2 fl oz/¼ cup) water and the remaining walnuts in a small saucepan. Bring to the boil over medium heat and stir until the sugar has dissolved, then reduce the heat to low and simmer for 10 minutes. The syrup will thicken. Using a slotted spoon, dip a few biscuits at a time in the hot syrup. Use another spoon to baste them, then transfer to a plate.

tsoureki tou paska (easter bread)

✳ ✳

Preparation time: **35 minutes**
   + 1 hour 40 minutes proving time
Cooking time: **45 minutes**
Makes **1** loaf

2 teaspoons dried yeast
125 ml (4 fl oz/½ cup) milk
60 g (2¼ oz) butter
55 g (2 oz/¼ cup) caster
   (superfine) sugar
1 teaspoon finely grated orange zest
375 g (13 oz/3 cups) strong white flour
1 teaspoon ground aniseed
1 egg, lightly beaten

TOPPING
1 egg, lightly beaten
1 tablespoon milk
1 tablespoon sesame seeds
1 tablespoon chopped slivered almonds
1 tablespoon caster (superfine) sugar

1 Place the yeast and 2 tablespoons warm water in a small bowl and stir well. Leave in a warm, draught-free place for 10 minutes, or until bubbles appear on the surface. The mixture should be frothy and slightly increased in volume. If your yeast doesn't foam, it is dead, so you will have to discard it and start again.

2 Combine the milk, butter, sugar, orange zest and ½ teaspoon salt in a small saucepan. Heat until the butter has melted and the milk is just warm. Sift 310 g (11 oz/2½ cups) of the flour and the ground aniseed into a large bowl. Make a well in the centre, add the yeast and the milk mixtures, then the egg. Gradually beat into the flour for 1 minute, or until a smooth dough forms.

3 Turn out onto a lightly floured surface. Knead for 10 minutes, incorporating the remaining flour, or until smooth and elastic. Place in an oiled bowl and brush the surface with oil. Cover with plastic wrap and leave in a warm, draught-free place for 1 hour, or until well risen.

4 Lightly grease a baking tray. Punch down the dough (one punch with your fist) and knead for 1 minute. Divide the dough into three equal pieces. Roll each portion into a sausage 35 cm (14 inches) long. Plait the strands and fold the ends under. Place on the tray.

5 To make the topping, combine the egg and milk and brush over the dough. Sprinkle with the sesame seeds, almonds and sugar (if using dyed eggs, push them into the dough — see Note). Cover with

lightly oiled plastic wrap and leave in a warm, draught-free place for 40 minutes, or until the dough is well risen.

6 Preheat the oven to 180°C (350°F/ Gas 4). Bake for 30–40 minutes, or until cooked. The bread should sound hollow when tapped on the base.

NOTE: Use Greek red dye, available in some Greek speciality food stores, which comes with easy-to-follow instructions for dyeing eggs.

halvas fourno (semolina cake)

✹ ✹

Preparation time: 20 minutes
Cooking time: 1 hour
Serves 6–8

125 g (4½ oz) unsalted butter, softened
185 g (6½ oz/¾ cup) caster (superfine)
    sugar
2 teaspoons finely grated lemon zest
3 eggs
185 g (6½ oz/1½ cups) semolina
125 g (4½ oz/1 cup) self-raising flour
125 ml (4 fl oz/½ cup) milk
80 g (2¾ oz/½ cup) blanched almonds,
    toasted and finely chopped
blanched flaked almonds,
    to decorate

SYRUP
625 g (1 lb 6 oz/2½ cups) sugar
2 tablespoons lemon juice

1 Preheat the oven to 170°C (325°F/
Gas 3). Grease a 20 x 30 cm (8 x 12 inch)
cake tin.
2 To make the syrup, dissolve the sugar
in 750 ml (26 fl oz/3 cups) water in a
saucepan over high heat. Add the lemon
juice and bring to the boil. Reduce the
heat and simmer for 20 minutes. Remove
from the heat and leave until cool.
3 Meanwhile, cream the butter, sugar
and lemon zest using electric beaters until
light and fluffy. Add the eggs one at a
time, beating well after each addition.
4 Sift together the semolina and
flour and fold into the butter mixture
alternately with the milk. Mix in the
chopped almonds, then spread the
mixture into the tin and arrange rows
of flaked almonds on top. Bake for
35–40 minutes, or until a skewer inserted
into the centre of the cake comes out
clean. Prick the surface with a fine skewer,
then pour the cooled syrup over the hot
cake. When the cake is cool, cut it into
squares or diamonds.

greek sweets

Fruit, rather than dessert, is usually served at the end of a Greek meal. The enormous selection of sweet pastries, biscuits and sweetmeats are instead eaten in the late afternoon, or for supper, before bed. They are a measure of hospitality as well as the cook's skill. Many, such as the Tsoureki tou paska (Easter bread), are associated with festive holidays. Greek halva differs from the halva you'll find in Middle Eastern countries, which is a confection that is made from ground sesame seeds and honey.

turkey

Turkish cuisine can hold its head up high as one of the foremost in the world. It owes this enviable reputation to the culinary expertise developed in the grand houses and palaces centuries ago. Here, a large number of chefs specialised in their own particular type of cooking and their skills were honed and passed down from generation to generation. Lamb is the basic meat and shish kebab and lamb pilaff are famous worldwide. Vegetables are very prominent in the cuisine and in some areas there is also abundant seafood. Staples are yoghurt and many breads, including pide and lavash. Coffee plays an important role in the culture, and coffee houses are a popular meeting place.

hummus (chickpea dip)

❋ ❋

Preparation time: 20 minutes
  + overnight soaking time
Cooking time: 1 hour 15 minutes
Makes 3 cups

220 g (7¾ oz/1 cup) dried chickpeas
2 tablespoons tahini
4 garlic cloves, crushed
2 teaspoons ground cumin
80 ml (2½ fl oz/⅓ cup) lemon juice
60 ml (2 fl oz/¼ cup) olive oil
large pinch of cayenne pepper
lemon juice, extra, optional
extra virgin olive oil, to garnish
paprika, to garnish
chopped flat-leaf (Italian) parsley,
  to garnish

1 Put the chickpeas in a bowl, add 1 litre (35 fl oz/4 cups) water and soak overnight. Drain and place in a large saucepan with 2 litres (70 fl oz/8 cups) water, or enough to cover the chickpeas by 5 cm (2 inches). Bring to the boil, then reduce the heat and simmer for 1 hour 15 minutes, or until the chickpeas are very tender. Skim any scum from the surface. Drain well, reserving the cooking liquid and leave until cool enough to handle. Pick through for any loose skins and discard them.
2 Combine the chickpeas, tahini, garlic, cumin, lemon juice, olive oil, cayenne pepper and 1½ teaspoons salt in a food processor until thick and smooth. With the motor running, gradually add enough of the reserved cooking liquid, about 185 ml (6 fl oz/¾ cup), to form a smooth creamy purée. Season with salt or some extra lemon juice, to taste.
3 Spread into shallow bowls or onto plates, drizzle with the extra virgin olive oil, sprinkle with the paprika and scatter the parsley over the top. Hummus is delicious served with warm pitta bread or pide (Turkish/flat bread).

walnut taratoor

❋

Preparation time: 5 minutes
Cooking time: nil
Serves 8

250 g (9 oz) walnuts
80 g (2¾ oz/1 cup) fresh white breadcrumbs
3 garlic cloves
60 ml (2 fl oz/¼ cup) white wine vinegar
250 ml (9 fl oz/1 cup) olive oil
chopped parsley, to garnish

1 Finely chop the walnuts in a blender or food processor. Set aside 1 teaspoon of the walnuts to garnish. Add the breadcrumbs, garlic, vinegar and 60 ml (2 fl oz/¼ cup) water to the rest and blend until the mixture is well combined.
2 With the motor running, gradually add the olive oil in a thin steady stream until smooth. Add a little more water if the sauce appears to be too thick. Season to taste, then transfer to a serving bowl and refrigerate until ready to serve.
3 Sprinkle with the combined reserved walnuts and parsley before serving.

NOTE: This is suitable for serving with seafood, salads, fried vegetables or bread. It can be made with almonds, hazelnuts or pine nuts instead of walnuts. Lemon juice can be substituted for the vinegar.

walnut taratoor

cucumber and yoghurt salad

Unlike the Greek tzatziki, this cucumber and yoghurt salad has only a small amount of garlic and is flavoured with dill instead of mint. It is very popular in Turkey. Coarsely grate or chop 1 large unpeeled cucumber into a colander, sprinkle with salt and set aside for 15–20 minutes. In a bowl, combine 500 g (1 lb 2 oz/2 cups) Greek-style yoghurt with 1 crushed garlic clove, 2 tablespoons chopped dill and 1 tablespoon white wine vinegar. Add the cucumber and season with salt and ground white pepper, to taste. Cover and refrigerate. If you are making this salad just before serving, you don't need to salt the cucumber. Serve drizzled with olive oil. Serves 6–8.

borek (turkish filo parcels)

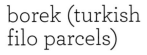

Preparation time: **30 minutes**
Cooking time: **20 minutes**
Makes **24**

400 g (14 oz) feta cheese
2 eggs, lightly whisked
2 large handfuls flat-leaf (Italian) parsley, chopped
375 g (13 oz) filo pastry
80 ml (2½ fl oz/⅓ cup) olive oil

1 Preheat the oven to 180°C (350°F/ Gas 4). Lightly grease a baking tray. Crumble the feta into a large bowl using your fingers. Mix in the egg and parsley and season with pepper.
2 Lay the filo pastry flat on a work surface and cover with a damp tea towel (dish towel) so it doesn't dry out. Remove one sheet at a time. Brushing each sheet lightly with olive oil, layer four sheets on top of one another. Cut the pastry into four 7 cm (2¾ inch) strips.
3 Put 2 heaped teaspoons of the feta mixture in one corner of each strip and fold diagonally, creating a triangular pillow. Put on the baking tray, seam side down, and brush with olive oil. Repeat with the remaining pastry and filling to make 24 parcels. Bake for 20 minutes, or until the pastry is golden and crisp.

feta

Feta cheese is traditionally made using sheep's or goat's milk, but these days milk from cows is more often used. Feta cheese is made in large blocks and cured and stored in brine. It develops a salty rich flavour and quite a crumbly texture.

reduce the heat and simmer for 20 minutes, or until reduced and pulpy. Stir in the parsley. Check the seasoning, and adjust according to your taste.
3 Meanwhile, cook the beans in a saucepan of boiling water for 3–4 minutes or until bright green and tender crisp. Drain, then serve immediately with the tomato mixture spooned over the top.

lubyi bi zayt

lubyi bi zayt (green beans with tomato and olive oil)

✤

Preparation time: **10 minutes**
Cooking time: **30 minutes**
Serves **4**

80 ml (2½ fl oz/⅓ cup) olive oil
1 large onion, chopped
3 garlic cloves, finely chopped

400 g (14 oz) tin chopped tomatoes
½ teaspoon sugar
3 tablespoons chopped flat-leaf
  (Italian) parsley
750 g (1 lb 10 oz) green beans, trimmed

1 Heat the olive oil in a large frying pan, add the onion and cook over medium heat for 4–5 minutes, until softened. Add the garlic and cook for another 30 seconds.
2 Add the tomatoes, sugar and 125 ml (4 fl oz/½ cup) water and season with salt and pepper. Bring to the boil, then

cauliflower fritters

✤ ✤

Preparation time: **10 minutes**
  + 30 minutes standing time
Cooking time: **15 minutes**
Serves **4–6**

600 g (1 lb 5 oz) cauliflower
55 g (2 oz/½ cup) besan flour
2 teaspoons ground cumin
1 teaspoon ground coriander
1 teaspoon ground turmeric
pinch of cayenne pepper
1 egg, lightly beaten
1 egg yolk
vegetable oil, for deep-frying

1 Cut the cauliflower into bite-sized florets. Sift the flour and spices into a bowl, then stir in ½ teaspoon salt.
2 Lightly whisk the beaten egg and egg yolk with 60 ml (2 fl oz/¼ cup) water in a jug. Make a well in the centre of the dry ingredients and then pour in the egg mixture, whisking until smooth. Stand for 30 minutes.
3 Fill a deep saucepan one-third full of oil and heat to 180°C (350°F), or until a cube of bread dropped into the oil browns in 15 seconds. Dip the florets in the batter, allowing the excess to drain back into the bowl. Deep-fry in batches for 3–4 minutes per batch, or until puffed and browned. Drain, sprinkle with salt and extra cayenne, if desired, and serve hot.

besan flour

This is made by very finely milling dried chickpeas. It originated in east Indian cuisine and is nutritious and high in protein. It has a fine texture and is a pale, creamy yellow.

It is used as an alternative to wheat flour in breads, noodles and dumplings, to thicken soups and sauces, and, most commonly, in batters for deep-fried foods.

sigara boregi (fried cigar pastries)

Preparation time: 30 minutes
Cooking time: 20 minutes
Makes 12

500 g (1 lb 2 oz) English spinach, trimmed
1 tablespoon olive oil
4 garlic cloves, crushed
200 g (7 oz) French shallots,
    finely chopped
75 g (2¾ oz/½ cup) crumbled
    feta cheese
1 egg, lightly whisked
3 tablespoons chopped flat-leaf (Italian)
    parsley
¼ teaspoon finely grated lemon zest
¼ teaspoon paprika
pinch of nutmeg
6 sheets filo pastry
125 g (4½ oz) butter, melted
light olive oil, for deep-frying

1 Wash the spinach, leaving a substantial amount of water on the leaves. Place in a large saucepan, cover and briefly cook over low heat until just wilted. Tip the spinach into a colander and press out most of the excess liquid with a wooden spoon. When cool, squeeze dry and chop.

2 Heat the olive oil in a frying pan, add the garlic and shallots and cook for 2 minutes, or until soft but not browned. Transfer to a bowl and add the feta, egg, parsley, spinach and lemon zest. Season with the paprika, nutmeg and salt and pepper, and mix well.

3 Remove a sheet of filo and cover the rest with a damp tea towel (dish towel) to prevent them drying out. Brush the filo sheet with melted butter, then fold it in half lengthways. It should measure about 12 x 32 cm (4½ x 13 inches). Cut it in half widthways. Brush with butter, place about 1 heaped tablespoon of filling at one end of each, shaping it to within 1 cm (½ inch) of each side. Fold the sides over to cover the ends of the filling, continuing the folds right up the length of the pastry. Brush with melted butter, then roll up tightly. Brush the outside with butter and seal well. Cover with a damp tea towel while you prepare the rest of the pastries.

4 Heat the light olive oil in a saucepan to 180°C (350°F), or until a cube of bread dropped into the oil browns in 15 seconds. Deep-fry the pastries in small batches until golden. Drain on paper towels and serve warm.

Place the filling on the filo pastry leaving a border.

Roll up the pastries tightly to enclose the filling.

imam bayildi (baked eggplant)

✹ ✹

Preparation time: **15 minutes**
Cooking time: **1 hour 10 minutes**
Serves **4–6**

185 ml (6 fl oz/¾ cup) olive oil
1 kg (2 lb 4 oz) eggplants (aubergines),
    cut in half lengthways
3 onions, thinly sliced
3 garlic cloves, finely chopped
400 g (14 oz) tin chopped tomatoes
2 teaspoons dried oregano
4 tablespoons chopped flat-leaf
    (Italian) parsley
35 g (1¼ oz/¼ cup) currants
¼ teaspoon ground cinnamon
2 tablespoons lemon juice
pinch of sugar
125 ml (4 fl oz/½ cup) tomato juice

1 Preheat the oven to 180° (350°F/
Gas 4). Heat half the oil in a large
heavy-based frying pan and cook the
eggplant, in batches, for 8–10 minutes,
until the cut sides are golden. Remove
from the pan and scoop out some of the
flesh, leaving the skins intact and some
flesh lining the skins. Finely chop the
scooped-out flesh and set aside.
2 Heat the remaining olive oil in the
same frying pan and cook the onion
over medium heat for 8 minutes, until
softened. Add the garlic and cook for
another minute. Add the tomatoes,
oregano, parsley, currants, cinnamon and
chopped eggplant and season to taste.
3 Place the eggplant shells in a large
ovenproof dish and fill each shell with
the tomato mixture.
4 Combine the lemon juice, sugar,
tomato juice and some salt and pour a
little over each eggplant. Cover with foil
and bake for 30 minutes, then uncover
and cook for 10 minutes more. To serve,
place the eggplants on a serving platter
and lightly drizzle with any remaining
juice. Serve at room temperature with
some crusty bread.

imam bayildi

Imam bayildi literally translates
as 'the priest fainted'. It is
possibly the most famous
eggplant dish and is eaten all
over the Arab world. Much
ambiguity surrounds the story
behind this dish. Did the priest
faint from over-indulging in his
sumptuous lunch or possibly
from the shock of the quantity
of expensive olive oil that is
used in the preparation of
the dish? This dish makes an
excellent first course.

chickpea salad with cumin dressing

✹ ✹

Preparation time: 20 minutes
 + 8 hours or overnight soaking time
Cooking time: 1 hour 30 minutes
Serves 6

220 g (7¾ oz/1 cup) dried chickpeas
3 tablespoons finely chopped flat-leaf
  (Italian) parsley
1 small red onion, finely chopped
1 garlic clove, finely chopped
60 ml (2 fl oz/¼ cup) lemon juice

2 tablespoons olive oil
½ teaspoon ground cumin
pinch of cayenne pepper

1 Soak the dried chickpeas in plenty
of cold water for 8 hours, or overnight.
Drain, put in a large saucepan, cover with
water and bring to the boil over high heat.
Reduce the heat to low and simmer for
1½ hours, topping up with water to keep
the chickpeas covered. Drain and cool.
2 Combine the chickpeas, parsley, onion,
garlic, lemon juice, olive oil, cumin,
cayenne pepper and ½ teaspoon each
of salt and freshly ground black pepper
in a large bowl.

zucchini patties

✹ ✹

Preparation time: 20 minutes
Cooking time: 15 minutes
Makes 16

300 g (10½ oz) zucchini (courgettes),
  coarsely grated
1 small onion, finely chopped
30 g (1 oz/¼ cup) self-raising flour
35 g (1¼ oz/⅓ cup) grated kefalotyri or
  parmesan cheese
1 tablespoon chopped mint
2 teaspoons chopped flat-leaf
  (Italian) parsley
pinch of ground nutmeg
25 g (¾ oz/¼ cup) dry breadcrumbs
1 egg, lightly beaten
olive oil, for shallow-frying

1 Put the zucchini and onion in the
centre of a clean tea towel (dish towel),
gather the corners together and twist as
tightly as possible to remove all the juices.
Combine the zucchini, onion, flour,
cheese, mint, parsley, nutmeg,
breadcrumbs and egg in a large bowl.
Season well with salt and cracked black
pepper, then mix with your hands to a
stiff mixture that clumps together.
2 Heat the oil in a large frying pan
over medium heat. When hot, drop
level tablespoons of the mixture into
the pan and shallow-fry in batches for
2–3 minutes, or until well browned all
over. Drain on paper towels and serve
hot, with lemon wedges or Cucumber
and yoghurt salad (page 55).

chickpea salad with cumin dressing

pomegranates

These are round fruit with a thin, leathery reddish skin. Each fruit has hundreds of tiny translucent rich red edible seeds. The seeds can be eaten as a fruit, or used as a beautiful garnish for either sweet or savoury dishes. They have a delicious and interesting sweet and tart flavour.

green olive, walnut and pomegranate salad

☀

Preparation time: 10 minutes
Cooking time: nil
Serves 4

1 large red onion, chopped
100 g (3½ oz/1 cup) walnut halves, lightly toasted
350 g (12 oz/2 cups) green olives, pitted and halved
175 g (6 oz/1 cup) pomegranate seeds
20 g (¾ oz) flat-leaf (Italian) parsley leaves

DRESSING
125 ml (4 fl oz/½ cup) olive oil
1½ tablespoons pomegranate syrup
½ teaspoon chilli flakes

1 To make the dressing, combine all the ingredients and mix thoroughly.
2 Put the onion, walnuts, olives, pomegranate seeds and parsley in a bowl and toss. Just before serving, pour over the dressing, season to taste, and toss well to combine.

creamy red lentil soup

☀ ☀

Preparation time: 25 minutes
Cooking time: 1 hour
Serves 6

1½ teaspoons cumin seeds
80 g (2¾ oz) butter
1 large brown onion, diced
185 g (6½ oz/¾ cup) red lentils, rinsed and drained
1.5 litres (52 fl oz/6 cups) vegetable stock
2 tablespoons plain (all-purpose) flour
2 egg yolks
185 ml (6 fl oz/¾ cup) milk

CROUTONS
4 thick bread slices, crusts removed
60 g (2¼ oz) butter
1 tablespoon vegetable oil

1 To make the croutons, cut the bread into 1 cm (½ inch) cubes. Heat the butter and oil in a frying pan and when the butter foams, add the bread and cook over medium heat until golden and crisp. Drain on crumpled paper towels.
2 In a small frying pan, dry roast the cumin seeds until aromatic. Leave to cool, then grind to a fine powder using a mortar and pestle.
3 Melt half the butter in a heavy-based saucepan and cook the onion over medium heat for 8 minutes, until softened. Add the lentils, cumin and stock and bring to the boil. Cover and simmer for 30–35 minutes, until the lentils are very soft. Allow to cool slightly before transferring to a food processor and blending, in batches, until smooth.
4 In a large heavy-based saucepan, melt the remaining butter over low heat. Stir in the flour and cook for 2–3 minutes, or until pale and foaming. Stirring constantly, add the lentil purée gradually, then simmer for 4–5 minutes.

green olive, walnut and pomegranate salad

5 In a small bowl, combine the egg yolks and milk. Whisk a small amount of the soup into the egg mixture, then return it all to the soup, stirring constantly. Season to taste. Don't let the soup boil as the egg will curdle. Heat the soup to just under boiling and serve with the croutons.

yoghurt soup

Preparation time: **15 minutes**
Cooking time: **20 minutes**
Serves 4–6

1.5 litres (52 fl oz/6 cups) vegetable stock
70 g (2½ oz/⅓ cup) medium-grain
    white rice
80 g (2¾ oz) butter
50 g (1¾ oz) plain (all-purpose) flour
250 g (9 oz/1 cup) plain yoghurt
1 egg yolk
1 tablespoon thinly sliced mint leaves
¼ teaspoon cayenne pepper

1 Put the stock and rice in a saucepan and bring to the boil over high heat. Reduce the heat to low–medium and simmer for 10 minutes, then remove from the heat and set aside.
2 Melt 60 g (2¼ oz) of the butter in another saucepan over low heat. Stir in the flour and cook for 2–3 minutes, or until pale and foaming. Gradually add the stock and rice mixture, stirring constantly, and cook over medium heat for 2 minutes, or until the mixture thickens slightly. Reduce the heat to low.
3 In a small bowl, whisk together the yoghurt and egg yolk, then gradually pour into the soup, stirring constantly. Remove from the heat and stir in the mint and ½ teaspoon salt.
4 Just before serving, melt the remaining butter in a small saucepan over medium heat. Add the cayenne pepper and cook until the mixture is lightly browned. Pour over the soup and serve.

yoghurt

Thousands of years ago, nomadic Balkan tribesmen accidentally developed yoghurt and it became a way of preserving milk. Today, yoghurt is made by introducing non-harmful bacteria to milk, which causes it to ferment and coagulate, resulting in a creamy-textured yoghurt with a slightly sharp flavour.

skewered swordfish

2 Thread the fish onto six metal skewers and cook on a hot chargrill or barbecue grill for 5 minutes, turning and brushing with the marinade several times, or until the fish is just cooked.

3 Meanwhile, to make the lemon sauce, combine all the ingredients in a screw-top jar, seal and then shake several times. Serve over the fish.

NOTE: You can substitute any firm fish such as blue eye, hake or mahi mahi, or use prawns (shrimp).

hunkar begendi (lamb braise with eggplant cream)

❀ ❀

Preparation time: **30 minutes**
Cooking time: **1 hour 50 minutes**
Serves **6–8**

2 tablespoons olive oil
1 kg (2 lb 4 oz) boneless lamb, cut into 2 cm (¾ inch) cubes
1 large onion, chopped
1 bay leaf
small pinch of ground cloves
2 garlic cloves, crushed
2 tablespoons tomato paste (concentrated purée)
400 g (14 oz) tin chopped tomatoes
30 g (1 oz/1 cup) chopped flat-leaf (Italian) parsley
750 ml (26 fl oz/3 cups) beef stock
125 g (4½ oz) vine-ripened tomatoes, chopped
chopped flat-leaf (Italian) parsley, to garnish

EGGPLANT CREAM
1 kg (2 lb 4 oz) eggplants (aubergines)
60 g (2¼ oz) butter
2½ tablespoons plain (all-purpose) flour
310 ml (10¾ fl oz/1¼ cups) pouring (whipping) cream
60 g (2¼ oz/⅔ cup) grated kasseri cheese (see Note)
large pinch of ground nutmeg

skewered swordfish

❀ ❀

Preparation time: **15 minutes**
 + 3 hours marinating time
Cooking time: **10 minutes**
Serves **6**

1.5 kg (3 lb 5 oz) swordfish, cut into 3 cm (1¼ inch) cubes

MARINADE
80 ml (2½ fl oz/⅓ cup) lemon juice
2 tablespoons olive oil
1 small red onion, thinly sliced
1 teaspoon paprika
2 fresh bay leaves, crumpled
10 sage leaves, torn

LEMON SAUCE
60 ml (2 fl oz/¼ cup) olive oil
60 ml (2 fl oz/¼ cup) lemon juice
3 tablespoons chopped flat-leaf (Italian) parsley

1 Combine the marinade ingredients with 1 teaspoon salt and some freshly ground black pepper in a bowl. Add the fish, toss to coat with the marinade, then cover and refrigerate for 3 hours, turning the fish occasionally.

1 Heat the olive oil in a large saucepan over high heat and cook the lamb in three batches for 4–5 minutes, or until well browned. Remove from the pan using a slotted spoon and set aside.

2 Add the onion to the pan and cook for 5 minutes or until golden, then stir in the bay leaf, cloves, garlic, tomato paste, tomatoes, parsley, stock and lamb. Bring to the boil, then reduce the heat to low, cover and simmer, stirring occasionally, for 1½ hours, or until the lamb is very tender and the sauce is thick. Season.

3 Meanwhile, preheat the oven to 200°C (400°F/Gas 6). Pierce the eggplants a few times with a fork and, using a long-handled fork, roast them over an open flame (either a gas stovetop or a barbecue) for about 5 minutes, turning occasionally, until blackened and blistered all over. This will give them a good smoky flavour. Place the eggplants in a baking tray and bake for about 30 minutes, or until shrivelled and the flesh is very soft. Transfer to a colander and leave to cool.

4 When they are cool, peel the eggplants, ensuring all the skin is removed and discarded. Chop the flesh and set aside. Melt the butter in a saucepan over medium heat and add the flour. Stir for 2–3 minutes, or until it has a toasty aroma and darkens slightly. Gradually pour in the cream, whisking until smooth, then add the eggplant and combine. Add the cheese and nutmeg and stir until the cheese has melted. Season.

5 Spread the eggplant cream over serving plates, then place the lamb braise in the centre and sprinkle with the chopped tomato and parsley. Serve immediately.

NOTE: Kasseri cheese, available at specialist delicatessens, is a sheep's or goat's milk cheese, often used on top of traditional Turkish lamb stews.

Peel the cooled eggplants, ensuring all the skin is removed.

Stir the butter and flour over medium heat until it has a toasty aroma and darkens slightly.

circassian chicken

Circassian chicken comes from the culinary legacy of the Circassian women who were part of the sultan's harem during the days of the Ottoman Empire. Noted for their gastronomic skills as well as their beauty, the Circassians contributed this dish, which bears their name and has become a classic fixture in Turkish cuisine.

cerkes tavugu (circassian chicken)

☀ ☀

Preparation time: 25 minutes
Cooking time: 1 hour
Serves 6

2 teaspoons paprika
¼ teaspoon cayenne pepper
1 tablespoon walnut oil
4 chicken breasts, on the bone
4 chicken wings
1 large onion, chopped
2 celery stalks, coarsely chopped
1 carrot, chopped

1 bay leaf
4 parsley sprigs
1 thyme sprig
6 black peppercorns
1 teaspoon coriander seeds
250 g (9 oz) walnuts, toasted (see Note)
2 slices of white bread, crusts removed
1 tablespoon paprika, extra
4 garlic cloves, crushed

1 Place the paprika and cayenne pepper in a small dry frying pan and heat over low heat for about 2 minutes, or until aromatic, then add the walnut oil to the pan and set aside until ready to use.
2 Put the chicken in a large saucepan with the onion, celery, carrot, bay leaf, parsley, thyme, peppercorns and coriander seeds. Add 1 litre (35 fl oz/4 cups) water and bring to the boil, then reduce the heat to low and simmer for 15–20 minutes, or until the chicken is tender. Remove from the heat and allow to cool in the stock. Remove the chicken and return the stock to the heat. Simmer for 20–25 minutes, or until the stock is reduced by half. Strain, skim off the fat and reserve the stock. Remove the chicken skin and shred the flesh into bite-sized pieces. Season well and ladle some stock over the chicken to moisten it. Set aside.
3 Reserve a few of the walnuts to use as a garnish and blend the rest in a food processor to form a rough paste. Combine the bread with 125 ml (4 fl oz/½ cup) stock, add to the food processor and mix in short bursts for several seconds. Add the extra paprika, the garlic and some salt and pepper and process until smooth. Gradually add 250 ml (9 fl oz/1 cup) warm chicken stock until the mixture is of a smooth pourable consistency, adding a little more stock if necessary.
4 Mix half the sauce with the chicken and place on a serving platter. Pour the rest over to cover, then sprinkle with the spiced oil and the remaining walnuts. Serve at room temperature.

NOTE: It is best to use Californian walnuts when making this recipe as they are much less bitter than some.

pistachio nuts

These nuts have a hard, pale shell enclosing a pink-blushed green kernel that is greatly prized around the world. As these nuts mature, the shells open slightly, revealing kernels with a delicate flavour. They are eaten roasted and salted, or used in cooking in both sweet and savoury dishes.

lamb pilaff

Preparation time: 25 minutes
+ 1 hour standing time
Cooking time: 45 minutes
Serves 4–6

1 large eggplant (aubergine), about 500 g (1 lb 2 oz), cut into 1 cm (½ inch) cubes
125 ml (4 fl oz/½ cup) olive oil
1 large onion, finely chopped
2 teaspoons ground cumin
1 teaspoon ground cinnamon
1 teaspoon ground coriander
300 g (10½ oz) long-grain white rice
500 ml (17 fl oz/2 cups) chicken or vegetable stock
500 g (1 lb 2 oz) minced (ground) lamb
½ teaspoon ground allspice
2 tablespoons olive oil, extra
2 vine-ripened tomatoes, cut into wedges
3 tablespoons toasted pistachio nuts
2 tablespoons currants
2 tablespoons chopped coriander (cilantro) leaves, to garnish (optional)

1 Place the eggplant in a colander, sprinkle generously with salt and leave for 1 hour. Rinse well and squeeze dry in a clean tea towel (dish towel). Heat 2 tablespoons of the oil in a large, deep frying pan with a lid, add the eggplant and cook over medium heat for 8–10 minutes, or until golden and cooked through. Drain on paper towels.

2 Heat the remaining oil, add the onion and cook for 4–5 minutes, or until soft but not brown. Stir in half of each of the cumin, cinnamon and ground coriander. Add the rice and stir to coat, then add the stock, season and bring to the boil.

Reduce the heat and simmer, covered, for 15 minutes or until the rice is tender, adding a little more water if the pilaff starts to dry out.

3 Meanwhile, place the lamb in a bowl with the allspice and the remaining cumin, cinnamon and ground coriander. Season and mix well. Roll into balls the size of macadamia nuts. Heat the extra oil in the frying pan and cook the meatballs in batches over medium–high heat for 5 minutes each batch, or until lightly browned and cooked through. Drain on paper towels. Add the tomato to the pan and cook, turning, for 3–5 minutes, or until lightly golden. Remove from the pan.

4 Gently stir the eggplant, pistachios, currants and meatballs through the rice. Serve the pilaff surrounded by the tomato wedges and sprinkled with the coriander leaves, if desired.

turkish bread

✳ ✳ ✳

Preparation time: 30 minutes
+ 1 hour 30 minutes proving time
Cooking time: 40 minutes
Makes 3 loaves

1 tablespoon dried yeast
½ teaspoon sugar
60 g (2¼ oz/½ cup) plain
   (all-purpose) flour
440 g (15½ oz/3½ cups) strong white flour

80 ml (2½ fl oz/⅓ cup) olive oil
1 egg, lightly beaten with 2 teaspoons
   water
nigella or sesame seeds, to sprinkle

1 Put the yeast, sugar and 125 ml
(4 fl oz/½ cup) warm water in a small
bowl and stir well. Add a little of the flour
and mix to a paste. Leave in a warm,
draught-free place for 10 minutes, or
until bubbles appear on the surface. The
mixture should be frothy and slightly
increased in volume.

turkish bread

2 Put the remaining flours in a large
bowl with 1½ teaspoons salt and make a
well in the centre. Add the yeast mixture,
olive oil and 250 ml (9 fl oz/1 cup) warm
water. Mix to a rough dough, then turn
out onto a floured surface and knead for
5 minutes. Add minimal flour as the
dough should remain damp and springy.
3 Shape the dough into a ball and place
in a large oiled bowl. Cover with plastic
wrap or a damp tea towel (dish towel)
and leave in a warm, draught-free place
for 1 hour to triple in size. Punch down
and divide into three. Knead each portion
for 2 minutes and shape each into a ball.
Cover with plastic wrap or a damp tea
towel and leave for 10 minutes.
4 Roll each portion of dough into a
rectangle 15 x 35 cm (6 x 14 inches).
Cover with damp tea towels and leave in
a warm place for 20 minutes. Indent all
over the surface with your fingers, brush
with egg glaze and sprinkle with seeds.
Preheat the oven to 220°C (425°F/Gas 7).
5 For the best results, bake each loaf
separately. Place a baking tray in the oven
for a couple of minutes until hot, remove
and sprinkle lightly with flour. Place one
portion of dough on the hot tray and bake
for 10–12 minutes, or until puffed and
golden brown. Wrap in a clean tea towel
to soften the crust and set aside to cool.
Meanwhile, repeat baking the remaining
portions of dough.

turkish pizza

✳ ✳ ✳

Preparation time: 25 minutes
+ 1 hour proving time
Cooking time: 45 minutes
Makes 8

1 teaspoon dried yeast
½ teaspoon sugar
225 g (8 oz) plain (all-purpose) flour
80 ml (2½ fl oz/⅓ cup) olive oil
250 g (9 oz) onions, finely chopped
500 g (1 lb 2 oz) minced (ground) lamb
2 garlic cloves, crushed
1 teaspoon ground cinnamon

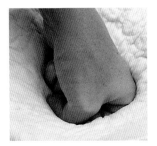

Knock down the dough, then turn onto a floured surface.

Divide the lamb among the ovals of dough and sprinkle the pine nuts over the top.

1½ teaspoons ground cumin
½ teaspoon cayenne pepper
60 g (2¼ oz/¼ cup) tomato paste (concentrated purée)
400 g (14 oz) tin chopped tomatoes
50 g (1¾ oz/⅓ cup) pine nuts
3 tablespoons chopped coriander (cilantro) leaves
Greek-style yoghurt, to serve

1 Mix the yeast, sugar and 60 ml (2 fl oz/ ¼ cup) warm water in a bowl. Leave in a warm, draught-free place for 10 minutes, or until bubbles appear on the surface. The mixture should be frothy and slightly increased in volume.
2 Sift the flour and 1 teaspoon salt into a bowl and stir in the yeast mixture, along with 1 tablespoon of the oil and 100 ml (3½ fl oz) warm water. Mix to form a soft dough, then turn onto a floured board and knead for 10 minutes, or until smooth. Place in an oiled bowl, cover and leave in a warm, draught-free place for 1 hour, or until doubled in size.
3 Heat 2 tablespoons of the oil in a frying pan over low heat and cook the onion for 5 minutes, or until soft but not golden. Add the lamb and cook for 10 minutes, or until brown. Add the garlic and spices, tomato paste and tomatoes. Cook for 15 minutes, until quite dry. Add half the pine nuts and 2 tablespoons of the coriander. Season, then leave to cool.
4 Preheat the oven to 210°C (415°F/ Gas 6–7). Grease two baking trays.

5 Knock down the dough, then turn out onto a floured surface. Form into eight portions and then roll each into a 12 x 18 cm (4½ x 7 inch) oval. Place on the trays. Divide the lamb mixture evenly among them and spread, leaving a small border. Sprinkle with the remaining pine nuts. Brush the edges with oil. Roll the uncovered dough over to cover the outer edges of the filling. Pinch the sides together at each end. Brush with oil. Bake for 15 minutes, or until golden. Sprinkle with the remaining coriander and serve with the yoghurt.

turkish delight

☀ ☀

Preparation time: 10 minutes
Cooking time: 1 hour
Makes 25

880 g (1 lb 15 oz/4 cups) sugar
125 g (4½ oz/1 cup) cornflour
    (cornstarch)
1 teaspoon cream of tartar
2 tablespoons rosewater
red food colouring
40 g (1½ oz/⅓ cup) icing
    (confectioners') sugar

1 Bring 625 ml (21½ fl oz/2½ cups) water to the boil in a large heavy-based saucepan. Add the sugar and stir until thoroughly dissolved. Remove from the heat and set aside.

2 In a large bowl, blend the cornflour, cream of tartar and 250 ml (9 fl oz/1 cup) cold water. Gradually add the blended cornflour to the sugar syrup, then return the saucepan to medium heat and stir until the mixture boils.

3 Reduce the heat and cook over low hear for 45 minutes, stirring often. The colour will change from cloudy to clear and golden, and the mixture will thicken.

4 Add the rosewater and a few drops of food colouring. Pour onto a lightly oiled 20 x 30 cm (8 x 12 inch) baking tray and leave to set. When firm and cool, cut into 2 cm (¾ inch) squares and toss in the icing sugar to coat.

figs in honey syrup

☀ ☀

Preparation time: 20 minutes
Cooking time: 1 hour
Serves 4

100 g (3½ oz) blanched whole almonds
12 fresh figs (about 750 g/1 lb 10 oz)
125 g (4½ oz/½ cup) sugar
115 g (4 oz/⅓ cup) honey
2 tablespoons lemon juice
6 cm (2½ inch) strip lemon zest
1 cinnamon stick
250 g (9 oz/1 cup) Greek-style yoghurt

1 Preheat the oven to 180°C (350°F/ Gas 4). Place the almonds on a baking tray and bake for 5 minutes, or until golden. Leave to cool. Cut the stems off the figs and make a small crossways incision 5 mm (¼ inch) deep on top of each. Push a blanched almond into the base of each fig. Roughly chop the remaining almonds.

2 Place 750 ml (26 fl oz/3 cups) water in a large saucepan, add the sugar and stir over medium heat until the sugar has dissolved. Increase the heat and bring to the boil. Stir in the honey, lemon juice, lemon zest and cinnamon stick. Reduce the heat to medium, place the figs in the pan and simmer gently for 30 minutes. Remove the figs with a slotted spoon and place on a large serving dish.

3 Boil the liquid over high heat for about 15–20 minutes, or until thick and syrupy. Remove the cinnamon stick and lemon zest. Cool the syrup slightly and pour over the figs. Sprinkle with chopped almonds and serve warm or cold with yoghurt.

yogurt tatlisi (yoghurt cake with syrup)

Preparation time: 20 minutes
Cooking time: 50 minutes
Serves 8–10

185 g (6½ oz) unsalted butter, softened
250 g (9 oz/1 cup) caster (superfine) sugar
5 eggs, separated
250 g (9 oz/1 cup) Greek-style yoghurt
2 teaspoons finely grated lemon zest
½ teaspoon natural vanilla extract
280 g (10 oz/2¼ cups) plain (all-purpose) flour
½ teaspoon bicarbonate of soda (baking soda)
2 teaspoons baking powder
whipped cream, to serve

SYRUP
250 g (9 oz/1 cup) caster (superfine) sugar
1 cinnamon stick
4 cm (1½ inch) strip lemon zest
1 tablespoon lemon juice

1 Preheat the oven to 180°C (350°F/ Gas 4) and lightly grease a 10 x 20 cm (4 x 8 inch) loaf (bar) tin.

2 Cream the butter and sugar in a bowl using electric beaters until light and fluffy. Add the egg yolks one at a time, beating well after each addition. Stir in the yoghurt, lemon zest and vanilla. Fold in the sifted flour, bicarbonate of soda and baking powder with a metal spoon.

3 Whisk the egg whites in a clean, dry bowl until stiff and gently fold into the mixture. Spoon into the tin and bake for 50 minutes, or until a skewer comes out clean when inserted into the centre of the cake. Cool in the tin for 10 minutes, then turn out onto a wire rack.

4 Meanwhile, for the syrup, place the sugar and cinnamon stick in a small saucepan with 185 ml (6 fl oz/¾ cup) cold water. Stir over medium heat until the sugar has dissolved. Bring to the boil, add the lemon zest and juice, then reduce the heat and simmer for 5–6 minutes. Strain, then pour the syrup all over the hot cake and wait for most of it to be absorbed before serving. Cut the cake into slices and serve warm with a dollop of whipped cream on top.

turkish coffee

Place 2 tablespoons finely ground coffee beans, 2 teaspoons caster (superfine) sugar, or to taste, and 1 lightly crushed cardamom pod in a small saucepan with 250 ml (9 fl oz/ 1 cup) cold water. Stir over medium heat until the coffee starts to rise to the surface. Remove from the heat immediately. Spoon the froth (or the crema) into 2 small cups and return the pan to the heat. When the coffee starts to rise to the top again, remove from the heat and fill the cups. The key sign of a good Turkish coffee is the creamy froth. Serves 2.

baklava

✹ ✹

Preparation time: **30 minutes**
Cooking time: **1 hour 15 minutes**
Makes **18 pieces**

540 g (1 lb 3 oz/2⅓ cups) caster (superfine) sugar, plus 2 tablespoons, extra
1½ teaspoons finely grated lemon zest
90 g (3¼ oz/¼ cup) honey
60 ml (2 fl oz/¼ cup) lemon juice
2 tablespoons orange flower water
200 g (7 oz) walnuts, finely chopped
200 g (7 oz) pistachio nuts, finely chopped
200 g (7 oz) blanched almonds, finely chopped
2 teaspoons ground cinnamon
200 g (7 oz) unsalted butter, melted
375 g (13 oz) filo pastry

1 Put the sugar, lemon zest and 375 ml (13 fl oz/1½ cups) water in a saucepan and stir over high heat until the sugar has dissolved, then boil for 5 minutes. Reduce the heat to low and simmer for a further 5 minutes, or until the syrup has thickened slightly and just coats the back of a spoon. Add the honey, lemon juice and orange flower water and cook for 2 minutes. Remove from the heat and leave to cool completely.
2 Preheat the oven to 170°C (325°F/ Gas 3). Combine the nuts, extra sugar and cinnamon in a bowl. Brush the base and sides of a 27 x 30 cm (10¾ x 12 inch) ovenproof dish or tin with the melted butter. Cover the base with a single layer of filo pastry and brush lightly with melted butter, folding in any overhanging edges. Keep the unused filo under a damp tea towel (dish towel). Continue layering

the filo, brushing each new layer with butter and folding in the edges until 10 sheets have been used.
3 Sprinkle half the nut mixture over the pastry and pat down evenly. Repeat the layering and buttering of five more filo sheets, sprinkle with the remaining nuts, then continue to layer and butter the remaining sheets, including the top layer. Press down with your hands so the pastry and nuts stick to each other. Using a large sharp knife, cut into diamond shapes, ensuring you cut through to the bottom layer. Pour any remaining butter evenly over the top and smooth with your hands. Bake for 30 minutes, then reduce the temperature to 150°C (300°F/Gas 2) and cook for another 30 minutes.
4 Immediately cut through the original diamond markings, then strain the syrup evenly over the top. Allow to cool

completely before lifting the diamonds out onto a serving platter.

NOTE: To achieve the right texture, it is important for the baklava to be piping hot and the syrup totally cooled when pouring the syrup over at the end.

semolina and nut diamonds

※ ※

Preparation time: 30 minutes
  + 30 minutes standing time
Cooking time: 25 minutes
Makes 12 pieces

115 g (4 oz) unsalted butter, softened
115 g (4 oz/½ cup) caster
  (superfine) sugar
125 g (4½ oz/1 cup) semolina
110 g (3¾ oz/1 cup) ground roasted
  hazelnuts
2 teaspoons baking powder
3 eggs, lightly beaten
1 tablespoon finely grated orange zest
2 tablespoons orange juice
whipped cream or honey-flavoured
  yoghurt, to serve

SYRUP
660 g (1 lb 7 oz/3 cups) sugar
4 cinnamon sticks
1 tablespoon thinly julienned
  orange zest
80 ml (2½ fl oz/⅓ cup) lemon juice
125 ml (4 fl oz/½ cup) orange flower water

TOPPING
60 g (2¼ oz/½ cup) slivered almonds
70 g (2½ oz/½ cup) roasted hazelnuts,
  roughly chopped

1 Preheat the oven to 210°C (415°F/ Gas 6–7). Lightly grease a 23 cm (9 inch) square baking tin and line the base with baking paper.
2 Cream the butter and caster sugar in a bowl until light and fluffy. Stir in the semolina, ground hazelnuts and baking powder. Add the egg, orange zest and orange juice and fold through until well combined. Spoon into the tin, smooth the surface and bake for 20 minutes, or until golden and just set. Leave in the tin.
3 Meanwhile, to make the syrup, put the sugar, cinnamon sticks and 800 ml (28 fl oz) water in a saucepan over low heat and stir until the sugar has dissolved. Increase the heat and boil rapidly, without stirring, for 5 minutes. Pour into a heatproof bowl, then return half to the saucepan. Boil for 15–20 minutes, or until the syrup has thickened and reduced to about 170 ml (5½ fl oz/⅔ cup). Stir in the julienned orange zest.

4 Add the lemon juice and orange flower water to the syrup in the bowl and pour it over the cake. When absorbed, turn the cake out onto a large flat plate. Slice into four equal strips, then slice each strip diagonally into three diamond-shaped pieces. Discard the end scraps but keep the pieces touching together.
5 To make the topping, combine the almonds and hazelnuts and scatter over the cake. Pour the thickened syrup and julienned orange zest over the nuts and set aside for 30 minutes before serving. Use a cake slice to transfer the diamonds to plates and serve with whipped cream or honey-flavoured yoghurt.

italy

Italians love good food. Friends and family often gather to share a feast. Their cooking is wonderfully uncomplicated and the versatile antipasto spreads have been embraced in many places outside Italy because of their simplicity. Italian cuisine has an interesting history as, traditionally, ingredients and cooking styles varied depending on the region. As recently as the 1950s, this was still the case. However, as people migrated within the country, so did food ideas and this has led to a wonderful mixed cuisine using polenta, risotto, fresh and dried pasta, olive oil, butter, pizza, tomatoes and eggplants (aubergines), as well as citrus, capers, parsley, basil and cheeses including the famous Parmigiano Reggiano.

zucchini (courgette) flowers

The delicate blossoms of the zucchini are very perishable and are best kept refrigerated on a plate under a moist paper towel. Choose flowers that are fresh and firm and check that they are clean and free of stray insects before use. There are male and female blossoms. The male is attached to the stem, while the female is attached to the zucchini.

bean and rosemary dip

☀

Preparation time: **5 minutes**
Cooking time: **5 minutes**
Makes **2 cups**

625 g (1 lb 6 oz) tin butterbeans
    (lima beans) or cannellini beans
60 ml (2 fl oz/¼ cup) olive oil
2 garlic cloves, crushed
1 tablespoon finely chopped rosemary
250 ml (9 fl oz/1 cup) chicken or
    vegetable stock
2 teaspoons lemon juice

1 Rinse and drain the beans and set aside. Heat the olive oil in a saucepan and cook the garlic and rosemary for 1 minute, or until the garlic is softened. Add the beans and stock and bring to the boil. Reduce the heat and simmer for 3–4 minutes. Allow to cool.
2 Blend or process the mixture in batches until smooth. Add the lemon juice and season, to taste. Serve with bread or grissini. This dip will keep, covered, in the refrigerator for several days.

stuffed zucchini (courgette) flowers

☀

Preparation time: **20 minutes**
Cooking time: **15 minutes**
Makes **20**

75 g (2½ oz) plain (all-purpose) flour
100 g (3½ oz) mozzarella cheese
10 anchovy fillets, halved lengthways
10 basil leaves, torn
20 zucchini (courgette) flowers, stems
    and pistils removed
olive oil, for shallow-frying
2 lemon wedges, to serve

1 In a bowl, combine the flour with about 250 ml (9 fl oz/1 cup) water, enough to obtain a creamy consistency. Add a pinch of salt and mix.
2 Cut the mozzarella into 20 matchsticks and pat dry the anchovies. Insert a piece of mozzarella, half an anchovy fillet and some basil into each zucchini flower. Press the petals closed.
3 Pour the oil into a heavy-based frying pan to a depth of 2.5 cm (1 inch). Heat until a drop of batter sizzles when dropped in the oil.
4 Dip one flower at a time in the batter, shaking off the excess. Cook in batches for 3 minutes, or until crisp and golden. Drain on paper towels. Season and serve immediately with lemon wedges.

bean and rosemary dip

roasted capsicums with anchovies

Preparation time: **15 minutes**
Cooking time: **50 minutes**
Serves **6**

3 yellow capsicums (peppers)
3 red capsicums (peppers)
2 tablespoons extra virgin olive oil
12 anchovy fillets, halved lengthways
3 garlic cloves, thinly sliced
2 tablespoons baby capers, rinsed and
    squeezed dry
25 g (1 oz/¼ cup) basil leaves, torn
extra virgin olive oil, extra, to serve
sea salt, for sprinkling

1 Preheat the oven to 180°C (350°F/ Gas 4). Cut each capsicum in quarters lengthways, leaving the stems intact. Remove the seeds and membrane. Drizzle a little of the oil in a baking dish and put the capsicums in, skin side down. Season.
2 Divide the anchovy fillets, garlic and capers among the capsicums. Sprinkle with some of the basil. Season and drizzle with the remaining oil.
3 Cover the dish with foil and bake the capsicums for 20 minutes. Remove the foil and cook for a further 25–30 minutes, or until the capsicums are tender. Drizzle with a little of the extra oil. Scatter the remaining basil over the capsicums, sprinkle with sea salt and serve warm or at room temperature.

mozzarella in carozza

Dip 8 thin slices of crustless, day-old white bread in 170 ml (5½ fl oz/⅔ cup) milk. Make 4 sandwiches, putting 2 slices of mozzarella between the bread. Lightly beat 2 eggs and season well with salt and pepper. Dip the sandwiches in the egg, then coat well with fresh breadcrumbs. Heat 250 ml (9 fl oz/1 cup) olive oil in a heavy-based frying pan over medium heat until hot and fry the sandwiches for 2–3 minutes on each side, or until the sandwiches are golden. Drain on crumpled paper towels and serve with lemon wedges. Makes 4.

arancini (fried stuffed rice balls)

☼ ☼

Preparation time: 30 minutes
  + 30 minutes chilling time
Cooking time: 40 minutes
Makes 12

500 g (1 lb 2 oz/2¼ cups) medium-grain
  white rice
¼ teaspoon saffron threads
2 eggs, beaten
100 g (3½ oz/1 cup) freshly grated
  parmesan cheese
plain (all-purpose) flour, for coating
2 eggs, beaten, extra
100 g (3½ oz/1 cup) dry breadcrumbs
vegetable oil, for deep-frying

FILLING
1 tablespoon olive oil
1 small onion, finely chopped
150 g (5½ oz) minced (ground) pork and
  veal or minced (ground) beef
170 ml (5½ fl oz/⅔ cup) white wine
1 tablespoon tomato paste
  (concentrated purée)
2 teaspoons thyme leaves

1 Bring 1 litre (35 fl oz/4 cups) water
to the boil in a large saucepan and add
the rice and saffron threads. Bring slowly
back to the boil, then reduce the heat to
low and simmer, covered, for 15 minutes,
or until the rice is tender. Transfer to a
large bowl and cool to room temperature.
Stir in the egg and parmesan.
2 Meanwhile, for the filling, heat the oil
in a small frying pan over medium heat.
Add the onion and cook for 2–3 minutes,
or until soft. Add the mince and cook
for 2 minutes, or until it changes colour,
pressing out any lumps. Add the wine
and tomato paste. Reduce the heat and
simmer for 3–4 minutes, or until the wine
has evaporated. Stir in the thyme and set
aside to cool.
3 With wet hands, divide the rice mixture
into 12 balls. Flatten each ball slightly,
make an indent in the centre and place

When cooking the mince, break up
any lumps with a wooden spoon.

Place 2 heaped teaspoons of filling
into the centre of each rice ball.

Enclose the rice around the filling,
gently pressing the rice back into
a ball shape.

Roll each ball in flour, then dip in
beaten egg before rolling in the
breadcrumbs.

2 heaped teaspoons of the filling into each ball. Close the rice around the filling.

4   Roll each ball in the flour, dip in the extra egg, then roll in the breadcrumbs. Refrigerate for 30 minutes.

5   Fill a deep, heavy-based saucepan one-third full of oil and heat to 180°C (350°F), or until a cube of bread dropped in the oil browns in 15 seconds. Deep-fry the balls in four batches for 2–3 minutes each, or until golden brown. Drain on crumpled paper towels. Serve warm or at room temperature.

asparagus

When buying fresh asparagus, make sure the tips of the spears are tightly closed and the stalk is firm and green with no tinges of yellow. Not all asparagus needs to be peeled, especially if thin, but if the stems are thick and woody, they should be trimmed and the bottom third of the stems peeled using a vegetable peeler. There is also a white asparagus, which takes longer to cook, and a purple variety called *viola*.

frittata di asparagi alla menta (asparagus and mint frittata)

Preparation time: **10 minutes**
Cooking time: **20 minutes**
Serves **4**

6 eggs
35 g (1¼ oz/⅓ cup) grated pecorino
   or parmesan cheese
1 handful mint leaves, finely shredded
200 g (7 oz) baby asparagus spears
2 tablespoons extra virgin olive oil

1   Put the eggs in a large bowl, beat well, then stir in the cheese and mint. Set aside.

2   Trim the woody parts from the asparagus, then cut the asparagus diagonally into 5 cm (2 inch) pieces. Heat the oil in a 20 cm (8 inch) frying pan. Add the asparagus and cook for 4–5 minutes, until tender and bright green. Season, then reduce the heat to low.

3   Pour the egg mixture over the asparagus and cook for 8–10 minutes. During cooking, use a spatula to gently pull the side of the frittata away from the side of the pan and tip the pan slightly so the egg runs underneath the frittata.

4   When the mixture is nearly set but still slightly runny on top, place the pan under a hot grill (broiler) for 1–2 minutes, until the top is set and just browned. Serve warm or at room temperature.

pancetta

Coming from the Italian word *pancia*, which means belly, pancetta is exactly the same cut of meat as bacon but it is not smoked. There are two types of pancetta: *pancetta stesa*, a flat type that is cured for about three weeks and then hung to air and dry for up to four months, and *pancetta arrotolata*, which is rolled into a salami-like shape. In the Italian kitchen, pancetta stesa is used to flavour sauces, stews and pastas, and the rolled pancetta is mainly used as part of an antipasto platter.

fried stuffed olives

✴ ✴ ✴

Preparation time: 45 minutes
Cooking time: 1 hour 15 minutes
Serves 6–8 (as part of an antipasto platter)

1 tablespoon olive oil
100 g (3½ oz) minced (ground) pork
   and veal
60 g (2¼ oz) pancetta, chopped
3 garlic cloves, crushed
½ tablespoon chopped flat-leaf (Italian)
   parsley
pinch of cayenne pepper
125 ml (4 fl oz/½ cup) dry white wine
500 ml (17 fl oz/2 cups) chicken stock
25 g (1 oz/⅓ cup) fresh white breadcrumbs
1 egg yolk
2 tablespoons grated provolone cheese
1 kg (2 lb 4 oz) extra-jumbo green olives
   (such as Gordal), pitted
60 g (2¼ oz/½ cup) plain (all-purpose) flour
1 egg, beaten
100 g (3½ oz/1 cup) dry breadcrumbs
vegetable oil, for deep-frying

1 Heat the oil in a frying pan over low heat and add the mince, pancetta, garlic and parsley. Cook, stirring, until the mince changes colour. Add the cayenne and season with salt and pepper. Increase the heat to high, pour in the wine and cook until almost evaporated. Add the stock, reduce the heat and simmer for 45 minutes, by which time the liquid should have evaporated. If not, increase the heat and reduce the mixture until dry.
2 Pass the meat mixture through a fine mincer, or process in a food processor until as smooth as possible. Stir in the fresh breadcrumbs, egg yolk and provolone. Using a piping (icing) bag fitted with a small round nozzle, pipe the filling into the olives. Roll the olives in the flour and shake off any excess. Roll in the beaten egg, then the dry breadcrumbs.
3 Fill a deep heavy-based saucepan one-third full of oil and heat to 180°C (350°F), or until a cube of bread dropped in the oil browns in 15 seconds. Deep-fry the olives in batches until golden. Drain on paper towels before serving.

stuffed sardines

✴ ✴

Preparation time: 20 minutes
Cooking time: 25 minutes
Serves 4–6

1 kg (2 lb 4 oz) butterflied fresh sardines
60 ml (2 fl oz/¼ cup) olive oil
40 g (1½ oz/½ cup) fresh white
   breadcrumbs
30 g (1 oz/¼ cup) sultanas (golden raisins)
40 g (1½ oz/¼ cup) pine nuts, toasted
20 g (¾ oz) tin anchovy fillets, drained
   and mashed
1 tablespoon finely chopped flat-leaf
   (Italian) parsley
2 spring onions (scallions), finely
   chopped

1 Preheat the oven to 200°C (400°F/ Gas 6). Grease a baking dish. Open out each sardine and place, skin side down, on a chopping board.

stuffed sardines

2 Heat half the oil in a frying pan. Add the breadcrumbs and cook over medium heat, stirring until light golden. Drain on paper towels.

3 Put half the fried breadcrumbs in a bowl and stir in the sultanas, pine nuts, anchovy, parsley and spring onion. Season with salt and pepper, to taste. Spoon about 2 teaspoons of the mixture into each sardine, then carefully fold up to enclose the stuffing.

4 Place the stuffed sardines in a single layer in the baking dish. Sprinkle any remaining stuffing over the top of the sardines, along with the remaining breadcrumbs. Drizzle with the remaining olive oil and bake for 15–20 minutes.

insalata caprese (tomato and bocconcini salad)

❋ ❋

Preparation time: **10 minutes**
Cooking time: **nil**
Serves **4**

3 large vine-ripened tomatoes
250 g (9 oz) bocconcini (fresh baby
    mozzarella cheese)
12 basil leaves
60 ml (2 fl oz/¼ cup) extra virgin olive oil

1 Slice the tomatoes into twelve 1 cm (½ inch) slices. Slice the bocconcini into 12 slices the same thickness as the tomato.

2 Arrange the tomato slices, basil leaves and bocconcini on a plate, alternating them as you go.

3 Drizzle with the extra virgin olive oil and season well.

NOTE: You could use whole cherry tomatoes and toss them with the bocconcini and basil.

tomato and bocconcini salad

This is a very popular summer salad in Italy. It is delicious made with buffalo mozzarella if you can find it. We've used bocconcini in this recipe as it is more readily available than very fresh mozzarella.

antipasto

Antipasto, probably the most modern aspect of the Italian table, means 'before the meal'. The variety and combinations of these small tasty, aromatic dishes are endless.

Antipasto dishes are still not usually part of the main family meal of the day, but a formal Italian dinner, particularly in wealthy households or at restaurants and weddings, usually begins with them. This flexibility and the fact that antipasto generally requires advance preparation makes it a perfect option when entertaining. You can mix and match to make an impressive banquet, a meal for two or a simple snack.

Antipasto dishes can range from a plate of sliced, cured meats, especially prosciutto and salamis, with fresh fruits in season such as figs or melons, to a warm frittata, a simple salad of tuna and beans or a plate of fried whitebait. Good-quality ingredients such as grilled marinated vegetables, fresh cheeses and marinated olives can supplement home-made dishes.

All of the dishes on pages 74 to 84 are classic antipasto recipes. It is easy to adjust the quantities to suit your needs. Although we have presented the following recipes in the book as main course side vegetables, they also make perfect choices for the antipasto table: Fennel fritters (page 104), Carciofi alla romana (page 107), Baked radicchio (page 109) and Green beans with garlic breadcrumbs (page 101).

The most important thing to remember when putting together a selection of antipasto is to use fresh seasonal produce. For example, to make the most of vine-ripened tomatoes, a typical summer selection might include Insalata caprese (page 79) and Panzanella (page 85). A winter selection might include such dishes as Bean and rosemary dip (page 74), Arancini (page 76), Roasted balsamic onions (page 82) and Shaved fennel salad (page 82). If you are including foods such as meats from the delicatessen, buy them from a reliable supplier with a good turnover.

Perhaps the most important ingredient on the antipasto table is olive oil. A drizzle of fruity extra virgin olive oil can transform even the most simple ingredient into a dish. Don't be tempted to compromise on the quality of the oil, because although they are significantly more expensive than regular olive oils, the difference in taste is enormous. If you use extra virgin olive oil only for dressing or drizzling over breads, and not for cooking, you will find that it goes a long way. Drizzle your good-quality extra virgin olive oil over a slice of rustic bread that has been rubbed with a piece of garlic and you have a simple yet flavoursome bruschetta. A plate of boiled vegetables such as globe artichokes becomes a meal when served with extra virgin olive oil, sea salt and cracked pepper.

The secret of all Italian cooking lies in the quality of the ingredients, rather than the complexity of the dish. Antipasto dishes reflect this only too well and are a perfect opportunity to make the most of really good quality, fresh seasonal produce with little (or no) fuss.

balsamic vinegar

This centuries-old speciality is produced in the province of Modena, just north of Bologna in Italy. It is made from boiled-down must, which is the concentrated sweet juice of white grapes. True balsamic vinegar is aged for decades in a succession of barrels, each made from a different wood to produce a syrupy sweet-and-sour liquid. Labelled *aceto balsamico tradizionale di Modena* and originally made only by wealthy families who could afford to wait for their vinegar to mature, much of what is available today is a far cry from the real thing and is consequently sold without the traditional label. True balsamic is used sparingly and in cooking should be put in at the very end so the aromas are present in the final dish.

roasted balsamic onions

Preparation time: 15 minutes
    + overnight marinating time
Cooking time: 1 hour 30 minutes
Serves 8 (as part of an antipasto platter)

1 kg (2 lb 4 oz) pickling onions, unpeeled (see Note)
185 ml (6 fl oz/¾ cup) balsamic vinegar
2 tablespoons soft brown sugar
185 ml (6 fl oz/¾ cup) olive oil

1 Preheat the oven to 160°C (315°F/ Gas 2–3). Bake the onions in a baking dish for 1½ hours. When cool enough to handle, trim off the stems and peel away the skin (the outer part of the root should come away but the onions will remain intact). Rinse a 1 litre (35 fl oz/4 cup) wide-necked jar with boiling water and then dry in a 120°C (235°F/Gas ½) oven (do not dry with a tea towel/dish towel). Add the onions to the jar.
2 Combine the vinegar and sugar in a small screw-top jar and stir to dissolve the sugar. Add the oil, seal the jar and shake vigorously until the mixture is combined.
3 Pour the vinegar mixture over the onions, seal, and turn upside down

to coat. Marinate overnight in the refrigerator, turning occasionally. Return to room temperature and shake to combine the dressing before serving.

NOTE: Pickling onions are very small. The ideal size is around 35 g (1¼ oz) each. Sizes will probably range from 20 g (¾ oz) up to 40 g (1½ oz). The cooking time given is suitable for this range and there is no need to cook the larger ones any longer than this. The marinating time given is a minimum time and the onions can be marinated for up to three days in the refrigerator. The marinade may separate after a few hours, which is fine — simply stir occasionally.

shaved fennel salad

Preparation time: 10 minutes
Cooking time: nil
Serves 4

2 fennel bulbs
extra virgin olive oil

1 Trim the fennel by cutting off the tops where they meet the bulb. Reserve any small green fronds and discard the tops. Remove any tough outer parts of the bulb that are bruised or discoloured. Remove 3 mm (⅛ inch) from the end and slice the bulb horizontally into paper-thin rings.
2 Soak the fennel slices in two changes of cold water for 5 minutes, then drain well and pat dry with paper towels or a clean tea towel (dish towel). Toss in a serving bowl with enough extra virgin olive oil to coat well. Season with salt and cracked black pepper, to taste.

roasted balsamic onions

seafood salad

✹ ✹

Preparation time: 45 minutes
   + 40 minutes marinating time
Cooking time: 25 minutes
Serves 4

500 g (1 lb 2 oz) small squid
1 kg (2 lb 4 oz) large clams (vongole)
1 kg (2 lb 4 oz) mussels
4 tablespoons chopped flat-leaf (Italian)
   parsley (reserve the stalks), plus extra,
   to garnish
500 g (1 lb 2 oz) raw prawns (shrimp),
   peeled and deveined, tails intact
2 tablespoons lemon juice
80 ml (2½ fl oz/⅓ cup) olive oil
1 garlic clove, crushed

1 To clean the squid, gently pull the tentacles away from the tube (the intestines should come away at the same time). Remove the intestines from the tentacles by cutting under the eyes, then remove the beak if it remains in the centre of the tentacles by using your fingers to push up the centre. Pull away the quill (the transparent cartilage) from inside the body and remove. Remove and discard any white membrane. Under cold running water, pull the skin from the tube. Rinse, then slice into 7 mm (⅜ inch) rings.
2 Scrub the clams and mussels and pull out the hairy beards. Discard any broken mussels, or open ones that don't close when tapped. Rinse well. Fill a large frying pan with 1 cm (½ inch) water, add the parsley stalks, cover the pan and bring the water to simmering point. Add the clams and mussels in batches, being careful not to overcrowd the pan. Cover and steam over high heat for 3–4 minutes, or until the shells begin to open. Remove with a slotted spoon and place in a colander over a bowl. Return any drained juices to the pan before cooking the next batch. Continue until all the clams and mussels are cooked. Reserve the cooking liquid. Allow the clams and mussels to cool before removing them from the shells. Discard any unopened ones.

3 Add 1 litre (35 fl oz/4 cups) water to the pan with the cooking liquid. Bring to the boil, then add the prawns and cook for 3–4 minutes, or until the water returns to the boil. Remove with a slotted spoon and drain in a colander. Add the squid and cook for 30–40 seconds, until the flesh becomes white and opaque. Remove immediately and drain.

4 Whisk the lemon juice, oil and garlic in a bowl, then season. Pour over the seafood with the chopped parsley, then toss. Adjust the seasoning if necessary. Marinate for 30–40 minutes to allow the flavours to develop. Sprinkle with extra parsley and serve with crusty bread.

mussels

Mussels attach themselves to rocks or, in the case of farmed mussels, to bags or ropes, with the tough brown fibres known as the 'beard'. Farmed mussels take up to two years to mature. When buying mussels, avoid any that have broken shells. Use soon after purchasing, or keep in a very cool place in a small amount of water, covered with a damp hessian bag. Do not use any mussels that are already open. When mussels are cooked, the shells should open. If they don't open after 3–4 minutes cooking, they should be thrown away.

baked eggplant with
tomato and mozzarella

baked eggplant with tomato and mozzarella

✹ ✹

Preparation time: 20 minutes
Cooking time: 40 minutes
Serves 6

6 large slender eggplants (aubergines),
   halved lengthways, leaving the stems
   attached
100 ml (3½ fl oz) olive oil
2 onions, finely chopped
2 garlic cloves, crushed
400 g (14 oz) tin chopped tomatoes
1 tablespoon tomato paste
   (concentrated purée)
3 tablespoons chopped flat-leaf
   (Italian) parsley
1 tablespoon chopped oregano
125 g (4½ oz) mozzarella cheese, grated

1   Preheat the oven to 180°C (350°F/
Gas 4). Score the eggplant flesh by cutting
a criss-cross pattern with a sharp knife,
being careful not to cut through the skin.
Heat 2 tablespoons of the oil in a large
frying pan, add half the eggplant and cook
for 2–3 minutes each side, or until the
flesh is soft. Remove. Repeat with another
2 tablespoons of the oil and the remaining
eggplant. Cool slightly and then scoop
out the flesh, leaving a 2 mm (1/16 inch)
border. Finely chop the eggplant flesh and
reserve the shells.

2   In the same pan, heat the remaining oil
and cook the onion over medium heat for
5 minutes. Add the garlic and cook for
30 seconds, then add the tomatoes,
tomato paste, herbs and eggplant flesh,
and cook, stirring occasionally, over low
heat for 8–10 minutes, or until the sauce
is thick and pulpy. Season well.
3   Arrange the eggplant shells in a lightly
greased baking dish and spoon in the
tomato filling. Sprinkle with mozzarella
and bake for 5–10 minutes, or until the
cheese has melted.

herbed baked ricotta

✹ ✹

Preparation time: 25 minutes
   + overnight chilling time
Cooking time: 30 minutes
Serves 6–8

1 kg (2 lb 4 oz) wedge full-fat ricotta
   (see Note)
2 tablespoons thyme leaves
2 tablespoons chopped rosemary
2 tablespoons chopped oregano
15 g (½ oz/¼ cup) chopped parsley
15 g (½ oz/¼ cup) snipped chives
2 garlic cloves, crushed
125 ml (4 fl oz/½ cup) olive oil

1   Pat the ricotta dry with paper towels
and place in a baking dish.
2   Combine the herbs, garlic, oil and
2 teaspoons of cracked pepper. Spoon
onto the ricotta, pressing down with the
spoon. Cover and refrigerate overnight.
3   Preheat the oven to 180°C (350°F/
Gas 4). Bake for 30 minutes, or until the
ricotta is golden. Delicious served with
crusty bread.

NOTE: If you can't buy a wedge, drain
the ricotta in a colander over a bowl
overnight. Spread half the herb mixture in
a greased 1.25 litre (44 fl oz/5 cup) loaf
(bar) tin, spoon in the ricotta and spread
with the remaining herbs before baking.

panzanella

Preparation time: 30 minutes
Cooking time: 5 minutes
Serves 6–8

1 small red onion, thinly sliced
250 g (9 oz) stale bread (such as ciabatta),
    crusts removed
4 ripe tomatoes
6 anchovy fillets, finely chopped
1 small garlic clove, crushed
1 tablespoon baby capers, rinsed,
    squeezed dry and chopped
2 tablespoons red wine vinegar
125 ml (4 fl oz/½ cup) extra virgin olive oil

2 small Lebanese (short) cucumbers,
    peeled and sliced
30 g (1 oz) basil leaves, torn

1   In a small bowl, cover the onion rings with cold water and leave for 5 minutes. Squeeze the rings in your hand, closing tightly and letting go and then repeating the process about five times. This removes the acid from the onion. Repeat the whole process twice more, using fresh water each time.

2   Tear the bread into roughly 3 cm (1¼ inch) squares and toast lightly under a medium–hot grill (broiler) for 4 minutes, or until the bread is crisp but not browned. Allow to cool. Set aside.

3   Score a cross in the base of each tomato. Put in a heatproof bowl and cover with boiling water. Leave for 30 seconds, then transfer to cold water and peel the skin away from the cross. Cut each tomato in half and scoop out the seeds. Roughly chop two of the tomatoes and purée the other two. Set aside.

4   Combine the anchovy, garlic and capers in a bowl. Add the vinegar and olive oil and whisk to combine. Season, then transfer to a large bowl and add the bread, onion, puréed and chopped tomato, cucumber and basil. Toss well and season, to taste. Leave to stand for at least 15 minutes to allow the flavours to develop. Serve at room temperature.

anchovies

In Italy, the preserved anchovies used in cooking are usually those preserved in salt. They are whole and much larger than the fillets preserved in oil, and have a far superior flavour and texture. All the recipes in this book, however, call for those preserved in oil because they are much more readily available outside Italy. If using salt-preserved anchovies, wash the salt off under running water and remove the fillets from the bone using your fingers. Remember that the salted anchovies are usually up to four times larger than those preserved in oil so you should adjust the recipe accordingly.

minestrone with pesto

✹ ✹

Preparation time: 25 minutes
+ overnight soaking time
Cooking time: 2 hours
Serves 6

125 g (4½ oz) dried borlotti (cranberry)
   beans
60 ml (2 fl oz/¼ cup) olive oil
1 large onion, finely chopped
2 garlic cloves, crushed
60 g (2¼ oz) pancetta, finely chopped
1 celery stalk, halved lengthways and
   thinly sliced
1 carrot, halved lengthways and sliced
1 potato, diced
2 teaspoons tomato paste (concentrated
   purée)
400 g (14 oz) tin chopped tomatoes
6 basil leaves, roughly torn
2 litres (70 fl oz/8 cups) chicken
   or vegetable stock
2 zucchini (courgettes), sliced
115 g (4 oz/¾ cup) shelled fresh peas
60 g (2¼ oz) green beans, cut into
   short lengths
80 g (2¾ oz) silverbeet (Swiss chard)
   leaves, shredded
3 tablespoons chopped flat-leaf
   (Italian) parsley
70 g (2½ oz) ditalini or other small pasta

PESTO
30 g (1 oz) basil leaves
20 g (¾ oz) lightly toasted pine nuts
   (see Note)
2 garlic cloves
100 ml (3½ fl oz) olive oil
25 g (1 oz/¼ cup) freshly grated
   parmesan cheese

1 Soak the borlotti beans in plenty of
cold water overnight. Drain and rinse
thoroughly under cold water.
2 Heat the oil in a large, deep saucepan,
add the onion, garlic and pancetta and
cook over low heat, stirring occasionally,
for 8–10 minutes, or until softened. Add

minestrone

Not all the ingredients for
minestrone go into the
saucepan at the same time, so
you can reduce the preparation
time by peeling and cutting up
one vegetable while another
is cooking. It is not even

necessary to make minestrone
entirely from scratch on the
same day you plan to serve it
because, like most vegetable
soups, the flavour improves
with standing.

the celery, carrot and potato and cook for 5 minutes. Stir in the tomato paste, tomatoes, basil and drained beans. Season with freshly ground black pepper. Add the stock and bring slowly to the boil. Cover and simmer, stirring occasionally, for 1½ hours. Add the zucchini, peas, green beans, silverbeet, parsley and the pasta. Simmer for a further 8–10 minutes, or until the vegetables are tender and the pasta is *al dente*. Taste and adjust the seasoning if necessary.

3 To make the pesto, combine the basil, pine nuts and garlic with a pinch of salt in a food processor. Process until finely chopped. With the motor running, slowly add the olive oil. Transfer to a bowl and stir in the parmesan and ground black pepper, to taste. Serve with the soup.

NOTE: Toast the pine nuts in a frying pan over medium heat, stirring constantly, until they are golden brown and aromatic. Watch carefully as they will burn easily.

pappa al pomodoro

pappa al pomodoro (tomato bread soup)

Preparation time: 25 minutes
Cooking time: 25 minutes
Serves 4

750 g (1 lb 10 oz) vine-ripened
    tomatoes
1 loaf (about 450 g/1 lb) day-old crusty
    Italian bread
1 tablespoon olive oil
3 garlic cloves, crushed
1 tablespoon tomato paste (concentrated
    purée)
1.25 litres (44 fl oz/5 cups) hot vegetable
    stock or water
1 tablespoon torn basil leaves
2–3 tablespoons extra virgin olive oil,
    plus extra, to serve

1 Score a cross in the base of each tomato. Put in a heatproof bowl and cover with boiling water. Leave for 30 seconds, then transfer to cold water and peel the skin away from the cross. Cut in half, scoop out the seeds and chop the flesh.
2 Discard most of the crust from the bread and tear the bread into roughly 3 cm (1¼ inch) pieces.
3 Heat the oil in a large saucepan. Add the garlic, tomato and tomato paste and simmer over low–medium heat, stirring occasionally, for 10–15 minutes, or until reduced. Add the stock and bring to the boil, stirring for about 3 minutes. Reduce the heat to medium, add the bread pieces and cook, stirring, for 5 minutes, or until it softens and absorbs most of the liquid. Add more stock or water if the soup is too thick. Remove from the heat.
4 Stir in the basil leaves and extra virgin olive oil, and leave for 5 minutes so the flavours have time to develop. Serve drizzled with a little extra virgin olive oil.

rocket and pecorino salad

Preparation time: 10 minutes
Cooking time: nil
Serves 4

60 ml (2 fl oz/¼ cup) extra virgin olive oil
2 tablespoons lemon juice
150 g (5½ oz) rocket (arugula) leaves
pecorino cheese, to serve

1 Combine the oil with the lemon juice and salt and pepper in a bowl. Add the rocket leaves and toss lightly to coat. Place in a serving dish.
2 Using a vegetable peeler, shave thin curls of pecorino over the salad. Adjust the seasoning and serve.

making pasta

Making pasta isn't difficult and the results are well worth the effort. Here are a few key tips: don't skimp on the kneading, as it makes the dough elastic and easier to roll, and use good-quality ingredients.

basic plain pasta dough

To serve six as a first course or four as a main course, you will need 300 g (10½ oz) plain (all-purpose) flour, 3 large (59 g/ 2¼ oz) eggs, 1½ tablespoons olive oil and a large pinch of salt.

1 Mound the flour on a work surface or place in a large bowl and make a well in the centre. Break the eggs into the well and add the oil and salt. Using a fork, begin to whisk the eggs and oil together, incorporating a little flour as you go. Gradually blend the flour with the eggs, working from the centre out.

2 Knead the dough on a lightly floured surface for 6 minutes, or until you have a soft, smooth elastic dough that is dry to touch. If it is sticky, knead in a little extra flour. Cover with plastic wrap and allow to rest for 30 minutes.

rolling by hand

1 Divide the dough into four portions and cover with plastic wrap. Lightly flour a work surface and use a floured rolling pin to roll out one portion from the centre to the edge. Continue, always rolling from in front, outwards. Rotate the dough often.

2 When a well-shaped rectangle has formed, fold the dough in half and roll it again. Continue this process seven or eight times to make a smooth rectangle of pasta about 5 mm (¼ inch) thick. Roll this sheet quickly and smoothly to 2.5 mm (⅛ inch) thick.

3 As each sheet is done, transfer it to a tea towel (dish towel). Keep the pasta sheets covered if making filled pasta, or leave uncovered to dry slightly if cutting into lengths or shapes.

4 To make lasagne sheets, cut the pasta into the required sizes.

5 For cutting lengths such as fettuccine, roll each pasta sheet up like a Swiss roll (jelly roll), then cut into uniform lengths with a long, sharp knife. Allow the lengths to dry in a single layer on a tea towel for a maximum of 10 minutes or hang on broom handles between two chairs.

6 To make farfalle (bow ties), using a fluted pastry wheel against a ruler, cut 2.5 x 5.5 cm (1 x 2¼ inch) rectangles from the 2.5-mm (⅛-inch) thick pasta sheets and pinch the centres together to form bow-tie shapes. Lay them on a tea towel to dry for 10–12 minutes.

7 To make ravioli, follow the recipe on page 94.

using a machine

1 Divide the pasta dough into four even portions. Keep the unworked portions covered with plastic wrap so they don't dry out. Lightly flour a work surface and use a floured rolling pin to roll out one portion from the centre to the edge as before, forming a rectangle roughly the same width as the machine. Lightly dust the dough and the pasta machine rollers with flour.

2 With the machine rollers set to the widest setting, pass the dough through the machine two or three times. Fold the dough into thirds, turn it by 90 degrees and feed it through again, repeating this process eight to 10 times, until the pasta dough is smooth and elastic and has a velvety appearance.

3 Reduce the roller width by one setting and pass the dough through. Repeat this process with the roller setting one notch closer each time until the dough is rolled to the required thickness. If using the cutting attachment on the machine, pass the lengths through immediately after rolling, then allow them to dry on a tea towel or over broom handles between two chairs for 10 minutes. Cover them if they are to be filled.

pesto

This famous Italian sauce goes especially well with pasta or fish. It requires a little patience when adding the oil, as it must be drizzled very slowly and gradually into the basil and pine nut mixture. Always stir in the cheese last, whether you are making the pesto in a food processor or by the traditional method using a mortar and pestle. Pesto should always be used raw at room temperature and should never be warmed up.

linguine pesto

Preparation time: 15 minutes
Cooking time: 15 minutes
Serves 4–6

100 g (3½ oz/2 cups) basil leaves
2 garlic cloves, crushed
40 g (1½ oz/¼ cup) pine nuts, toasted
185 ml (6 fl oz/¾ cup) olive oil
50 g (1¾ oz/½ cup) grated parmesan cheese, plus extra, to serve
500 g (1 lb 2 oz) linguine

1 Finely chop the basil, garlic and pine nuts together in a food processor. With the motor running, add the oil in a steady stream until mixed to a smooth paste. Transfer to a bowl, stir in the parmesan and season, to taste.

2 Cook the pasta in a large saucepan of rapidly boiling salted water until *al dente*. Drain and return to the pan. Toss enough of the pesto through the pasta to coat it well. Serve sprinkled with the extra parmesan, grated or shaved.

NOTE: Refrigerate any leftover pesto in an airtight jar for up to a week. Cover the surface with a layer of oil. Freeze for up to a month.

orecchiette with broccoli

Preparation time: 5 minutes
Cooking time: 20 minutes
Serves 6

750 g (1 lb 10 oz) broccoli, cut into florets
450 g (1 lb) orecchiette
60 ml (2 fl oz/¼ cup) extra virgin olive oil
8 anchovy fillets
½ teaspoon chilli flakes
30 g (1 oz/⅓ cup) grated pecorino or parmesan cheese

1 Blanch the broccoli in a large saucepan of boiling salted water for 5 minutes, or until just tender. Remove with a slotted spoon, drain well and return the water to the boil. Cook the pasta in the boiling water until *al dente*, then drain well and return to the pan.

2 Meanwhile, heat the oil in a frying pan and cook the anchovies over very low heat for 1 minute. Add the chilli flakes and broccoli. Increase the heat to medium and cook, stirring, for 5 minutes, or until the broccoli is well-coated and beginning to break apart. Season. Add to the pasta, add the cheese and toss.

orecchiette with broccoli

tomatoes

Unless tomatoes have been allowed to ripen on the vine, they are, more often than not, tasteless and watery and impart very little to cooking apart from acid. Outside the summer months, most tomatoes available to the consumer are very poor in quality. For this reason it is important to consider the season when planning a meal that calls for fresh tomatoes. If you can't get good-quality fresh tomatoes, it is better to use tinned tomatoes, preferably whole peeled or chopped roma (plum) tomatoes from Italy.

bucatini amatriciana

Place 1 finely chopped onion in a heavy-based frying pan with 2 tablespoons olive oil and cook over medium heat until golden. Add 150 g (5½ oz) chopped pancetta and stir for 1 minute. Add a 400 g (14 oz) tin of chopped tomatoes, salt and pepper and ½ teaspoon chilli flakes. Simmer for 20–25 minutes. Meanwhile, cook 450 g (1 lb) bucatini in a large pan of boiling water until *al dente*. Drain and add to the sauce with 3 tablespoons of freshly grated parmesan cheese. Toss well and serve immediately. Serves 4.

penne alla napolitana

※

Preparation time: 20 minutes
Cooking time: 25 minutes
Serves 4–6

2 tablespoons olive oil
1 onion, finely chopped
2–3 garlic cloves, finely chopped
1 small carrot, finely diced
1 celery stalk, finely diced
800 g (1 lb 12 oz) tin chopped tomatoes or 1 kg (2 lb 4 oz) ripe tomatoes, peeled and chopped
1 tablespoon tomato paste (concentrated purée)
3 tablespoons shredded basil
500 g (1 lb 2 oz) penne
freshly grated parmesan cheese, to serve (optional)

1　Heat the oil in a large frying pan. Add the onion and garlic and cook for 2 minutes, or until golden. Add the carrot and celery and cook for a further 2 minutes. Add the tomatoes and tomato paste. Simmer for 20 minutes, or until the sauce thickens, stirring occasionally. Stir in the shredded basil and season to taste.
2　While the sauce is cooking, cook the pasta in a large saucepan of rapidly boiling salted water until *al dente*. Drain well and return to the pan. Add the sauce to the pasta and mix well. Serve with freshly grated parmesan cheese, if desired.

spaghetti puttanesca

Preparation time: **15 minutes**
Cooking time: **20 minutes**
Serves 6

80 ml (2½ fl oz/⅓ cup) olive oil
2 onions, finely chopped
3 garlic cloves, finely chopped
½ teaspoon chilli flakes
6 large ripe tomatoes, diced
4 tablespoons capers, rinsed and
  squeezed dry
8 anchovy fillets in oil, drained and
  chopped
150 g (5½ oz) kalamata olives
3 tablespoons chopped flat-leaf
  (Italian) parsley
375 g (13 oz) spaghetti

1 Heat the olive oil in a saucepan, add the onion and cook over medium heat for 5 minutes. Add the garlic and chilli flakes to the saucepan and cook for 30 seconds.
2 Add the tomato, capers and anchovy. Simmer over low heat for 10–15 minutes, or until the sauce is thick and pulpy. Stir the olives and parsley through the sauce.
3 While the sauce is cooking, cook the spaghetti in a large saucepan of rapidly boiling salted water until *al dente*. Drain and return to the pan.
4 Add the sauce to the pasta and stir it through. Season with salt and pepper, to taste, and serve immediately.

spaghettini with garlic and chilli

Cook 500 g (1 lb 2 oz) spaghettini in a large saucepan of rapidly boiling salted water until *al dente*. Drain and return to the pan. Meanwhile, heat 125 ml (4 fl oz/½ cup) extra virgin olive oil in a large frying pan. Add 2–3 finely chopped garlic cloves and 1–2 seeded, finely chopped, fresh red chillies, and cook over very low heat for 2–3 minutes, or until the garlic is golden. Take care not to burn the garlic or chillies as this will make the sauce bitter. Toss 3 tablespoons chopped flat-leaf (Italian) parsley and the warmed oil, garlic and chilli mixture through the pasta. Season with salt and freshly ground black pepper. Serve with grated parmesan cheese. Serves 4–6.

puttanesca

The name puttanesca is a derivation of the word *puttana*, which in Italian means whore. There are many stories surrounding this dish and according to one of them, the name comes from the fact that the intense flavours of the sauce were like a siren call to the men who visited such 'ladies of pleasure'. Another story claims the dish got its name because these wayward women were forbidden to shop for groceries during regular hours and were left to rely upon the pantry staples such as olives, capers and anchovies.

sardines

These small fish have an oily, soft flesh with a fine texture. The backbone is easy to remove and the small remaining bones are edible. Sardines are sold whole, butterflied and filleted. They have a strong, distinctive flavour and are suitable for baking, grilling, pan-frying and barbecuing.

spaghetti with sardines, fennel and tomato

Preparation time: 30 minutes
Cooking time: 45 minutes
Serves 4–6

3 roma (plum) tomatoes
80 ml (2½ fl oz/⅓ cup) olive oil
3 garlic cloves, crushed
80 g (2¾ oz/1 cup) fresh white breadcrumbs
1 red onion, thinly sliced
1 fennel bulb, quartered and thinly sliced
40 g (1½ oz/¼ cup) raisins
40 g (1½ oz/¼ cup) pine nuts, toasted
4 anchovy fillets, chopped
125 ml (4 fl oz/½ cup) dry white wine
1 tablespoon tomato paste (concentrated purée)
4 tablespoons finely chopped flat-leaf (Italian) parsley
350 g (12 oz) butterflied sardine fillets
500 g (1 lb 2 oz) spaghetti

1 Score a cross in the base of each tomato. Place the tomatoes in a bowl of boiling water for 30 seconds, then transfer to cold water and peel the skin from the cross. Cut the tomatoes in half and scoop out the seeds. Roughly chop the flesh.
2 Heat 1 tablespoon of the oil in a large frying pan over medium heat. Add a third of the garlic and the breadcrumbs and stir for about 5 minutes, until golden and crisp. Transfer to a plate.
3 Heat the remaining oil in the same frying pan and cook the onion, fennel and remaining garlic for 8 minutes, or until soft. Add the tomato, raisins, pine nuts and anchovy and cook for 3 minutes. Add the wine, tomato paste and 125 ml (4 fl oz/½ cup) water. Simmer for 10 minutes, or until the mixture thickens slightly. Stir in the parsley and set aside.
4 Pat the sardines dry with paper towels. Cook the sardines in batches in a lightly greased frying pan over medium heat for 1 minute, or until cooked through. Take care not to overcook them or they will break up. Set aside.
5 Cook the pasta in a large saucepan of rapidly boiling salted water until al dente. Drain and return to the pan.
6 Stir the sauce through the pasta until the pasta is well coated and the sauce evenly distributed. Add the sardines and half the breadcrumbs and toss gently. Sprinkle the remaining breadcrumbs over the top and serve immediately.

Place heaped teaspoons of the filling at even intervals along the pasta sheets.

Use a pastry wheel or sharp knife to cut the ravioli.

herb-filled ravioli with sage butter

✳ ✳ ✳

Preparation time: 1 hour + 30 minutes standing time
Cooking time: 15 minutes
Serves 4

250 g (9 oz/1 cup) ricotta cheese
2 tablespoons freshly grated parmesan cheese, plus extra, shaved, to garnish
2 teaspoons snipped chives
1 tablespoon chopped flat-leaf (Italian) parsley
2 teaspoons chopped basil
1 teaspoon chopped thyme

PASTA
300 g (10½ oz) plain (all-purpose) flour
3 eggs, beaten
60 ml (2 fl oz/¼ cup) olive oil

SAGE BUTTER
200 g (7 oz) butter
12 sage leaves

1   To make the pasta, sift the flour into a bowl and make a well in the centre. Gradually mix in the eggs and oil. Turn onto a lightly floured surface and knead for 6 minutes, or until smooth. Cover with plastic wrap and leave for 30 minutes.
2   Divide the dough into four even portions. Lightly flour a large work surface and use a floured long rolling pin to roll out one portion from the centre to the edge. Continue, always rolling from in front of you outwards and rotating the dough often. Fold the dough in half and roll it out again. Continue this process seven times to make a smooth circle of pasta about 5 mm (¼ inch) thick. Roll this sheet out quickly and smoothly to a thickness of 2.5 mm (⅛ inch). Make four sheets, two slightly larger than the others. Cover with a tea towel (dish towel).
3   Mix together the ricotta, parmesan and herbs. Season with salt and pepper. Spread one of the smaller pasta sheets out on a work surface and place heaped teaspoons of filling at 5 cm (2 inch) intervals. Brush a little water between the filling along the cutting lines. Place

a larger sheet on top and press it down along the cutting lines. Cut the ravioli with a pastry wheel or knife and transfer to a lightly floured baking tray. Repeat with the remaining dough and filling.

4   To make the sage butter, melt the butter over low heat in a small saucepan, without stirring or shaking. Carefully pour the clear butter into another container and discard the remaining white sediment. Return the clarified butter to a clean pan and heat gently over medium heat. Add the sage leaves and cook until crisp, but not brown. Remove and drain on paper towels. Reserve the warm butter.

5   Cook the ravioli in batches in a large saucepan of salted simmering water for 5–6 minutes, or until tender. Top with warm sage butter and leaves and garnish with shaved parmesan.

NOTE: Don't cook the ravioli in rapidly boiling water or the squares will split and lose the filling.

gnocchi romana

✳ ✳

Preparation time: 20 minutes
  + 1 hour chilling time
Cooking time: 40 minutes
Serves 4

750 ml (26 fl oz/3 cups) milk
½ teaspoon freshly grated nutmeg
85 g (3 oz/⅔ cup) semolina
1 egg, beaten
150 g (5½ oz/1½ cups) freshly grated
    parmesan cheese
60 g (2¼ oz) butter, melted
125 ml (4 fl oz/½ cup) pouring
    (whipping) cream
70 g (2½ oz/½ cup) freshly grated
    mozzarella cheese

1   Line a deep Swiss roll (jelly roll) tin with baking paper. Combine the milk and half the nutmeg in a saucepan and season to taste. Bring to the boil, then reduce the heat and gradually stir in the semolina. Cook, stirring occasionally, for a further

5–10 minutes, or until the semolina becomes very stiff.

2   Remove the pan from the heat, add the egg and 100 g (3½ oz/1 cup) of the parmesan. Stir to combine and then spread the mixture in the prepared tin. Refrigerate for 1 hour, or until the mixture is firm. Preheat the oven to 180°C (350°F/ Gas 4). Lightly grease a shallow casserole dish. Cut the semolina into rounds using

a floured 4 cm (1½ inch) cutter and arrange in the dish.

3   Pour the melted butter over the top, followed by the cream. Combine the remaining grated parmesan with the mozzarella cheese and sprinkle over the semolina rounds. Sprinkle the remaining nutmeg evenly over the top. Bake for 20–25 minutes, or until the cheese is melted and golden.

seafood risotto

✵ ✵

Preparation time: 25 minutes
Cooking time: 45 minutes
Serves 4

2 ripe tomatoes
500 g (1 lb 2 oz) black mussels
310 ml (10¾ fl oz/1¼ cups) white wine
1.25 litres (44 fl oz/5 cups) fish stock
pinch of saffron threads
2 tablespoons olive oil
30 g (1 oz) butter
500 g (1 lb 2 oz) raw prawns (shrimp),
    peeled and deveined, tails intact
225 g (8 oz) squid tubes, sliced into
    thin rings
200 g (7 oz) scallops
3 garlic cloves, crushed
1 onion, finely chopped
370 g (13 oz/2 cups) risotto rice (arborio,
    vialone nano or carnaroli)
2 tablespoons chopped parsley

1   Score a cross in the base of each tomato. Place in a bowl of boiling water for 30 seconds, then plunge into cold water and peel the skin away from the cross. Chop the tomato flesh.

2   Scrub the mussels with a stiff brush and remove the hairy beards. Discard any broken mussels or any that do not close when tapped. Pour the wine into a large saucepan and bring to the boil. Add the mussels and cook, covered, over medium heat for 3–5 minutes, or until the mussels open. Discard any that do not open. Strain, reserving the liquid. Remove the mussels from their shells.

3   Combine the mussel liquid, stock and saffron in a saucepan, cover and keep at a low simmer.

4   Heat the oil and butter in a large saucepan over medium heat. Add the prawns and cook until they curl up and change colour. Remove from the pan and set aside. Cook the squid and scallops for about 1–2 minutes, until white. Remove. Add the garlic and onion and cook for 3 minutes, or until golden. Add the rice and stir until coated.

5   Add 125 ml (4 fl oz/½ cup) of the hot liquid to the pan, stirring constantly until it is all absorbed. Continue adding liquid, 125 ml (4 fl oz/½ cup) at a time, stirring constantly, for 25 minutes, or until all of the liquid is absorbed. Stir in the tomato, seafood and parsley and cook just until heated through. Season with salt and pepper, to taste.

NOTE: You can use almost any combination of seafood for this risotto. Try using small pieces of firm, white fish, clams (vongole) or octopus.

Cook the prawns until they curl up and change colour.

Continue adding hot liquid, stirring constantly until it is all absorbed.

mushroom risotto

✳ ✳

Preparation time: 10 minutes
  + 30 minutes soaking time
Cooking time: 1 hour
Serves 4–6

20 g (¾ oz) dried porcini mushrooms
1 litre (35 fl oz/4 cups) chicken or
    vegetable stock
2 tablespoons olive oil
100 g (3½ oz) butter, chopped
650 g (1 lb 7 oz) small cap or Swiss brown
    mushrooms, stems trimmed, sliced
3 garlic cloves, crushed
80 ml (2½ fl oz/⅓ cup) dry white vermouth
1 onion, finely chopped
440 g (15½ oz/2 cups) risotto rice (arborio,
    vialone nano or carnaroli)
150 g (5½ oz/1½ cups) grated parmesan
    cheese

1 Soak the porcini mushrooms in 500 ml (17 fl oz/2 cups) warm water for 30 minutes. Drain, reserving the liquid. Chop the mushrooms and set aside. Pour the liquid through a fine sieve lined with a paper towel.

2 Put the stock and mushroom liquid in a saucepan, bring to the boil, then reduce the heat, cover and keep at a low simmer.

3 Heat half the oil and 40 g (1½ oz) of the butter in a large frying pan over high heat. Add all the mushrooms and the garlic and cook, stirring, for 10 minutes, or until soft and the juices have been released. Reduce the heat to low and cook for another 5 minutes, or until all the juices have evaporated. Increase the heat, add the vermouth and cook for 2–3 minutes, until evaporated. Set aside.

4 Heat the remaining oil and 20 g (¾ oz) butter in a large saucepan over medium heat. Add the onion and cook, stirring

often, for 10 minutes, or until soft. Add the rice and stir for 1–2 minutes, or until well coated. Add 125 ml (4 fl oz/ ½ cup) stock and stir constantly over medium heat until all the liquid is absorbed. Continue adding more stock, 125 ml (4 fl oz/½ cup) at a time, stirring constantly for 20–25 minutes, or until tender and creamy.

5 Remove from the heat and stir in the mushrooms, parmesan and remaining butter. Season with salt and freshly ground black pepper, to taste.

NOTE: It is important that the porcini mushrooms are soaked for at least 30 minutes in warm water and that the soaking liquid is passed through a paper towel to ensure all the grit is removed.

risotto

A common misconception surrounding risotto is that it should be eaten piping hot, straight from the stove. However, unlike pasta, risotto benefits from resting on your plate for a minute or so to allow the flavours to settle and the steam to disperse. Italians often spread the risotto on their plate from the centre out, then eat from the rim to the centre.

making pizzas

Pizza has transcended its rustic origins in Naples to become an international symbol of Italian food. It usually combines three to five toppings, so the character and flavour of each shines through.

pizza margherita

The margherita pizza, with its trio of tomato, cheese and basil, represents the colours of the Italian flag. For a medium pizza, you will need 225 g (8 oz) strong white flour; 1 teaspoon sugar; 2 teaspoons dried yeast; 2 tablespoons olive oil; 90 ml (3 fl oz) milk; 1 crushed garlic clove; 400 g (14 oz) tin chopped tomatoes; 1 bay leaf; 1 teaspoon chopped thyme; polenta, to sprinkle; 150 g (5½ oz) thinly sliced bocconcini; some extra olive oil, to drizzle; and 6 torn basil leaves.

1 Place the flour, sugar, yeast and ½ teaspoon salt in a large bowl. Stir half the olive oil with the milk and 80 ml (2½ fl oz/ ⅓ cup) warm water and add to the bowl. Stir with a wooden spoon until the mixture comes together to form a dough.

2 Place on a lightly floured work surface and knead for 5 minutes, or until soft and smooth. Lightly oil a bowl, add the dough and turn to coat in the oil. Leave in a warm, draught-free place for 1 hour, or until doubled in size. Preheat the oven to 210°C (415°F/Gas 6–7).

3 Heat the remaining oil in a saucepan over medium heat, add the garlic and stir for 30 seconds. Add the tomatoes, bay leaf and thyme and simmer, stirring occasionally, for 20–25 minutes, or until thick. Cool, then remove the bay leaf.

4 Place the dough on a floured work surface, punch down to expel the air and knead for 5 minutes. Shape into a ball and roll to 28–30 cm (11¼–12 inch) diameter. Oil a pizza tray the same size, sprinkle it with polenta and place the dough on it. Spread with the tomato sauce, leaving a 3 cm (1¼ inch) border. Arrange the bocconcini on top, drizzle with olive oil and top with the basil. Bake for 15 minutes, or until crisp and bubbling.

thick base

To make a thick base for a medium pizza, you will need 2 teaspoons dried yeast; ½ teaspoon each of salt and sugar; 310 g (10 oz/2½ cups) strong white flour; semolina or polenta, to sprinkle; 1 quantity cooled tomato sauce, as described for Pizza margherita; and olive oil, to drizzle.

1 Combine the yeast, salt, sugar and 250 ml (9 fl oz/1 cup) water in a bowl. Cover with plastic wrap and leave in a warm, draught-free place for 10 minutes, or until frothy. Sift the flour into a large bowl. Make a well in the centre, add the yeast mixture and mix to a soft dough.

2 Place the dough on a lightly floured work surface and knead for 5 minutes, or until smooth and elastic. Lightly oil a bowl, add the dough and turn to coat in the oil. Leave in a warm, draught-free place for 1 hour, or until doubled in size.

3 Preheat the oven to 210°C (415°F/Gas 6–7). Roll out dough to 35 cm (14 inch) diameter. Oil a 30 cm (12 inch) pizza tray, sprinkle with semolina or polenta and place the dough on the tray, folding in the edges to form a rim. Spread the sauce over the dough, leaving a 3 cm (1¼ inch) border. Arrange toppings of your choice over the sauce, drizzle with olive oil and bake for 25 minutes, or until the crust is golden.

topping suggestions

Prosciutto e rucola: Brush with olive oil, scatter with cheese, season. Lay thinly shaved slices of prosciutto on top. When cooked, scatter with rocket and drizzle with olive oil.

Quattro formaggio: Brush with olive oil, season, then scatter with mozzarella, parmesan, fontina, and gorgonzola or pecorino.

pizza rustica

✳ ✳ ✳

Preparation time: **35 minutes + 30 minutes**
   chilling time
Cooking time: **50 minutes**
Serves **6**

PASTRY
375 g (13 oz/3 cups) plain (all-purpose) flour
1 teaspoon icing (confectioners') sugar
150 g (5½ oz) butter, chilled and chopped
1 egg
1 egg yolk
2 tablespoons iced water

FILLING
500 g (1 lb 2 oz/2 cups) ricotta cheese
6 eggs, separated
100 g (3½ oz) lean bacon, cut into
   thin strips
80 g (2¾ oz) thickly sliced salami,
   cut into 5 mm (¼ inch) pieces
100 g (3½ oz) mozzarella cheese, grated
100 g (3½ oz) smoked mozzarella cheese or
   other naturally smoked cheese, cut into
   1 cm (½ inch) cubes
25 g (1 oz/¼ cup) freshly grated
   parmesan cheese
1 tablespoon chopped flat-leaf
   (Italian) parsley
½ teaspoon chopped oregano
pinch of freshly grated nutmeg
1 egg, beaten with 1 tablespoon cold water,
   to glaze

1 To make the pastry, sift the flour, icing sugar and 1 teaspoon salt into a bowl. Using your fingertips, rub in the butter until the mixture resembles fine breadcrumbs. Add the egg and egg yolk, then add the iced water, ½ teaspoon at a time. Mix with a flat-bladed knife, using a cutting action, to form a dough. Turn out onto a lightly floured surface and gather into a smooth ball. Cover with plastic wrap and refrigerate for 30 minutes.
2 Preheat the oven to 190°C (375°F/ Gas 5) and place a baking tray on the centre shelf. Grease a pie dish with a 23 cm (9 inch) base, 25 cm (10 inch) rim and depth of 4 cm (1½ inches).

Fold the beaten egg whites
through the ricotta mixture.

Spread the filling evenly over
the pastry base, then smooth the
surface with the back of a spoon.

3 To make the filling, beat the ricotta until smooth. Gradually add the egg yolks, beating well after each addition. Add the bacon, salami, cheeses, parsley, oregano and nutmeg. Season well. Beat the egg whites in a large bowl until stiff, then fold through the ricotta mixture.

4 Divide the pastry into two portions, one slightly larger than the other. Roll out the larger portion on a lightly floured surface to a size big enough to fit the base and sides of the dish. Line the dish with the pastry. Roll out the second pastry portion to the same thickness for the pie lid. Spread the filling over the base and smooth the surface. Brush the pastry edges with the egg glaze and position the lid on top. Press the edges together firmly, then trim with a sharp knife. Press a fluted pattern around the rim with your fingers to further seal in the filling. Brush the surface well with the egg glaze, then prick the surface all over with a fork. Place the pie dish on the heated tray.

5 Bake the pie for 45–50 minutes, or until the pastry is golden. Cover loosely with foil if it browns too quickly. Set aside for 20 minutes before serving.

sweet and sour liver

Preparation time: **10 minutes**
Cooking time: **10 minutes**
Serves **4**

40 g (1½ oz) butter
80 ml (2½ fl oz/⅓ cup) olive oil
600 g (1 lb 5 oz) calves' livers, cut into long thin slices
80 g (2¾ oz/1 cup) fresh white breadcrumbs
1 tablespoon sugar
2 garlic cloves, crushed
60 ml (2 fl oz/¼ cup) red wine vinegar
1 tablespoon chopped flat-leaf (Italian) parsley

1 Heat the butter and half the oil in a large heavy-based frying pan over medium–high heat. Coat the liver in breadcrumbs, pressing them on firmly with your hands. Shake off the excess and when the butter begins to foam, cook the liver in batches, for 1 minute each side, or until the crust is brown and crisp. Remove from the pan and keep warm.

2 Add the remaining oil to the frying pan and cook the sugar and garlic over low heat until golden. Add the vinegar and cook for 30 seconds, or until almost evaporated. Add the parsley, then pour over the liver. Serve the liver hot or at room temperature.

green beans with garlic breadcrumbs

Preparation time: **10 minutes**
Cooking time: **15 minutes**
Serves **4**

600 g (1 lb 5 oz) trimmed baby green beans
60 ml (2 fl oz/¼ cup) olive oil
4 garlic cloves, peeled
40 g (1½ oz/½ cup) fresh white breadcrumbs
2 tablespoons chopped flat-leaf (Italian) parsley

1 Cook the beans in a large saucepan of boiling salted water until tender but still firm. Drain and refresh under cold running water. Drain again and pat dry with paper towels.

2 Heat the olive oil in a heavy-based frying pan and cook the garlic cloves until golden brown. Remove and discard.

3 Add the breadcrumbs to the oil and cook over low heat, stirring constantly for 3–4 minutes, or until brown and crunchy. Add the beans and parsley to the pan, then season to taste. Stir to mix with the breadcrumbs and warm the beans. Serve warm or at room temperature.

green beans with garlic breadcrumbs

chicken cacciatora

Preparation time: **15 minutes**
Cooking time: **1 hour**
Serves **4**

60 ml (2 fl oz/¼ cup) olive oil
1 large onion, finely chopped
3 garlic cloves, crushed
150 g (5½ oz) pancetta, finely chopped
125 g (4½ oz) button mushrooms,
    thickly sliced
1 large chicken (at least 1.6 kg/3 lb 8 oz),
    cut into 8 pieces
80 ml (2½ fl oz/⅓ cup) dry vermouth or
    dry white wine
800 g (1 lb 12 oz) tin chopped tomatoes
¼ teaspoon soft brown sugar
¼ teaspoon cayenne pepper
1 oregano sprig
1 thyme sprig
1 bay leaf

1 Heat half the olive oil in a large
flameproof casserole dish. Add the onion
and garlic and cook for 6–8 minutes
over low heat, stirring, until the onion is
golden. Add the pancetta and mushrooms,
increase the heat and cook, stirring, for
4–5 minutes. Transfer to a bowl.
2 Add the remaining oil to the casserole
dish and brown the chicken pieces, a few
at a time, over medium heat. Season as
they brown. Spoon off the excess fat and
return all the chicken to the casserole
dish. Increase the heat, add the vermouth
to the dish and cook until the liquid has
almost evaporated.
3 Add the tomatoes, sugar, cayenne and
herbs, and stir in 80 ml (2½ fl oz/⅓ cup)
water. Bring to the boil, then stir in the
reserved onion mixture. Reduce the heat,
cover and simmer for 25 minutes, or until
the chicken pieces are tender but not
falling off the bone.
4 If the liquid is too thin, remove the
chicken from the casserole dish, increase
the heat and boil until the liquid has
thickened. Discard the herbs and adjust
the seasoning.

cacciatora

Cacciatora means 'in the style
of the hunter'. Like many dishes
throughout Italy, there are
countless variations, with each
region adding its own twist to
the dish. Generally, the dish
consists of a chicken or rabbit
fricassée with tomato, onion
and other vegetables.

grilled squid with salsa verde

Preparation time: 30 minutes
+ 30 minutes marinating time
Cooking time: 10 minutes
Serves 6

1 kg (2 lb 4 oz) squid
250 ml (9 fl oz/1 cup) olive oil
2 tablespoons lemon juice
2 garlic cloves, crushed
2 tablespoons chopped oregano
2 tablespoons chopped flat-leaf (Italian)
    parsley, to serve
lemon wedges, to serve

SALSA VERDE
4 anchovy fillets, drained
1 tablespoon capers
1 garlic clove, crushed
3 tablespoons chopped flat-leaf (Italian)
    parsley
1 small handful basil leaves
1 small handful mint leaves
2 teaspoons red wine vinegar
60 ml (2 fl oz/¼ cup) extra virgin
    olive oil
1 teaspoon dijon mustard

semi-dried roma tomatoes

Preheat the oven to 160°C (315°F/ Gas 2–3). Quarter 16 roma (plum) tomatoes lengthways and lay, skin side down, on a wire rack in a baking dish. Combine 1 teaspoon each of salt and pepper with 3 tablespoons chopped thyme. Sprinkle over the tomatoes. Bake for 2½ hours, checking occasionally to avoid burning. Put in a bowl and toss with 2 tablespoons olive oil. Cool, then refrigerate in an airtight container for 24 hours. Eat within 3–4 days. Fills a 500 ml (16 fl oz) container.

1 To clean the squid, gently pull the tentacles away from the tube (the intestines should come away at the same time). Remove the intestines from the tentacles by cutting under the eyes, then remove the beak if it remains in the centre of the tentacles by using your fingers to push up the centre. Pull away the quill (the transparent cartilage) from inside the body and remove. Remove and discard any white membrane. Under cold running water, pull the skin away from the tube. Cut into 1 cm (½ inch) rings and place in a bowl with the tentacles. Add the oil, lemon juice, garlic and oregano to the bowl, and toss to coat the squid. Leave to marinate for 30 minutes.

2 To make the salsa verde, put the anchovies, capers, garlic, parsley, basil and mint in a food processor and chop in short bursts until roughly blended. Transfer to a bowl and stir in the vinegar. Slowly mix in the extra virgin olive oil, then the mustard. Season.

3 Heat a barbecue or chargrill pan until hot. Drain the squid rings and cook them in batches for 1–2 minutes each side.

4 Season the squid rings and sprinkle with the parsley. Serve with the salsa verde and lemon wedges.

marsala

This fortified wine comes from a small town of the same name in Sicily. Made from local grapes, Marsalas can range from the very dry to the very sweet. While the dry Marsala is used more frequently in the kitchen and also drunk as an aperitif, sweet Marsala is used for sweet dishes such as the famous Zabaglione (page 116) and is also drunk as a dessert wine. There are also special Marsala blends with added ingredients such as cream, eggs and almonds.

fennel fritters

Preparation time: **15 minutes**
Cooking time: **20 minutes**
Serves **4**

1 kg (2 lb 4 oz) fennel bulbs (see Note)
30 g (1 oz/⅓ cup) grated pecorino cheese
80 g (2¾ oz/1 cup) fresh white breadcrumbs
60 g (2¼ oz/½ cup) plain (all-purpose) flour
3 eggs, lightly beaten
olive oil, for pan-frying
lemon wedges, to serve

1 Remove the tough outer leaves from the fennel, then trim the base and small stalks. Slice the fennel lengthways at 5 mm (¼ inch) intervals and blanch in boiling salted water for 3 minutes, or until tender. Drain and pat dry. Leave to cool.
2 Mix together the cheese and breadcrumbs and season.
3 Coat the fennel in the flour and shake off the excess, then dip in the egg and coat in the crumb mix. Heat the oil in a large heavy-based frying pan until it begins to sizzle. Fry the fennel in batches, being careful not to overcrowd the pan, for 2–3 minutes each side, until golden brown and crisp. Drain on paper towels, season and serve with lemon wedges.

NOTE: Use the rounder, 'male' fennel bulbs, rather than the flatter 'female' bulbs, as they have more flavour.

saltimbocca (veal escalopes with prosciutto)

Preparation time: **15 minutes**
Cooking time: **20 minutes**
Serves **4**

4 thin veal steaks, fat and sinew trimmed
2 garlic cloves, crushed
4 prosciutto slices
4 sage leaves, plus extra, to garnish
30 g (1 oz) butter
170 ml (5½ fl oz/⅔ cup) Marsala

saltimbocca

1 Flatten each steak to 5 mm (¼ inch) thick, nick the edges to prevent curling and pat the meat dry with paper towels. Combine the garlic with ¼ teaspoon salt and ½ teaspoon freshly ground black pepper and rub some of the mixture over one side of each steak. Place a slice of prosciutto on each and top with a sage leaf. The prosciutto should cover the veal completely but not overlap the edge.

2 Melt the butter in a large heavy-based frying pan, add the veal, prosciutto side up, and cook over medium heat for 5 minutes, or until the underside is golden brown. Do not turn the veal. Add the Marsala, without wetting the top of the veal. Reduce the heat and simmer very slowly for 10 minutes. Transfer the veal to warm serving plates. Boil the sauce for 2–3 minutes, or until syrupy, then spoon it over the veal. Garnish with sage and serve with rocket leaves, if desired.

fritto misto di mare (fried seafood salad)

✹ ✹

Preparation time: **15 minutes**
Cooking time: **10 minutes**
Serves **4**

2 cuttlefish tubes
8 red mullet fillets
½ teaspoon paprika
75 g (2½ oz) plain (all-purpose) flour
12 raw medium prawns (shrimp), peeled and
    deveined, tails intact
good-quality olive oil, for deep-frying
lemon wedges, to serve

1 Preheat the oven to 150°C (300°F/ Gas 2). Line a large tray with baking paper. Place the cuttlefish bone-side down on a board and gently cut lengthways through the body. Open out, remove the cuttlebone, then gently remove the insides. Cut the flesh in half. Under cold running water, pull the skin away. Cut the cuttlefish and mullet into even-sized pieces. Season well. Combine the paprika

cuttlefish

Cuttlefish belong to the *cephalopod* family (molluscs without shells) along with squid, calamari and octopus. Almost all cephalopods rely on a brownish or black blanket of ink to hide from their predators. Many Mediterranean countries use this ink to colour and flavour pasta and seafood stews. Some insist that only cuttlefish ink should be used to cook with as it is sweeter than other varieties, but many cooks also use squid ink. Small cuttlefish are usually very tender but the larger varieties are similar to octopus in that they need special treatment to tenderise them prior to cooking.

and flour in a bowl, add all the seafood and toss to coat. Shake off any excess.

2 Fill a deep, heavy-based saucepan one-third full of oil and heat to 190°C (375°F), or until a cube of bread dropped into the oil browns in 10 seconds. Cook the seafood in batches, for 1–2 minutes each, or until crisp and golden. Keep warm in the oven.

3 Place the seafood on a serving platter. Sprinkle with extra salt and serve immediately with lemon wedges.

pork chops with marsala sauce

Preparation time: 10 minutes
Cooking time: 15 minutes
Serves 4

4 pork loin chops
2 tablespoons olive oil
125 ml (4 fl oz/½ cup) Marsala
2 teaspoons grated orange zest
60 ml (2 fl oz/¼ cup) orange juice
3 tablespoons chopped flat-leaf (Italian)
  parsley

1 Pat dry the chops with paper towels
and season well. Heat the olive oil in a
heavy-based frying pan over medium
heat and cook the chops for 5 minutes
each side, or until brown and just cooked
through. Remove and keep warm.
2 Add the Marsala, orange zest and juice
to the pan and cook for 4–5 minutes,
or until the sauce has reduced and
thickened. Add the parsley and serve with
the pork chops and vegetables, if desired.

pork chops with marsala sauce

polenta squares with mushroom ragu

Preparation time: 30 minutes
Cooking time: 35 minutes
Serves 4

500 ml (17 fl oz/2 cups) vegetable stock
  or water
150 g (5½ oz/1 cup) polenta
20 g (¾ oz) butter
100 g (3½ oz/1 cup) grated parmesan
  cheese
5 g (⅛ oz) dried porcini mushrooms
125 ml (4 fl oz/½ cup) boiling water
200 g (7 oz) Swiss brown mushrooms
300 g (10½ oz) field mushrooms
125 ml (4 fl oz/½ cup) olive oil
1 onion, finely chopped
3 garlic cloves, finely chopped

1 fresh bay leaf
2 teaspoons finely chopped thyme
2 teaspoons finely chopped oregano
15 g (½ oz/½ cup) finely chopped flat-leaf
  (Italian) parsley
1 tablespoon balsamic vinegar

1 Grease a shallow 20 cm (8 inch) square
cake tin. Place the stock and a pinch of
salt in a large saucepan and bring to the
boil. Add the polenta in a steady stream,
stirring constantly. Reduce the heat and
simmer, stirring often, for 15–20 minutes.
Remove from the heat and stir in the
butter and 75 g (2¾ oz/¾ cup) of the
parmesan. Spread the mixture into the tin
and refrigerate for 20 minutes.
2 Soak the porcini mushrooms in the
boiling water for 10 minutes, or until
softened, then drain, reserving 80 ml
(2½ fl oz/⅓ cup) liquid. Pass the liquid
through a sieve lined with a paper towel.

3 Thickly slice the Swiss brown
mushrooms and coarsely chop the field
mushrooms. Heat 80 ml (2½ fl oz/
⅓ cup) of the oil in a large frying pan,
add all the mushrooms and cook for
4–5 minutes, then remove from the pan.
Heat the remaining oil in the pan and
cook the onion and garlic over medium
heat for 2–3 minutes, or until softened.
4 Add the reserved liquid, bay leaf,
thyme and oregano to the pan, season
and cook for 2 minutes. Return the
mushrooms to the pan, add the parsley
and vinegar and cook over medium heat
for 1 minute, or until nearly dry. Remove
the bay leaf and check the seasoning.
5 Meanwhile, sprinkle the remaining
parmesan over the polenta. Heat under a
medium grill (broiler) for 10 minutes, or
until browned and the cheese has melted.
Cut into four 10 cm (4 inch) squares and
serve topped with the mushroom ragu.

carciofi alla romana (roman-style artichokes)

✳ ✳

Preparation time: 25 minutes
Cooking time: 1 hour 30 minutes
Serves 4 as an entrée

60 ml (2 fl oz/¼ cup) lemon juice
4 globe artichokes
1 tablespoon fresh breadcrumbs, toasted
1 large garlic clove, crushed
3 tablespoons finely chopped flat-leaf (Italian) parsley
3 tablespoons finely chopped mint
1½ tablespoons olive oil
60 ml (2 fl oz/¼ cup) dry white wine

1 Preheat the oven to 190°C (375°F/ Gas 5). Add the lemon juice to a large bowl of cold water to make acidulated water. Remove the tough outer leaves from the artichokes and trim the stalks to 5 cm (2 inches) long. Peel the stalks with a potato peeler. Slice off the top quarter of each artichoke with a sharp knife to give a level surface. Gently open out the leaves and scrape out the hairy choke using a teaspoon or small sharp knife. Drop each artichoke into the lemon water as you go.
2 Combine the breadcrumbs, garlic, parsley, mint and olive oil in a bowl and season well. Fill the centre of each artichoke with the mixture, pressing it in well. Close the leaves as tightly as possible to prevent the filling from falling out.
3 Arrange the artichokes with the stalks up in a deep casserole dish just large enough to fit them so they are tightly packed. Sprinkle with salt and pour in the wine. Cover with a lid, or a double sheet of kitchen foil secured tightly at the edges. Bake for about 1½ hours, until very tender. Serve hot as a first course or side vegetable, or at room temperature as part of an antipasto platter.

NOTE: Check the artichokes halfway through cooking and, if necessary, add a little water to prevent them burning.

artichokes

This is the common name given to three unrelated plants: Jerusalem artichokes, Chinese artichokes and globe artichokes. However, the latter is the only one considered to be a true artichoke. Globe artichokes are a member of the thistle family and are natives of the Mediterranean region. When buying artichokes, make sure the centres are well closed and avoid any that are heavily browned as they are beyond their prime. Artichokes are best used on the day of purchase, but can be stored in a plastic bag in the refrigerator for up to three days. An interesting fact about artichokes is that they sweeten the flavour of the next thing that you eat. This is due to the presence of the chemical cynarin and has a most marked effect upon the taste of wine, making it taste quite unpleasant. This reaction is much less pronounced in crumbed or fried artichokes. Jerusalem artichokes are a variety of sunflower, whose name derives from 'girasole', the Italian word for sunflower, rather than Jerusalem the city.

parmesan and rosemary crusted veal chops

☀

Preparation time: **15** minutes
Cooking time: **15** minutes
Serves **4**

4 veal chops, excess fat trimmed
150 g (5½ oz) fresh white
   breadcrumbs
75 g (2¾ oz/¾ cup) freshly grated
   parmesan cheese
1 tablespoon rosemary leaves, finely
   chopped, plus sprigs, for garnish
2 eggs, lightly beaten, seasoned
60 ml (2 fl oz/¼ cup) olive oil
60 g (2¼ oz) butter
4 garlic cloves

1 Flatten the chops to 1 cm (½ inch) thickness. Pat the meat dry with paper towels. Combine the breadcrumbs, parmesan and rosemary in a dish.

2 Dip each chop in the egg, draining off the excess. Press both sides of the chops firmly in the crumb mixture.

3 Heat the oil and butter in a large heavy-based frying pan over low heat, add the garlic cloves and cook until golden. Discard the garlic.

4 Increase the heat to medium and cook the chops for 4–5 minutes on each side, until golden and crisp. Season with salt and pepper, then transfer to serving dishes, garnish with rosemary sprigs and serve with salad, if desired.

salsa rossa

This is usually paired with Salsa verde when served with boiled meats, but it is also delicious with crumbed meats such as the veal chops on this page. Cut 3 large red capsicums (peppers) in half lengthways. Discard the membrane and seeds, then slice the flesh into 1 cm (½ inch) wide strips. Heat 60 ml (2 fl oz/¼ cup) olive oil in a heavy-based frying pan and cook 3 large onions, thinly sliced, over medium heat until soft but not browned. Add the capsicum and cook until the vegetables are very soft and the bulk has been reduced by half. Add ¼ teaspoon chilli flakes, a 400 g (14 oz) tin of tomatoes and season with salt. Simmer for another 25 minutes, or until the sauce has thickened and the oil has separated from the tomatoes. Check the seasoning and adjust if necessary. Serve warm. Serves 4.

parmesan

Parmesan is a hard, crumbly cheese made from skimmed or partially skimmed cow's milk. Buy parmesan in a wedge or, if possible, ask that it be cut from the wheel. Grate it as you need it because when cut, the cheese becomes dry and the flavour is altered. For this reason, never buy pre-grated cheese as it bears little resemblance in flavour and texture to the real thing. Select parmesan with the rind still attached and with no evidence of whitening at the rim. To store, wrap tightly in greaseproof or baking paper and then in foil.

caponata with tuna

✳

Preparation time: 25 minutes
  + 1 hour standing time
Cooking time: 50 minutes
Serves 6

olive oil, for brushing
6 x 200 g (7 oz) tuna steaks

CAPONATA
500 g (1 lb 2 oz) ripe tomatoes
750 g (1 lb 10 oz) eggplants (aubergines),
  cut into 1 cm (½ inch) cubes
125 ml (4 fl oz/½ cup) olive oil
1 onion, chopped
3 celery stalks, thinly sliced
2 tablespoons capers, rinsed and
  squeezed dry
125 g (4½ oz/⅔ cup) green olives, pitted
1 tablespoon sugar
125 ml (4 fl oz/½ cup) red wine vinegar

1   To make the caponata, score a cross
in the base of each tomato. Place in a
heatproof bowl, cover with boiling water
and leave for 30 seconds. Transfer to cold
water and peel the skin from the cross.
Cut the flesh into 1 cm (½ inch) cubes.
2   Sprinkle the eggplant with salt and
leave in a colander for 1 hour. Rinse well
and pat dry with paper towels. Heat
2 tablespoons of the oil in a frying pan
over medium heat and cook half the
eggplant for 4–5 minutes, or until golden
and soft. Remove from the pan and drain
on crumpled paper towels. Repeat with
more oil and the remaining eggplant.
3   Heat the remaining oil in the same
pan, add the onion and celery, and cook
for 5–6 minutes, or until softened. Reduce
the heat to low, add the tomato and
simmer for 15 minutes. Stir in the capers,
olives, sugar and vinegar, season and
continue to simmer for 10 minutes, or
until slightly reduced. Stir in the eggplant.
Remove from the heat and cool.
4   Heat a chargrill plate and brush it
lightly with olive oil. Cook the tuna for
2–3 minutes each side, or to your liking.
Serve with the caponata.

caponata with tuna

baked radicchio

✳

Preparation time: 10 minutes
Cooking time: 35 minutes
Serves 4

1 kg (2 lb 4 oz) radicchio
2 tablespoons olive oil
100 g (3½ oz) bacon, thinly sliced

1   Preheat the oven to 180°C (350°F/
Gas 4). Remove the tough outer leaves of
the radicchio, then cut into four wedges.

2   Heat the oil in a flameproof casserole
dish large enough to fit all the radicchio
in a single layer (but do not add the
radicchio yet). Add the bacon and cook
over medium heat until the fat has just
melted but the meat is not crisp. Add the
radicchio wedges and turn gently to coat
well. Bake, covered, for 25–30 minutes,
turning the radicchio occasionally, until it
is tender when pierced with a sharp knife.
Season and transfer to a warm dish with
all the liquid. Serve immediately.

involtini of swordfish

Preparation time: **35 minutes**
Cooking time: **10 minutes**
Serves **4**

1 kg (2 lb 4 oz) piece swordfish, skin
  removed, cut into four 4 x 5 cm
  (1½ x 2 inch) pieces
3 lemons
80 ml (2½ fl oz/⅓ cup) olive oil
1 small onion, chopped
3 garlic cloves, chopped
2 tablespoons chopped rinsed capers
2 tablespoons chopped kalamata olives
35 g (1¼ oz/⅓ cup) freshly grated
  parmesan cheese
120 g (4¼ oz/1½ cups) fresh white
  breadcrumbs
2 tablespoons chopped flat-leaf (Italian)
  parsley
1 egg, lightly beaten
24 fresh bay leaves
4 small white onions, each cut into 6 wedges

1 Cut each swordfish piece horizontally
into four slices to give you 16 slices. Place
each piece between two pieces of plastic
wrap and roll with a rolling pin to flatten
the fish. Cut each piece in half.
2 Thinly peel the zest from the lemons
and cut it to make 24 pieces. Squeeze
60 ml (2 fl oz/¼ cup) of lemon juice.
3 Heat 2 tablespoons of the olive oil
in a frying pan over medium heat. Add
the chopped onion and garlic and cook
for 2 minutes. Place in a bowl with the
capers, olives, parmesan, breadcrumbs
and parsley. Season, add the egg and mix.
Divide the stuffing among the fish pieces
and roll up the fish to form neat parcels.
Thread four rolls onto each of eight
skewers, alternating with the bay leaves,
lemon zest and onion wedges.
4 Mix the remaining olive oil with the
lemon juice. Barbecue the skewers for
3–4 minutes each side, basting with the
oil and lemon mixture.

NOTE: To prevent wooden skewers from
burning, soak for 20 minutes before using.

Roll the fish slices between two
pieces of plastic wrap to flatten.

Thread the rolls, bay leaves, lemon
zest and onion onto skewers.

rabbit with rosemary and white wine

✻

Preparation time: **25 minutes**
Cooking time: **2 hours**
Serves **4**

1 large rabbit (about 1.6 kg/3 lb 8 oz)
30 g (1 oz/¼ cup) seasoned flour
60 ml (2 fl oz/¼ cup) olive oil
2 onions, thinly sliced
1 large rosemary sprig
1 small sage sprig
2 garlic cloves, crushed
500 ml (17 fl oz/2 cups) dry white wine
400 g (14 oz) tin chopped tomatoes
pinch of cayenne pepper
125 ml (4 fl oz/½ cup) chicken stock
12 small black olives (such as niçoise or
    ligurian) (optional)
3 small rosemary sprigs, extra (optional)

1 Cut the rabbit into large pieces and dredge the pieces in the flour. Heat the oil in a large heavy-based saucepan over medium heat. Brown the rabbit pieces on all sides, then remove and set aside.
2 Reduce the heat and add the onion, rosemary and sage to the pan. Cook gently for 10 minutes, then stir in the garlic and return the rabbit to the pan.
3 Increase the heat to high, add the wine and cook for 1 minute. Stir in the tomatoes, cayenne pepper and stock. Reduce the heat, cover and simmer over low heat for about 1½ hours, or until the rabbit is tender.
4 Halfway through cooking, check the sauce and if it seems too dry, add 60 ml (2 fl oz/¼ cup) water. Discard the herb sprigs. Season to taste. Garnish with the olives and extra rosemary, if desired.

rabbit

There are two types of rabbit, domestic and wild, with the latter being the more flavoursome because it feeds on wild herbs, bay leaves and juniper berries. The quality of the domestic rabbit depends upon its feed, breeding and age, but in general they are plumper than their wild counterparts.

Ideally, a rabbit should weigh between 1 and 1.25 kg (2 lb 4 oz and 2 lb 12 oz) and have light-coloured flesh. These are the most tender and can be cooked in any manner suitable for young chicken. Older or wild rabbits benefit from longer, more moist cooking methods such as braising.

olive oils

Like wine, the flavour, colour and taste of olive oil varies according to the type of fruit used and the climate, soil and area of cultivation.

The type and ripeness of the olive influences the colour of the oil, so green olives give grassy, green oils, while ripe black olives produce rich yellow oils. Black olives that are less ripe produce a rich, green oil that pales after three months and is considered superior. However, riper olives yield more oil. Some olive trees are grown to produce olives for eating and some for oil — they are not harvested from the same trees.

what does the label mean?

Olive oils can be divided into four major groups that are distinguished by their level of acidity.

• Extra virgin olive oil is the highest quality oil, made from the first pressing of olives, with the lowest acidity level at less than 1 per cent. It has an intense, fruity flavour. It can only be extracted mechanically or manually cold pressed, without using heat or chemicals, so the oil is not altered.

• Virgin olive oil has a good flavour and is treated and extracted in the same way as extra virgin. However, it has an acidity level of less than 2 per cent.

• Olive oil, once known as pure olive oil, is a blend of unrefined virgin olive oil and refined virgin olive oil which has an acidity level of less than 3.3 per cent. The use of heat to aid extraction contributes to the higher level of acidity.

• Light olive oil is made from the filtered combination of refined olive oil with very small amounts of virgin olive oil. It is not light in kilojoules as it has exactly the same amount as other oils. It is lighter than other olive oils in texture and taste, however, making it ideal for baking. Filtration leads to a higher smoke point so it is also suitable for deep-frying.

Olive oils that are infused with Mediterranean flavours, such as lemon, basil, garlic, rosemary, truffle, tarragon and porcini mushrooms, are becoming more readily available.

The better-quality infused oils are made by pressing the flavouring with the olives to simultaneously extract both of their essential oils. Otherwise, the essential oil is extracted separately and infused into the olive oil, often with some of the flavouring ingredient put in the bottle.

which type to use?

Undoubtedly the best oil to use when preparing Mediterranean food, olive oil's diversity lends itself to most cooking methods and many dishes, including salad dressings, pasta making and baking. Olive oil is excellent for frying as it reaches high temperatures without breaking down and forms a seal around the food, minimising fat absorption and imparting a golden glow.

While there are some classic rules, such as using olive oil for general cooking purposes and extra virgin olive oil for making salad dressings and drizzling on food before serving, the choice of the type of olive oil used is equally a matter of personal taste. Connoisseurs identify four flavour categories: gentle-flavoured oil with a hint of olive taste is light; delicate, buttery-flavoured oil is mild; oils with a stronger, more distinct olive taste are semi-fruity; and the fully fledged, strongest olive-flavoured oils are fruity or peppery. There are now so many olive oils on the market that it is best to try different varieties from different countries and regions to find those that you prefer.

Like all oils, olive oil should be stored in a cool, dark place. Do not store it in the refrigerator because it will solidify, and never keep it near the stovetop. If the olive oil container is left open, exposure to air will oxidise the oil and make it rancid.

Olive oil can generally be kept for up to six months when opened and up to two years unopened. Some boutique oils, however, only last for three months. Bear in mind that unlike many wines, olive oils do not improve with age.

olive bread

✳ ✳

Preparation time: 30 minutes + 2 hours
30 minutes proving time
Cooking time: 35 minutes
Makes 1 loaf

375 g (13 oz/3 cups) strong white
flour, plus 2 teaspoons extra
2 teaspoons dried yeast
2 teaspoons sugar
2 tablespoons olive oil

110 g (3¾ oz/⅔ cup) pitted and halved
kalamata olives
1 small oregano sprig, leaves removed and
torn into small pieces (optional)
olive oil, to glaze

1 Put one-third of the flour in a large bowl and stir in 1 teaspoon salt. Put the yeast, sugar and 250 ml (9 fl oz/1 cup) warm water in a small bowl and stir well. Leave in a warm, draught-free place for 10 minutes, or until bubbles appear on the surface. The mixture should be frothy and slightly increased in volume. If your yeast doesn't foam, it is dead, so you will have to discard it and start again.

2 Add the yeast mixture to the salted flour and stir to make a thin, lumpy paste. Cover with a tea towel (dish towel) and set aside in a warm, draught-free place for 45 minutes, or until doubled in size.

3 Stir in the remaining flour, the oil and 125 ml (4 fl oz/½ cup) warm water. Mix with a wooden spoon until a rough dough forms. Transfer to a lightly floured work surface and knead for 10–12 minutes, incorporating as little extra flour as possible to keep the dough soft and moist, but not sticky. Form into a ball. Oil a clean large bowl and roll the dough around in it to lightly coat in the oil. Cut a cross on top, cover the bowl with a tea towel and set aside in a warm, draught-free place for 1 hour, or until doubled in size.

4 Lightly grease a baking tray and dust with flour. Punch down the dough on a lightly floured surface. Roll the dough out to 25 x 30 cm (10 x 12 inches) and 1cm (½ inch) thick. Squeeze any excess liquid from the olives and toss in the extra 2 teaspoons of flour to coat. Scatter over the dough and top with the oregano. Roll up tightly lengthways, pressing firmly to expel any air pockets as you roll. Press the ends together to form an oval, 25 cm (10 inches) long. Transfer to the prepared tray, join side down. Make three shallow diagonal slashes across the top. Slide the tray into a large plastic bag and leave in a warm place for 45 minutes, or until doubled in bulk.

5 Preheat the oven to 220°C (425°F/ Gas 7). Brush the top of the loaf with olive oil and bake for 30 minutes. Reduce the temperature to 180°C (350°F/Gas 4) and bake for another 5 minutes. Cool on a wire rack. Serve warm or cold.

NOTE: Instead of oregano, you can use 2 teaspoons finely chopped rosemary. Fold through the dough and sprinkle whole leaves on top after brushing with olive oil.

focaccia

✹ ✹

Preparation time: 50 minutes + 1 hour
  50 minutes proving time
Cooking time: 25 minutes
Makes 1 flat loaf

2 teaspoons dried yeast
1 teaspoon caster (superfine) sugar
2 tablespoons olive oil
405 g (14¼ oz/3¼ cups) strong white flour
1 tablespoon full-cream milk powder

TOPPING
1 tablespoon olive oil
1–2 garlic cloves, crushed
black olives
rosemary sprigs or leaves
1 teaspoon dried oregano
1–2 teaspoons coarse sea salt

1 Lightly grease an 18 x 28 cm
(7 x 11¼ inch) baking tray. Put the yeast,
sugar and 250 ml (9 fl oz/1 cup) warm
water in a small bowl and stir well. Leave
in a warm, draught-free place for 10
minutes, or until bubbles appear on the
surface. The mixture should be frothy and
slightly increased in volume. If your yeast
doesn't foam, it is dead, so you will have
to discard it and start again. Add the oil.
2 Sift 375 g (13 oz/3 cups) of the flour,
the milk powder and ½ teaspoon salt into
a large bowl. Make a well in the centre
and add the yeast mixture. Beat with a
wooden spoon until the mixture is well
combined. Add enough of the remaining
flour to form a soft dough, and then turn
onto a lightly floured surface.
3 Knead the dough for 10 minutes, or
until smooth and elastic. Place in a large,
lightly oiled bowl and brush the surface
with oil. Cover with plastic wrap or a
damp tea towel (dish towel) and leave
in a warm place for 1 hour, or until well
risen. Punch down the dough and knead
for 1 minute. Roll into a rectangle,
18 x 28 cm (7 x 11¼ inches) and place in
the prepared tray. Cover with plastic wrap
and leave in a warm place for 20 minutes.
Using the handle of a wooden spoon, form
indents 1 cm (½ inch) deep all over the
dough at regular intervals. Cover with
plastic wrap and set aside for 30 minutes,
or until the dough is well risen. Preheat
the oven to 180°C (350°F/Gas 4).
4 To make the topping, brush the
combined olive oil and garlic over the
surface of the dough. Top with the olives
and rosemary sprigs, and then sprinkle
with the oregano and salt.
5 Bake for 20–25 minutes, or until
golden and crisp. Cut into large squares
and serve warm.

NOTE: Focaccia is best eaten on the day of
baking. It can be reheated if necessary.

zabaglione

Zabaglione is a whisked custard traditionally made in a copper bowl. Usually, it is served as soon as it is made, although sometimes it is chilled for several hours before serving. It is also delicious poured over fruit in a gratin dish and browned under the grill. It can be made using sweet Marsala or dessert wine.

strawberries with balsamic vinegar

strawberries with balsamic vinegar

Preparation time: 10 minutes
   + 1 hour standing time
Cooking time: nil
Serves 4

750 g (1 lb 10 oz) ripe small strawberries
55 g (2 oz/¼ cup) caster (superfine) sugar
2 tablespoons balsamic vinegar
125 g (4½ oz/½ cup) mascarpone cheese, to serve

1 Wipe the strawberries with a clean damp cloth and hull them. If there are any large strawberries, cut them in half.
2 Place the strawberries in a glass bowl, sprinkle the sugar evenly over the top and toss gently to coat. Leave for 30 minutes to macerate. Sprinkle the vinegar over the strawberries, toss gently to coat and set aside for a further 30 minutes.
3 Spoon the strawberries into four glasses, drizzle with the syrup and top with a dollop of mascarpone.

zabaglione

Preparation time: 5 minutes
Cooking time: 5 minutes
Serves 4

4 egg yolks
80 g (2¾ oz/⅓ cup) caster (superfine) sugar
80 ml (2½ fl oz/⅓ cup) Marsala

1 Combine all the ingredients in a large heatproof bowl set over a saucepan of barely simmering water. Make sure the base of the bowl does not touch the water.

Whisk with a balloon whisk or electric beaters for 5 minutes, or until the mixture is smooth and foamy and has tripled in volume. Do not stop whisking and do not allow the bowl to become too hot or the eggs will scramble. The final result should be creamy, pale and mousse-like.

2 Pour the zabaglione into four glasses and serve immediately.

NOTE: Sometimes zabaglione is served chilled. If you want to do this, cover the glasses with plastic wrap and refrigerate for at least 1 hour. You must make sure the zabaglione is properly cooked or it may separate when left to stand.

cassata alla siciliana

✹ ✹

Preparation time: 25 minutes
    + overnight chilling time
Cooking time: 2 minutes
Serves 6

60 g (2¼ oz) blanched almonds, halved
650 g (1 lb 7 oz) fresh ricotta (see Note)
80 g (2¾ oz/½ cup) icing (confectioners') sugar
1½ teaspoons natural vanilla extract
2 teaspoons finely grated lemon zest
60 g (2¼ oz) cedro, chopped (see Note)
60 g (2¼ oz) glacé orange, chopped
60 g (2¼ oz) red glacé cherries, halved
30 g (1 oz) pistachio nuts
375 g (13 oz) unfilled, ready-made round sponge cake
125 ml (4 fl oz/½ cup) Madeira
sweetened whipped cream
6 blanched almonds, extra
red glacé cherries, extra, halved
icing (confectioners') sugar, for dusting

1 Place the almonds in a small frying pan and dry-fry, tossing, over medium heat for 2 minutes, or until just starting to change colour. Remove and cool.
2 Press the ricotta through a sieve over a bowl. Stir in the icing sugar, vanilla, lemon zest, cedro, glacé orange, glacé cherries, almonds and pistachios. Mix together well.
3 Grease a 1.5 litre (52 fl oz/6 cup) pudding bowl. Cut the cake horizontally into 1 cm (½ inch) thick slices. Set aside 1 round and cut the remaining rounds into wedges, trimming the bases to make triangles. Lightly sprinkle the cut side of the triangles with Madeira and arrange around the base and side of the bowl, cut side down, trimming if necessary to fit. Spoon the ricotta mixture into the centre. Top with the reserved round of sponge cake. Press down firmly and neaten the rough edges, if necessary. Refrigerate overnight.
4 Carefully unmould onto a serving plate. Spoon some of the cream on top and arrange the extra almonds and cherries around it. Dust with icing sugar just before serving and serve with more sweetened cream.

NOTE: Fresh ricotta from delicatessens is best for this recipe as it can be successfully moulded. Cedro is the candied fruit of the citron tree. If it is not available, you can use glacé citrus instead. The cream can be piped in patterns over the cassata for a true Sicilian look.

cassata alla siciliana

Arrange the pieces of cake around the base and side of the bowl.

Spoon the ricotta mixture into the cake-lined bowl.

Top with the reserved round of sponge cake, press down firmly and neaten any edges.

zuppa inglese

❋

Preparation time: 25 minutes
Cooking time: 5 minutes
Serves 6

500 ml (17 fl oz/2 cups) milk
1 vanilla bean, halved lengthways
4 egg yolks
115 g (4 oz/½ cup) caster (superfine) sugar
2 tablespoons plain (all-purpose) flour
300 g (10½ oz) Madeira cake, cut into
    1 cm (½ inch) slices
80 ml (2½ fl oz/⅓ cup) dark (bittersweet)
    rum
30 g (1 oz) dark chocolate, coarsely grated
50 g (1¾ oz) flaked almonds, toasted

1   Heat the milk and vanilla bean in a
saucepan over low heat until bubbles
appear around the edge of the pan.
Whisk the egg yolks, sugar and flour
together in a bowl until thick and pale.
2   Discard the vanilla bean and whisk the
warm milk slowly into the egg mixture,
then blend well. Return to a clean pan
and stir over medium heat until it boils
and thickens. Allow to cool slightly.
3   Line the base of a 1.5 litre (52 fl oz/
6 cup) serving dish with one-third of
the cake slices and brush well with the
rum combined with 1 tablespoon water.
Spread one-third of the custard over the
cake. Repeat this process, finishing with a
layer of custard. Cover and refrigerate for
3 hours. Sprinkle with the chocolate and
almonds just before serving.

almond semifreddo

Place the biscuits in a plastic bag and crush them with a rolling pin.

Beat the egg yolks and sugar together using electric beaters.

Carefully spoon the mixture into the lined loaf tin.

almond semifreddo

❋

Preparation time: 30 minutes
    + 4 hours freezing time
Cooking time: nil
Serves 8–10

8 amaretti biscuits
310 ml (10¾ fl oz/1¼ cups) pouring
    (whipping) cream
4 eggs, at room temperature, separated

85 g (3 oz/⅔ cup) icing (confectioners')
    sugar
60 ml (2 fl oz/¼ cup) amaretto
80 g (2¾ oz/½ cup) toasted almonds,
    chopped
fresh fruit or extra amaretto, to serve

1   Place the biscuits in a plastic bag and
crush with a rolling pin. Set aside. Whip
the cream until firm peaks form, then
cover and refrigerate. Line a 10 x 21 cm
(4 x 8¼ inch) loaf (bar) tin with plastic
wrap, extending it over the long sides.
2   Beat the egg yolks and icing sugar
in a large bowl until pale and creamy.

Whisk the egg whites in a separate bowl
until firm peaks form. Stir the amaretto,
almonds and crushed biscuits into the egg
yolk mixture, then carefully fold in the
chilled cream and egg whites until well
combined. Carefully spoon into the lined
tin and cover with the overhanging plastic
wrap. Freeze for 4 hours, or until frozen
but not rock hard. Serve slices with the
fresh fruit or a sprinkling of amaretto.

NOTE: Semifreddo means semi-frozen,
so if you are leaving it in the freezer
overnight, put it in the refrigerator for
30 minutes before serving.

pesche ripiene (stuffed peaches)

Preparation time: 15 minutes
Cooking time: 25 minutes
Serves 6

6 ripe peaches
60 g (2¼ oz) amaretti biscuits, crushed
1 egg yolk
2 tablespoons caster (superfine) sugar
20 g (¾ oz) ground almonds
1 tablespoon amaretto
60 ml (2 fl oz/¼ cup) sweet white wine
1 teaspoon caster (superfine) sugar, extra
20 g (¾ oz) unsalted butter

1 Preheat the oven to 180°C (350°F/
Gas 4) and lightly grease a 25 x 30 cm
(10 x 12 inch) ovenproof dish with butter.
2 Cut each peach in half and remove
the stones. Scoop a little of the pulp out
from each and combine in a small bowl
with the biscuit, egg yolk, sugar, ground
almonds and amaretto.
3 Spoon some of the mixture into each
peach half and then place them, cut
side up, in the dish. Sprinkle with the
wine and the extra sugar. Place a dot
of butter on top of each and bake for
20–25 minutes, or until golden.

macerated oranges

Preparation time: 10 minutes
    + 2 hours chilling time
Cooking time: nil
Serves 4

4 oranges
1 teaspoon finely grated lemon zest
55 g (2 oz/¼ cup) caster (superfine) sugar
1 tablespoon lemon juice
2 tablespoons Cointreau or Maraschino
    (optional)

1 Cut a thin slice off the top and bottom
of each orange. Using a small sharp knife,
slice off the skin and pith. Slice down the
side of an orange segment between the
flesh and the membrane. Repeat on the
other side and lift the segment out. Do
this over a bowl to catch the juice. Repeat
with all the orange segments. Squeeze out
any juice remaining in the membranes.

2 Place the orange segments on a
shallow dish and sprinkle with the lemon
zest, sugar and lemon juice. Toss carefully.
Cover and refrigerate for at least 2 hours.
Toss again. Serve chilled and drizzle with
the Cointreau or Maraschino just before
serving, if desired.

macerated oranges

sicilian cannoli

✹ ✹ ✹

Preparation time: 30 minutes
  + 30 minutes chilling time
Cooking time: 5 minutes
Makes 12

300 g (10½ oz) plain (all-purpose)
  flour
1 tablespoon caster (superfine) sugar
1 teaspoon ground cinnamon
40 g (1½ oz) unsalted butter
60 ml (2 fl oz/¼ cup) Marsala
vegetable oil, for deep-frying
icing (confectioners') sugar,
  to dust

FILLING
100 g (3½ oz/½ cup) cedro (see Note)
500 g (1 lb 2 oz) ricotta cheese
1 teaspoon orange flower water
60 g (2¼ oz) bittersweet chocolate,
  coarsely grated or chopped
1 tablespoon grated orange zest
60 g (2¼ oz/½ cup) icing
  (confectioners') sugar

1 To make the filling, finely chop the
cedro and combine with the other
ingredients in a bowl. Add 2 tablespoons
water and mix well to form a dough.
Cover with plastic wrap and refrigerate.
2 Combine the flour, sugar and cinnamon
in a bowl, rub in the butter and add the
Marsala. Mix until the dough comes
together in a loose clump, then knead on
a lightly floured surface for 4–5 minutes,
or until smooth. Wrap in plastic wrap and
refrigerate for at least 30 minutes.
3 Cut the dough in half and roll each
portion on a lightly floured surface into
a thin sheet about 5 mm (¼ inch) thick.
Cut each portion into six 9 cm (3½ inch)
squares. Place a metal cannoli tube (see
Note) diagonally across the middle of
each square. Fold the sides over the tube,
moistening the overlap with water, then
press together to seal.
4 Heat the oil in a large, deep saucepan
to 180°C (350°F), or until a cube of
bread dropped into the oil browns in

Knead the dough on a lightly
floured surface until it is smooth.

Fold the dough over the metal
tube, moisten the overlap with
water and press the dough
together to seal.

15 seconds. Drop one or two tubes at a time into the hot oil. Fry gently until golden brown and crisp. Remove from the oil, gently remove the moulds and drain on crumpled paper towels. When the tubes have cooled, fill a piping (icing) bag with the ricotta mixture and fill the shells. Dust with icing sugar and serve.

NOTE: Cedro is the candied fruit of the citron tree. You can use glacé citrus as a substitute. Metal cannoli tubes are available at kitchenware shops. You can also use 2 cm (¾ inch) diameter wooden dowels cut into 12 cm (4½ inch) lengths.

sicilian rice fritters

✹ ✹

Preparation time: **20 minutes**
    + 1 hour standing time
Cooking time: **40 minutes**
Serves **8**

110 g (3¾ oz/½ cup) arborio rice
330 ml (11¼ fl oz/1⅓ cups) milk
10 g (¼ oz) unsalted butter
1 tablespoon caster (superfine) sugar
1 vanilla bean, halved lengthways, scraped
1 teaspoon dried yeast
2 tablespoons cedro (see Note above), finely chopped
2 teaspoons grated lemon zest
vegetable oil, for deep-frying
plain (all-purpose) flour, for rolling
2 tablespoons fragrant honey

1 Combine the rice, milk, butter, sugar, vanilla bean and scraped seeds, and a pinch of salt in a heavy-based saucepan. Bring to the boil over medium heat, then reduce the heat to very low. Cover and cook for 15–18 minutes, or until most of the liquid has been absorbed. Remove from the heat, cover and set aside.
2 Dissolve the yeast in 2 tablespoons warm water and set aside for 5 minutes, or until frothy. If your yeast doesn't foam, it is dead and you will have to start again.
3 Discard the vanilla bean from the rice mixture. Add the yeast mixture, cedro and lemon zest to the rice. Mix well, cover and allow to stand for 1 hour.
4 Fill a deep-fryer or heavy-based saucepan one-third full of oil and heat to 180°C (350°F), or until a spoonful of the batter dropped into the oil browns in 15 seconds.
5 Shape the rice into croquettes, about 2.5 x 8 cm (1 x 3¼ inches), and roll them in flour. Deep-fry in batches for 5–6 minutes, or until golden brown on all sides. Remove with a slotted spoon and drain on crumpled paper towels. Drizzle with honey and serve immediately.

biscotti

✻ ✻

Preparation time: **25 minutes**
Cooking time: **55 minutes**
Makes **45**

250 g (9 oz/2 cups) plain (all-purpose) flour
1 teaspoon baking powder
230 g (8 oz/1 cup) caster (superfine) sugar
3 eggs
1 egg yolk
1 teaspoon natural vanilla extract
1 teaspoon grated orange zest
110 g (3¾ oz/¾ cup) pistachio nuts

1 Preheat the oven to 180°C (350°F/
Gas 4). Line two baking trays with baking
paper and lightly dust with flour.
2 Sift the flour and baking powder into
a large bowl. Add the sugar and mix
well. Make a well in the centre and add
2 whole eggs, the egg yolk, vanilla
and orange zest. Using a large metal
spoon, stir until just combined. Mix in
the pistachios. Knead for 2–3 minutes
on a floured surface. The dough will be
stiff at first. Sprinkle a little water onto
the dough. Divide the mixture into two
portions and roll into logs about 25 cm
(10 inches) long and 8 cm (3¼ inches)
wide. Slightly flatten the tops.
3 Place the logs on the trays, allowing
room for spreading. Beat the remaining
egg and brush over the logs to glaze. Bake
for 35 minutes, then remove from the
oven and allow to cool slightly.
4 Reduce the temperature to 150°C
(300°F/Gas 2). Use a serrated knife to cut
each log into 5 mm (¼ inch) slices. Place,
flat side down, on the trays and bake for
8 minutes. Turn the biscuits over and cook
for a further 8 minutes, or until slightly
coloured, crisp and dry. Transfer to a
wire rack to cool completely. Store in an
airtight container.

biscotti

Meaning 'twice cooked',
biscotti originally referred to
ships' biscuits, which were very
dry, rock-hard little slabs of
cooked flour and water paste
made to last indefinitely for
the long voyages in old sailing
ships. The biscuits were so hard
that they had to be soaked
before eating and only weevils
and sea water could destroy
them. Nowadays, biscotti
generally refers to the sweet
Italian biscuits that are first
shaped into a loaf and baked,
then thinly sliced and baked
again. The result is a very
crunchy biscuit that is perfect
for dipping into coffee or a
sweet dessert wine.

honey and pine nut tart

✸ ✸

Preparation time: 25 minutes
+ 30 minutes chilling time
Cooking time: 1 hour
Serves 6

235 g (8½ oz/1½ cups) pine nuts
175 g (6 oz/½ cup) honey
115 g (4 oz) unsalted butter, softened
115 g (4 oz/½ cup) caster (superfine) sugar
3 eggs, lightly beaten
¼ teaspoon natural vanilla extract
1 tablespoon almond liqueur
1 teaspoon finely grated lemon zest
1 tablespoon lemon juice
icing (confectioners') sugar, to dust
crème fraîche or mascarpone cheese,
   to serve

PASTRY
250 g (9 oz/2 cups) plain (all-purpose) flour
1½ tablespoons icing (confectioners') sugar
115 g (4 oz) unsalted butter, chilled and
   chopped
1 egg, lightly beaten

1 Preheat the oven to 190°C (375°F/
Gas 5) and place a baking tray on the
middle shelf. Lightly grease a 23 cm
(9 inch) loose-based tart (flan) tin.
2 To make the pastry, sift the flour and
icing sugar into a large bowl and add the
butter. Rub the butter into the flour with
your fingertips until it resembles fine
breadcrumbs. Make a well in the centre
and add the egg and 2 tablespoons cold
water. Mix with a flat-bladed knife, using
a cutting action, until the mixture comes
together in beads.
3 Gather the dough and lift onto a lightly
floured work surface. Press into a ball,
roll out to a 3 mm (⅛ inch) thick circle
and invert into the tin. Use a small ball
of pastry to press it into the tin, allowing
any excess to hang over the sides. Roll a
rolling pin over the tin, cutting off any
excess pastry. Prick the base all over with
a fork and chill for 15 minutes. Roll out
the pastry scraps and cut out three leaves.
Cover and refrigerate for 15 minutes.
4 Line the pastry with baking paper and
fill with baking beads or uncooked rice.
Bake on the heated tray for 10 minutes,
then remove the tart tin, leaving the tray
in the oven. Reduce the temperature to
180°C (350°F/Gas 4).
5 To make the filling, roast the pine nuts
in the oven for 3 minutes, or until golden.
Heat the honey in a small saucepan until
runny, then allow to cool. Cream the
butter and sugar until smooth and pale.
Gradually add the egg, beating well after
each addition. Mix in the honey, vanilla,
liqueur, lemon zest and juice and a pinch
of salt. Stir in the pine nuts. Spoon into
the pastry case and smooth the surface.
Arrange the pastry leaves in the centre.
6 Place the tin on the hot tray and bake
for 40 minutes, or until golden and set.
Cover the top with foil after 25 minutes.
Serve warm or at room temperature,
dusted with icing sugar. Serve with the
crème fraîche or mascarpone.

chimneysweep's gelato

This simple, yet unexpectedly
wonderful, dessert can be made
using home-made gelato, or equally
well using a premium-quality bought
vanilla ice cream. For each portion
of vanilla gelato or ice cream,
sprinkle 1 teaspoon of finely ground
espresso coffee over the top. Pour on
1 tablespoon of whisky or bourbon
and serve immediately.

france

Think of France and you immediately think of food and wine. French cooking is famous for its simplicity — a few herbs, a little wine and some garlic are used in subtle ways to flavour meat, chicken or seafood that is cooked to perfection. Accompanying sauces, another feature of French cuisine, are often strongly flavoured as with the garlicky aïoli. Long, slow cooking is commonly utilised to produce melt-in-the-mouth dishes such as Chicken with forty cloves of garlic. Olives, olive oil, eggplants (aubergines), zucchini (courgettes) and tomatoes fresh from the vine are very popular in the Provençal region. French desserts, many of which are based on fruits such as pears, cherries, figs and apricots, are renowned.

salad niçoise

Preparation time: 20 minutes
Cooking time: 15 minutes
Serves 4

3 eggs
2 vine-ripened tomatoes
175 g (6 oz) baby green beans, trimmed
125 ml (4 fl oz/½ cup) olive oil
2 tablespoons white wine vinegar
1 large garlic clove, halved

325 g (11½ oz) iceberg lettuce heart
1 small red capsicum (pepper)
1 Lebanese (short) cucumber
1 celery stalk
¼ large red onion, thinly sliced
425 g (15 oz) tin tuna, drained and
    broken into chunks
12 kalamata olives
45 g (1¾ oz) tin anchovy fillets,
    drained
2 teaspoons baby capers, rinsed and
    squeezed dry
12 small basil leaves

1 Put the eggs in a saucepan of cold water. Bring to the boil, then reduce the heat and simmer for 10 minutes. Stir during the first few minutes to centre the yolks. Cool under cold water, then peel and cut into quarters. Cut each tomato into eight wedges.

2 Cook the beans in a saucepan of boiling water for 2 minutes, rinse under cold water, then drain.

3 To make the dressing, whisk together the oil and vinegar.

4 Rub the garlic over the base and sides of a platter. Cut the lettuce into eight wedges and arrange over the base of the platter. Remove the seeds and membrane from the capsicum, then thinly slice. Cut the cucumber and celery into thin 5 cm (2 inch) lengths. Layer the egg, tomato, beans, capsicum, cucumber and celery over the lettuce. Scatter the onion and tuna over them, then the olives, anchovies, capers and basil. Drizzle with dressing and serve.

anchovy butter

Mash 50 g (1¾ oz) drained anchovies using a mortar and pestle. Cream 125 g (4½ oz) softened unsalted butter until smooth. Gradually beat in the anchovy, then mix in 1 teaspoon lemon juice, or to taste, a few drops at a time. Season with ground black pepper. You can also stir in 1 tablespoon chopped mixed thyme and parsley. Serve with grilled fish or beef. Serves 4–6.

salad niçoise

This dish literally has dozens of interpretations, although the most traditional is not always instantly recognised. It does not contain modern additions such as cooked ingredients, except for hard-boiled eggs.

Ingredients depend on what is seasonally available, although the staples are black olives such as niçoise, anchovy fillets, tomatoes and garlic. Tuna often makes an appearance.

fresh beetroot and goat's cheese salad

✻

Preparation time: 20 minutes
Cooking time: 30 minutes
Serves 4

1 kg (2 lb 4 oz) fresh beetroot (4 bulbs
    with leaves)
200 g (7 oz) green beans
1 tablespoon red wine vinegar
2 tablespoons extra virgin olive oil
1 garlic clove, crushed
1 tablespoon drained capers, rinsed and
    coarsely chopped
100 g (3½ oz) goat's cheese

1 Trim the leaves from the beetroot.
Scrub the bulbs and wash the leaves well.
Add the whole bulbs to a large saucepan
of salted water, bring to the boil, then
reduce the heat and simmer, covered, for
30 minutes, or until tender when pierced
with the point of a knife.
2 Meanwhile, bring a saucepan of water
to the boil, add the beans and cook for
3 minutes, or until just tender. Remove
with a slotted spoon and plunge into a
bowl of cold water. Drain well. Add the
beetroot leaves to the same saucepan of
water and cook for 3–5 minutes, or until
the leaves and stems are tender. Drain,
plunge into cold water, then drain well.
3 Drain and cool the beetroot bulbs, then
peel the skins off and cut the beetroot
into thin wedges.
4 For the dressing, put the vinegar, oil,
garlic, capers and ½ teaspoon each of salt
and pepper in a screw-top jar and shake
well to combine.
5 To serve, divide the beans, beetroot
leaves and wedges among serving plates.
Crumble the goat's cheese over the top
of each and drizzle with the dressing.
Delicious served with fresh crusty bread.

NOTE: Wear rubber gloves while peeling
the beetroot to avoid staining your hands.

potato and anchovy salad

potato and anchovy salad

 ✻

Preparation time: 20 minutes
Cooking time: 25 minutes
Serves 6

1 kg (2 lb 4 oz) waxy potatoes (such as
    pink fir apple or kipfler/fingerling)
60 ml (2 fl oz/¼ cup) dry white wine
1 tablespoon cider vinegar
60 ml (2 fl oz/¼ cup) olive oil
4 spring onions (scallions), finely chopped
35 g (1¼ oz) anchovy fillets
1 tablespoon chopped flat-leaf (Italian)
    parsley
1 tablespoon snipped chives

1 Cook the potatoes in their skins in
boiling salted water for 20 minutes, or
until just tender. Drain and peel away the
skins while the potatoes are still warm.
Cut into 1 cm (½ inch) thick slices.
2 Put the wine, vinegar, olive oil and
spring onion in a large heavy-based frying
pan over low heat and add the potato
slices. Shake the pan to coat the potato,
then reheat gently.
3 When hot, remove from the heat and
season with salt and pepper. Roughly chop
half the anchovies and toss them through
the potatoes along with the parsley and
chives. Transfer to a platter and put the
remaining anchovies on top. Serve warm
or at room temperature.

pan bagnat

brandade de morue

✳ ✳

Preparation time: 25 minutes
  + 24 hours soaking time
Cooking time: 40 minutes
Serves 6 as an entrée

450 g (1 lb) salt cod (this is the dried weight
  and is about half a cod)
200 g (7 oz) roasting potatoes, cut into
  3 cm (1¼ inch) chunks
150 ml (5 fl oz) olive oil
250 ml (9 fl oz/1 cup) milk
4 garlic cloves, crushed
2 tablespoons lemon juice
olive oil, extra, to drizzle

1 Put the salt cod in a large bowl, cover
with cold water and soak for 24 hours,
changing the water frequently. Drain the
cod and place in a large saucepan of clean
water. Bring to the boil over medium heat,
reduce heat and simmer for 30 minutes.
Drain, then cool for 15 minutes.
2 Meanwhile, cook the potato in a
saucepan of boiling, salted water for
12–15 minutes, or until tender. Drain well
and keep warm.
3 Remove the skin from the fish and
break the flesh into large flaky pieces,
discarding any bones. Put the flesh in
a food processor. Using two separate
saucepans, gently warm the oil in one,
and the milk and garlic in another.
4 Start the food processor and, with
the motor running, alternately add small
amounts of the milk and oil until you
have a thick, paste-like mixture. Add the
potato and process this in short bursts
until combined, being careful not to
overwork the mixture once the potato
has been added. Transfer to a bowl and
gradually add the lemon juice, to taste,
and plenty of freshly ground black pepper.
Gently lighten the mixture by fluffing it
up with a fork. Drizzle with the extra oil
just before serving. Serve warm or cold
with fried bread.

pan bagnat

✳

Preparation time: 15 minutes
  + 1 hour standing time
Cooking time: nil
Serves 4

4 crusty bread rolls, or 1 baguette
  cut into 4 portions
1 garlic clove
60 ml (2 fl oz/¼ cup) olive oil
1 tablespoon red wine vinegar
3 tablespoons torn basil leaves
2 ripe tomatoes, sliced
2 hard-boiled eggs, sliced
95 g (3¼ oz) tin tuna in oil, drained

8 anchovy fillets
1 Lebanese (short) cucumber, sliced
½ green capsicum (pepper), thinly sliced
1 French shallot, thinly sliced

1 Slice the bread rolls or baguette
portions in half and remove some of the
soft centre from the tops. Cut the garlic
clove in half and rub the insides of the
bread with the cut sides. Sprinkle both
sides of the bread with olive oil, vinegar,
and salt and pepper.
2 Put the remaining ingredients on the
base of the rolls, cover with the other half
and wrap each roll in foil. Press firmly
with a light weight and stand in a cool
place for 1 hour before serving.

anchoiade

This classic Provençal sauce is often served as a dip for crudités or toasts. Place 75 ml (2½ fl oz) olive oil in a small saucepan with 150 g (5½ oz) anchovy fillets and cook over very low heat for 10 minutes, or until the anchovies have 'melted'. Remove from the heat and allow to cool. Mash the anchovy into a paste and then add 2 crushed garlic cloves, 2 tablespoons of red wine vinegar and 1 tablespoon of dijon mustard and combine well. Add 50 ml (1½ fl oz) olive oil in a slow steady stream, whisking constantly. Taste and adjust the seasoning if necessary. Makes about 250 ml (9 fl oz/1 cup).

frisée and garlic crouton salad

✹ ✹

Preparation time: 20 minutes
Cooking time: 10 minutes
Serves 4–6

1 tablespoon olive oil
250 g (9 oz) speck, rind removed, cut into 5 mm x 2 cm (¼ x ¾ inch) pieces
½ baguette, sliced
4 garlic cloves
1 baby frisée (curly endive)
100 g (3½ oz) walnuts, toasted

VINAIGRETTE
1 French shallot, finely chopped
1 tablespoon dijon mustard
60 ml (2 fl oz/¼ cup) tarragon vinegar
170 ml (5½ fl oz/⅔ cup) extra virgin olive oil

1 To make the vinaigrette, whisk together the shallot, mustard and vinegar in a bowl. Slowly add the oil, whisking constantly until thickened. Set aside.
2 Heat the oil in a large frying pan, add the speck, bread and garlic and cook over medium–high heat for 5–8 minutes, or until the bread and speck are both crisp. Remove the garlic from the pan.
3 Put the frisée, bread, speck, walnuts and vinaigrette in a large bowl. Toss together and serve.

dressings & sauces

Provençal sauces and dressings are based on herbs, vegetables and oil, rather than the typical butter, cream and flour. This reflects a key element in Provençal cuisine — letting natural flavours shine.

basic vinaigrette

Dissolve a pinch of salt in 2 tablespoons red wine vinegar and very slowly beat in 125 ml (4 fl oz/½ cup) extra virgin olive oil. Season with pepper. To vary this recipe you can add any of the following: 1 crushed garlic clove, 1 teaspoon dijon mustard, 2 tablespoons chopped chives, parsley or mint. You can use lemon juice or another wine vinegar instead of red wine vinegar.

fresh tomato dressing

Peel, seed and finely dice 900 g (2 lb) ripe tomatoes. Place in a bowl and mix with 1 tablespoon each of chopped basil and flat-leaf (Italian) parsley, 2 finely chopped French shallots and 3 tablespoons extra virgin olive oil. Season and stir well. Serve at room temperature. Makes 625 ml (21½ fl oz/2½ cups).

sauce vierge

Combine 700 g (1 lb 9 oz) peeled, seeded and chopped tomatoes, 170 ml (5½ fl oz/⅔ cup) extra virgin olive oil, 3 tablespoons lemon juice, 2 crushed garlic cloves and salt and pepper. Set aside for 2 hours. Just before serving, stir in 6 pitted, finely chopped black olives and 1 tablespoon each of finely chopped chives, parsley and tarragon. Makes 450 ml (16 fl oz).

sauce verte

Blanch and drain 280 g (10 oz) English spinach. Cool slightly, then squeeze to remove excess moisture. Alternatively, use 140 g (5 oz) frozen spinach, thawed and drained well. Put in a blender or food processor. Add 1 slice of bread that has been moistened with a little water, 1 chopped hard-boiled egg, 6 anchovy fillets, 2 tablespoons red wine vinegar and 125 ml (4 fl oz/½ cup) olive oil. Process until smooth. Stir in 1 tablespoon finely chopped cornichons and 1 teaspoon finely chopped capers. Season, to taste. Makes 220 ml (7½ fl oz).

sauce ravigote

Dissolve a pinch of salt in 2 tablespoons red wine vinegar. Stir in 6 tablespoons olive oil; 3 tablespoons chopped parsley, tarragon or chives; 1 small finely chopped onion; 2 tablespoons finely chopped gherkins or cornichons; and 2 tablespoons capers. Season, to taste. Makes 185 ml (6 fl oz/¾ cup).

classic mayonnaise

Bring all the ingredients to room temperature. Use a whisk to whisk 2 egg yolks and 1 teaspoon of dijon mustard for 1 minute. Slowly add 450 ml (16 fl oz) olive oil in a thin stream while continuing to whisk. When the mayonnaise begins to thicken, you can add the oil more rapidly, still whisking well after each addition. When all the oil is added, whisk in 2 tablespoons lemon juice, salt and pepper. If the mayonnaise separates, place a fresh yolk in a clean bowl and start adding the curdled mixture very slowly, whisking continuously until the mixture is silky and firm. Makes 450 ml (16 fl oz).

For a herb mayonnaise: stir in 3 tablespoons chopped herbs such as chives, parsley, basil, chervil or tarragon.

For a remoulade sauce: stir in 2 tablespoons each of capers and chopped gherkins, 2 teaspoons dijon mustard, 2 finely chopped French shallots, 3 finely chopped anchovy fillets, 1 tablespoon chopped tarragon and 2 tablespoons chopped parsley.

goat's cheese galette

✳ ✳

Preparation time: **20 minutes**
  + 30 minutes chilling time
Cooking time: **1 hour 15 minutes**
Serves 6

PASTRY
125 g (4½ oz/1 cup) plain (all-purpose) flour
60 ml (2 fl oz/¼ cup) olive oil

FILLING
1 tablespoon olive oil
2 onions, thinly sliced
1 teaspoon thyme
125 g (4½ oz) ricotta cheese
100 g (3½ oz) soft goat's cheese
2 tablespoons pitted niçoise olives, chopped
1 egg, beaten
60 ml (2 fl oz/¼ cup) pouring (whipping)
  cream

1 To make the pastry, sift the flour and
a pinch of salt into a bowl and make
a well in the centre. Add the olive oil
and mix with a flat-bladed knife until
crumbly. Gradually add 60–80 ml (2–2½
fl oz/¼–⅓ cup) water until the mixture
comes together. Remove and pat together
to form a disc. Refrigerate for 30 minutes.
2 Meanwhile, to make the filling, heat
the oil in a frying pan. Add the onion,
cover and cook for 30 minutes. Season
and stir in half the thyme. Cool.
3 Preheat the oven to 180°C (350°F/
Gas 4). Lightly flour the work surface and
roll out the pastry to 30 cm (12 inch) in
diameter. Put on a heated baking tray.
Evenly spread the onion over the pastry,
leaving a 2.5 cm (1 inch) border. Sprinkle
the ricotta and goat's cheese evenly over
the onion. Scatter the olives over the
cheeses, then sprinkle with the remaining
thyme. Fold the pastry border in to the
edge of the filling, pleating as you go.
4 Combine the egg and cream, then pour
over the filling. Bake in the lower half
of the oven for 45 minutes, or until the
pastry is golden.

goat's cheese
Commonly called chevre, the
French word for goat, goat's
cheeses are prized for their
distinct tart, nutty flavours,
ranging from strong to mild
depending on the altitude and
locality the milk has come from
and ripeness of the cheese.

panisses
(chickpea chips)

Preparation time: 20 minutes + cooling time
Cooking time: 30 minutes
Serves 6

170 g (5¾ oz) besan (chickpea flour)
1½ tablespoons olive oil
vegetable oil, for frying

1   Spray six saucers with cooking oil spray. Place the flour in a bowl and stir in 685 ml (23½ fl oz/2¾ cups) cold water. Whisk with a wire whisk for roughly 2 minutes, or until smooth. Stir in the olive oil and season, to taste, with salt and finely ground black pepper.

2   Pour into a heavy-based saucepan and cook over low heat for about 8 minutes, stirring constantly, until thickened. Cook and stir until the mixture becomes lumpy and starts to pull away from the sides of the pan, about 10–12 minutes more. Remove from the heat and beat until smooth. Working quickly, distribute among the saucers and spread to an even thickness. Allow to cool and set.

3   Preheat the oven to 120°C (235°F/ Gas ½). Remove the mixture from the saucers and cut into sticks 5 cm (2 inches) long and 2 cm (¾ inch) wide. Pour the vegetable oil into a large heavy-based saucepan to a depth of about 2.5 cm (1 inch). Heat to very hot and fry the chips in batches until crisp and golden, about 2 minutes on each side. Remove with a slotted spoon and drain on crumpled paper towels. Transfer cooked batches to trays and keep warm in the oven while the rest are being fried. Serve hot, sprinkled with salt and freshly ground black pepper and perhaps some grated parmesan cheese.

NOTE: For a sweet snack, sprinkle with sugar while still hot.

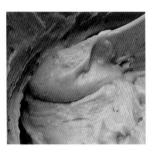

Cook and stir the mixture until it becomes lumpy and starts to pull away from the sides of the pan.

Working quickly, divide the mixture among the saucers and spread to an even thickness.

bourride

While there are numerous versions of this French Riviera classic, with Provençe and Languedoc claiming it as their own, the one defining characteristic of all bourride is the addition of aïoli, as this gives it the customary smooth texture, pale-yellow colour and hearty garlic flavour.

bourride (garlic seafood soup)

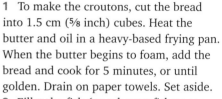

Preparation time: 25 minutes
Cooking time: 1 hour 10 minutes
Serves 8

4 slices white bread, crusts removed
1 tablespoon butter
1 tablespoon olive oil
2 kg (4 lb 8 oz) assorted firm white fish
   (such as bass, whiting and cod)
5 egg yolks
4 garlic cloves, crushed
3–5 teaspoons lemon juice
250 ml (9 fl oz/1 cup) olive oil, extra

STOCK
80 ml (2½ fl oz/⅓ cup) olive oil
1 large onion, chopped
1 carrot, sliced
1 leek, white part only, chopped
420 ml (14½ fl oz/1⅔ cups) dry white wine
1 teaspoon fennel seeds
2 garlic cloves, bruised
2 bay leaves
1 large strip orange zest
2 thyme sprigs

1 To make the croutons, cut the bread into 1.5 cm (⅝ inch) cubes. Heat the butter and oil in a heavy-based frying pan. When the butter begins to foam, add the bread and cook for 5 minutes, or until golden. Drain on paper towels. Set aside.

2 Fillet the fish (or ask your fishmonger to do it), reserving the heads and bones for the stock.

3 To make the aïoli, put 2 of the egg yolks, the garlic and 3 teaspoons lemon juice in a food processor and blend until creamy. With the motor still running, slowly drizzle in the extra oil. Season and add the remaining lemon juice, to taste. Set aside until needed.

4 To make the stock, heat the oil in a large saucepan or stockpot and cook the onion, carrot and leek over low heat for 12–15 minutes, or until the vegetables are soft. Add the fish heads and bones, wine, fennel seeds, garlic, bay leaves, orange zest, thyme, pepper and ½ teaspoon salt. Cover with 2 litres (70 fl oz/8 cups) water. Bring to the boil and skim off the froth. Reduce the heat and simmer for 30 minutes. Strain into a clean pan, crushing the bones to release as much flavour as possible. Return to the heat.

5 Preheat the oven to 120°C (235°F/ Gas ½). Cut the fish fillets into large pieces about 9 cm (3½ inches) long. Add to the stock and bring to a simmer, putting the heavier pieces in first and the more delicate pieces later. Poach for 6–8 minutes, until the flesh becomes translucent and begins to flake easily. Transfer the fish pieces to a serving platter and moisten with a little stock. Cover with foil and keep warm in the oven.

6 Place 8 tablespoons of the aïoli in a large bowl and slowly add the remaining 3 egg yolks, stirring constantly. Ladle a little stock into the aïoli mixture, blend well and return slowly to the rest of the stock. Stir continuously with a wooden spoon for 8–10 minutes over low heat, or until the soup has thickened and coats the back of a spoon. Do not boil or the mixture will curdle.

7 To serve, place the fish in bowls, spoon over the soup and scatter with croutons.

soup au pistou (vegetable soup with basil sauce)

❋

Preparation time: 45 minutes
Cooking time: 35 minutes
Serves 8

2 ripe tomatoes
3 flat-leaf (Italian) parsley sprigs
1 large rosemary sprig
1 large thyme sprig
1 large marjoram sprig
60 ml (2 fl oz/¼ cup) olive oil
2 onions, thinly sliced
1 leek, white part only, thinly sliced
1 bay leaf
375 g (13 oz) pumpkin (winter squash),
    cut into small pieces
250 g (9 oz) potatoes, cut into small pieces
1 carrot, halved lengthways and thinly sliced
2 litres (70 fl oz/8 cups) vegetable stock
    or water
90 g (3¼ oz) fresh or frozen broad (fava)
    beans
80 g (2¾ oz/½ cup) fresh or frozen peas
2 small zucchini (courgettes), finely chopped
80 g (2¾ oz/½ cup) short macaroni or
    shell pasta

PISTOU
25 g (1 oz/½ cup) basil leaves
2 large garlic cloves, crushed
80 ml (2½ fl oz/⅓ cup) olive oil
35 g (1¼ oz/⅓ cup) freshly grated
    parmesan cheese

1 Score a cross in the base of each tomato. Put in a heatproof bowl and cover with boiling water. Leave for 30 seconds, then transfer to cold water, peel the skin away from the cross and chop the flesh. Tie the parsley, rosemary, thyme and marjoram together with kitchen string.
2 Heat the oil in a heavy-based saucepan and add the onion and leek. Cook over low heat for 10 minutes, or until soft. Add the herb bunch, bay leaf, pumpkin, potato, carrot, 1 teaspoon salt and the stock. Cover and simmer for 10 minutes.

3 Add the broad beans, peas, zucchini, tomatoes and pasta. Cover and cook for 15 minutes, or until the vegetables are very tender and the pasta is *al dente*. Add more water if necessary. Remove the herbs, including the bay leaf.
4 To make the pistou, finely chop the basil and garlic in a food processor.

Pour in the oil gradually, processing until smooth. Stir in the parmesan and ½ teaspoon freshly ground black pepper and serve spooned over the soup.

NOTE: This soup's flavour improves if refrigerated overnight (minus the pistou). Reheat and spoon the pistou over to serve.

bouillabaisse with rouille

✳ ✳

Preparation time: 35 minutes
Cooking time: 1 hour 10 minutes
Serves 6

500 g (1 lb 2 oz) ripe tomatoes
60 ml (2 fl oz/¼ cup) olive oil
1 large onion, chopped
2 leeks, white part only, sliced
4 garlic cloves, crushed
2 tablespoons tomato paste (concentrated purée)
6 flat-leaf (Italian) parsley sprigs
2 bay leaves
2 thyme sprigs
1 fennel sprig
2 pinches of saffron threads
2 kg (4 lb 8 oz) fish trimmings (such as heads, bones, shellfish shells)
1 tablespoon Pernod or Ricard
4 potatoes, cut into 1.5 cm (⅝ inch) slices
1.5 kg (3 lb 5 oz) mixed fish fillets (such as rascasse, snapper, blue eye and bream), cut into large chunks (see Note)
2 tablespoons chopped flat-leaf (Italian) parsley

TOASTS
12 baguette slices
2 large garlic cloves, halved

ROUILLE
3 slices white bread, crusts removed
1 red capsicum (pepper), seeded, membrane removed and quartered
1 small red chilli, seeded and chopped
3 garlic cloves, crushed
1 tablespoon shredded basil
80 ml (2½ fl oz/⅓ cup) olive oil

1 Score a cross in the base of each tomato. Put in a heatproof bowl and cover with boiling water. Leave for 30 seconds, then transfer to cold water, drain and peel the skin away from the cross and roughly chop the flesh.
2 Heat the oil in a large saucepan over medium heat, add the onion and leek and

Cook the firmer-fleshed fish pieces slightly longer than the more delicate pieces.

Rub the halved garlic cloves over the toasted bread.

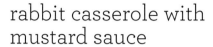
cook for 5 minutes without browning. Add the garlic, tomato and 1 tablespoon of the tomato paste, reduce the heat and simmer for 5 minutes. Stir in 2 litres (70 fl oz/8 cups) cold water, then add the parsley, bay leaves, thyme, fennel, saffron and fish trimmings. Bring to the boil, then reduce the heat and simmer for 30 minutes. Strain into a large saucepan, pressing out the juices and reserving 2 tablespoons of stock for the rouille.

3 Add the Pernod to the pan and stir in the remaining tomato paste. Season, bring to the boil and add the potato. Reduce the heat and simmer for 5 minutes.

4 Add the firmer-fleshed fish to the pan and cook for 2–3 minutes, then add the more delicate pieces of fish and cook for a further 5 minutes.

5 Meanwhile, toast the baguette slices until golden on both sides. While warm, rub the surfaces with the garlic.

6 To make the rouille, soak the bread in cold water for 5 minutes. Cook the capsicum pieces, skin side up, under a hot grill (broiler) until the skin blackens and blisters. Cool in a plastic bag, then peel. Roughly chop the flesh. Squeeze the bread dry and place in a food processor with the capsicum, chilli, garlic and basil. Process to a smooth paste. With the motor running, gradually add the oil until the consistency resembles mayonnaise. Thin it a little with 1–2 tablespoons of the stock. Season to taste.

7 To serve, place 2 baguette slices in each soup bowl. Spoon over the soup and fish. Sprinkle with parsley and serve the rouille on the side.

NOTE: Use at least four different fish with a range of textures and flavours. Shellfish such as lobster, crab, scallops and mussels can be used.

rabbit casserole with mustard sauce

✳ ✳ ✳

Preparation time: **30 minutes**
Cooking time: **2 hours**
Serves **4–6**

2 rabbits (800 g/1 lb 12 oz each)
2 tablespoons olive oil
2 onions, sliced
4 bacon slices, cut into 3 cm
    (1¼ inch) pieces
2 tablespoons plain (all-purpose) flour
375 ml (13 fl oz/1½ cups) chicken stock
125 ml (4 fl oz/½ cup) white wine
1 teaspoon thyme leaves, plus sprigs,
    to garnish
125 ml (4 fl oz/½ cup) pouring (whipping)
    cream
2 tablespoons dijon mustard

1 Preheat the oven to 180°C (350°F/ Gas 4). Remove any fat from the rabbits and wash the rabbits under cold water. Pat dry with paper towels. Cut along both sides of the backbones with kitchen scissors and discard. Cut each rabbit into 8 even-sized pieces and pat dry again.

2 Heat half the oil in a 2.5-litre (87 fl oz/ 10-cup) flameproof casserole dish. Brown the rabbit in batches, adding oil as necessary, then remove from the dish.

3 Add the onion and bacon to the casserole, and cook, stirring, for 5 minutes, or until lightly browned. Sprinkle with the flour and stir with a wooden spoon to scrape the sediment from the base. Add the stock and wine, and stir until the sauce comes to the boil. Return the rabbit to the casserole dish and add the thyme leaves.

4 Cover and bake for 1¼–1½ hours, or until the rabbit is tender and the sauce has thickened. Stir in the combined cream and mustard. Garnish with thyme sprigs. Delicious with steamed vegetables.

fish cooked in paper

✹

Preparation time: 20 minutes
Cooking time: 20 minutes
Serves 4

4 skinless fish fillets, 200 g/7 oz each
   (such as john dory, orange roughy,
   snapper or bream)
1 leek, white part only, julienned
4 spring onions (scallions), julienned
30 g (1 oz) butter, softened
1 lemon, very thinly sliced
2–3 tablespoons lemon juice

1 Preheat the oven to 180°C (350°F/
Gas 4). Place each fish fillet in the centre
of a piece of baking paper large enough to
enclose the fish. Season lightly.
2 Scatter with the leek and spring onion.
Top each with a teaspoon of butter and
3 slices of lemon. Sprinkle with the lemon
juice. Bring the paper together and fold
over several times. Fold the ends under.
Bake on a baking tray for 20 minutes (the
steam will make the paper puff up). Check
to see that the fish is cooked (it should be
white and flake easily when tested with a
fork). Serve as parcels or lift the fish out
and then pour the juices over.

poached salmon

✹ ✹

Preparation time: 40 minutes
Cooking time: 1 hour
Serves 8–10

2 litres (70 fl oz/8 cups) good-quality
   white wine
60 ml (2 fl oz/¼ cup) white wine vinegar
2 onions
10 whole cloves
4 carrots, chopped
1 lemon, cut into quarters
2 bay leaves
1 teaspoon whole black peppercorns
4 parsley sprigs
2.5 kg (5 lb 8 oz) whole Atlantic salmon,
   cleaned and scaled
watercress and lemon slices, to garnish

DILL MAYONNAISE
1 egg, at room temperature
1 egg yolk, at room temperature
1 tablespoon lemon juice
1 teaspoon white wine vinegar
375 ml (13 fl oz/1½ cups) light olive oil
1 tablespoon chopped dill

1 Put the wine, vinegar and 2.5 litres
(87 fl oz/10 cups) water in a large
heavy-based saucepan. Stud the onions
with the cloves. Add to the pan with the

Put a teaspoon of butter and
3 slices of lemon over the leek
and spring onion.

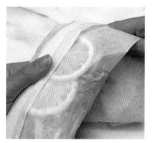

Fold the paper into a parcel around
the fish, tucking the ends under.

fish cooked in paper

carrot, lemon, bay leaves, peppercorns and parsley. Bring to the boil, reduce the heat and simmer for 30–35 minutes. Cool. Strain into a fish kettle large enough to hold the salmon.

2 Place the whole fish in the fish kettle and cover. Bring to the boil, reduce the heat and poach gently for 10–15 minutes, until the fish flakes when tested in the thickest part. Remove from the heat and cool the fish in the liquid.

3 To make the dill mayonnaise, process the egg, egg yolk, juice and vinegar in a food processor for 10 seconds, or until blended. With the motor running, add the oil in a thin, steady stream, blending until all the oil is added and the mayonnaise is thick and creamy. Transfer to a bowl and stir in the dill and salt and pepper.

4 Remove the fish from the liquid, place on a work surface or serving platter and peel back the skin. Garnish with the watercress and lemon slices and serve with the dill mayonnaise.

scallops provençal

Preparation time: **20 minutes**
Cooking time: **30 minutes**
Serves **4 as an entrée**

scallops provençal

600 g (1 lb 5 oz) ripe tomatoes
60 ml (2 fl oz/¼ cup) olive oil
1 onion, finely chopped
4 French shallots, finely chopped
60 ml (2 fl oz/¼ cup) dry white wine
60 g (2¼ oz) butter
20 fresh scallops, cleaned and dried, with shells
4 garlic cloves, crushed
2 tablespoons finely chopped parsley
½ teaspoon thyme leaves
2 tablespoons fresh white breadcrumbs

1 Score a cross in the base of each tomato. Place the tomatoes in boiling water for 30 seconds, then plunge into cold water and peel the skin away from the cross. Cut in half, scoop out the seeds and discard, then finely dice the flesh.

2 Heat 2 tablespoons of the oil in a frying pan over medium heat until hot, add the onion and shallots, then reduce the heat to low and cook slowly for 5 minutes, or until soft. Add the wine and simmer for several minutes until reduced slightly, then add the tomato. Season with salt and pepper and cook, stirring occasionally, for 20 minutes, or until thick and pulpy. Preheat the oven to 180°F (350°F/Gas 4).

3 Heat the butter and remaining oil in a frying pan over high heat until foamy. Cook half the scallops for 1–2 minutes each side, or until lightly golden and cooked to your liking. Remove and repeat with the remaining scallops. Set aside.

4 Add the garlic to the hot scallop pan and cook, stirring, for 1 minute. Remove from the heat and stir in the parsley, thyme and breadcrumbs.

5 To serve, warm the scallop shells on a baking tray in the oven. Place a small amount of tomato mixture on each shell, top with a scallop and sprinkle with the breadcrumb and herb mixture.

NOTE: If the shells are not available, serve the scallops on a small plate. Place them on a bed of the tomato mixture and top with the breadcrumb and herb mixture.

roast duck with olives

Preparation time: **30 minutes**
Cooking time: **1 hour 30 minutes**
Serves **4**

1.8 kg (4 lb) duck
2 bay leaves

SAUCE
1 tablespoon olive oil
1 onion, chopped
1 garlic clove, crushed
2 ripe roma (plum) tomatoes, peeled
    and chopped
250 ml (9 fl oz/1 cup) riesling
2 teaspoons thyme leaves
1 bay leaf
24 niçoise olives, pitted

STUFFING
60 g (2¼ oz/⅓ cup) medium-grain white
    rice, cooked
1 garlic clove, crushed
100 g (3½ oz) frozen chopped spinach,
    defrosted
2 ducks' livers (about 100 g/3½ oz),
    chopped
1 egg, lightly beaten
1 teaspoon thyme leaves

1 Preheat the oven to 200°C (400°F/ Gas 6). For the sauce, heat the oil in a frying pan, add the onion and cook for 5 minutes, or until translucent. Add the garlic, tomato, wine, herbs and season with salt and pepper. Cook for 5 minutes, add the olives and remove from the heat.
2 For the stuffing, mix all the ingredients in a bowl and season well. Rinse the duck cavity with cold water and pat dry, inside and out, with paper towels. Put the bay leaves in the cavity, then fill with stuffing.
3 Tuck the wings under the duck, then close the flaps of fat over the parson's nose and secure with a skewer or toothpick. Place in a deep baking dish and rub 1 teaspoon of salt into the skin. Prick the skin all over with a skewer.
4 Roast the duck on the top shelf of the oven for 35–40 minutes, then carefully

duck

Duck is available whole (head off or on), portioned, fresh and frozen. When selecting a fresh duck, look for those with an adequate layer of fat beneath the skin of the breast and have pearly, creamy white skin. If you are not intending to cook the fresh duck within two or three days of purchasing, it is preferable to buy a properly blast-frozen duck than to put a fresh duck in a domestic freezer where it may take days to freeze solid and will progressively deteriorate. Thaw frozen ducks or other poultry in the refrigerator, uncovered and placed on paper towels. Do not cook partially frozen poultry, because while the outside may appear crisp and browned, the interior temperature may not have reached a level at which dangerous bacteria are killed.

pour off the excess fat. Roast for another 35–40 minutes. To check that the duck is cooked, gently pull one leg out a little from the side. The flesh should be pale brown with no blood in the juices. Remove from the oven, then carve, serving a spoonful of the stuffing next to the duck and topping with the sauce.

lamb and artichoke fricassée

☼ ☼

Preparation time: 50 minutes
Cooking time: 1 hour 50 minutes
Serves 8

6 globe artichokes
60 ml (2 fl oz/¼ cup) lemon juice
2 ripe large tomatoes
80 ml (2½ fl oz/⅓ cup) olive oil
2 kg (4 lb 8 oz) diced lamb
750 g (1 lb 10 oz) brown onions, thinly sliced
1 tablespoon plain (all-purpose) flour
2 garlic cloves, crushed
185 ml (6 fl oz/¾ cup) white wine
375 ml (13 fl oz/1⅓ cups) chicken stock
1 bouquet garni
chopped flat-leaf parsley, to garnish
lemon wedges, to serve

1 To prepare the artichokes, bring a large saucepan of water to the boil and add the lemon juice. Trim the stems from the artichokes and remove the tough outer leaves. Cut off the hard tips of the remaining leaves using scissors. Blanch the artichokes for 5 minutes. Remove and turn upside down to drain. When cool enough to handle, use a small spoon to remove the hairy choke from the centre of each. Scrape the bases well to remove all the membrane. Cut the artichokes into quarters and set aside.

2 Score a cross in the base of each tomato and place in a bowl of boiling water for 30 seconds. Plunge into cold water and peel the skin away from the cross. Cut the tomatoes in half and scoop out the seeds. Chop the tomato flesh.

3 Heat half the oil in a deep flameproof casserole and fry the lamb in batches until golden. Add the remaining oil and cook the onion for about 8 minutes, until soft and caramelised. Add the flour and cook for 1 minute. Add the garlic, tomato, wine and chicken stock. Return the lamb to the pan, add the bouquet garni and simmer, covered, for 1 hour.

4 Place the artichokes in the casserole and simmer, uncovered, for another 15 minutes. Remove the meat and artichokes with a slotted spoon and place in a serving dish. Keep warm. Discard the bouquet garni. Cook the sauce over high heat until it thickens. Pour the sauce over the lamb and garnish with the parsley. Serve with the lemon wedges.

NOTE: If fresh artichokes are not available, you can use 270 g (9½ oz/ 1 cup) marinated artichokes. Drain them well and pat dry with paper towels.

bouquet garni

This is a small bundle of herbs used to flavour casseroles, soups and fricassées. It usually includes a few stalks of parsley, a sprig of thyme and a bay leaf. The herbs can be tied together with kitchen string or in a knot of muslin (cheesecloth). Other herbs can be added if they are appropriate to the dish you are making. Ready-made bouquet garni are also available.

niçoise olives

Niçoise olives are small and ripe, ranging in colour from purple to brown to black. Cured in brine and often packed in olive oil, they are an integral ingredient in Provençal cuisine, where they are eaten as a table olive and also added to beef stews, poultry stuffing, savoury tarts and as an addition to Niçoise salad.

beef provençal

✳ ✳

Preparation time: 20 minutes
  + overnight marinating time
Cooking time: 2 hours 25 minutes
Serves 6

1.5 kg (3 lb 5 oz) chuck steak, cut into
    3 cm (1¼ inch) cubes
2 tablespoons olive oil
1 small onion, sliced
375 ml (13 fl oz/1½ cups) red wine
2 tablespoons chopped flat-leaf
    (Italian) parsley
1 tablespoon chopped rosemary
1 tablespoon chopped thyme
2 fresh bay leaves
250 g (9 oz) speck, rind removed, cut into
    1 x 2 cm (½ x ¾ inch) pieces
400 g (14 oz) tin chopped tomatoes
250 ml (9 fl oz/1 cup) beef stock
500 g (1 lb 2 oz) baby carrots
45 g (1½ oz/⅓ cup) niçoise olives

1 In a bowl, combine the beef with 1 tablespoon of the oil, the onion, 250 ml (9 fl oz/1 cup) of wine and half the herbs. Cover with plastic wrap and marinate in the refrigerator overnight.

2 Drain the beef, reserving the marinade. Heat the remaining oil in a large, heavy-based saucepan and brown the beef and onion in batches. Remove from the pan.

3 Add the speck to the pan and cook for 3–5 minutes, until crisp. Return the beef to the pan with the remaining wine and the marinade and cook, scraping the residue from the base of the pan, for 2 minutes, or until the wine has slightly reduced. Add the tomatoes and stock and bring to the boil. Reduce the heat and add the remaining herbs. Season well, cover and simmer for 1½ hours.

4 Add the carrots and olives to the pan and cook, uncovered, for 30 minutes more, or until the meat and carrots are tender. Before serving, check the seasoning and adjust if necessary.

asparagus vinaigrette

Preparation time: 10 minutes
Cooking time: 5 minutes
Serves 4

2 teaspoons dijon mustard
2 tablespoons sherry vinegar
80 ml (2½ fl oz/⅓ cup) extra virgin
    olive oil
½ teaspoon finely snipped chives
24 asparagus spears, woody ends trimmed
60 ml (2 fl oz/¼ cup) olive oil
2 garlic cloves, peeled
80 g (2¾ oz/1 cup) fresh white breadcrumbs

1 Whisk together the mustard, vinegar, extra virgin olive oil and chives in a small bowl. Set aside.
2 Cook the asparagus in a large saucepan of boiling salted water over medium heat for 2–4 minutes, or until just tender.
3 While the asparagus is cooking, heat the olive oil in a frying pan, add the garlic and cook over low heat until golden. Discard the garlic, then add the breadcrumbs and increase the heat to medium. Cook until the breadcrumbs are crisp and golden. Season and drain on paper towels.
4 Drain the asparagus and place on a platter. Drizzle with the vinaigrette and sprinkle with the breadcrumbs.

asparagus vinaigrette

ratatouille

Preparation time: 25 minutes
Cooking time: 40 minutes
Serves 4–6

6 vine-ripened tomatoes
500 g (1 lb 2 oz) eggplants (aubergines)
375 g (13 oz) zucchini (courgettes)
1 green capsicum (pepper)
1 red onion
100 ml (3½ fl oz) olive oil
3 garlic cloves, finely chopped
¼ teaspoon cayenne pepper
2 teaspoons chopped thyme
2 bay leaves
1 tablespoon red wine vinegar
1 teaspoon caster (superfine) sugar
3 tablespoons shredded basil

1 Score a cross in the base of each tomato. Put the tomatoes in a heatproof bowl and cover with boiling water. Leave for 30 seconds, then transfer to cold water and peel the skin away from the cross. Cut the tomatoes in half, scoop out the seeds with a teaspoon and chop the flesh.
2 Cut the eggplants and zucchini into 2 cm (¾ inch) cubes. Cut the capsicum in half, remove the seeds and membrane and cut into 2 cm (¾ inch) squares. Cut the onion into 2 cm (¾ inch) wedges.
3 Heat 2 tablespoons of the oil in a large saucepan, add the eggplant and cook over medium heat for 4–5 minutes, or until softened but not browned. Remove the eggplant from the pan. Add another 2 tablespoons of the oil to the pan, add the zucchini and cook for 3–4 minutes, or until softened. Remove. Add the capsicum, cook for 2 minutes and remove.
4 Heat the remaining oil, add the onion and cook for 2–3 minutes, or until softened. Add the garlic, cayenne pepper, thyme and bay leaves and cook, stirring, for 1 minute.
5 Return the eggplant, zucchini and capsicum to the pan and add the tomato, vinegar and sugar. Simmer gently for 20 minutes, stirring occasionally. Stir in the basil and season with salt and pepper. Serve hot or at room temperature.

NOTE: You can also serve ratatouille as a starter with bread.

potato and oil purée

☀

Preparation time: 5 minutes
Cooking time: 20 minutes
Serves 4

1 kg (2 lb 4 oz) floury potatoes (such as
    russet, spunta and pontiac), peeled,
    cut into large chunks
200 ml (7 fl oz) stock (choose the flavour
    according to the dish the potatoes
    will be served with)
2 garlic cloves, peeled and bruised
2 thyme sprigs
150 ml (5 fl oz) extra virgin olive oil

1   Cook the potatoes in boiling salted
water until tender but still firm. While the
potatoes are cooking, heat the stock in a
small saucepan with the garlic and thyme.
Bring to simmering point, then remove
from the heat and allow to infuse.
2   Drain the potatoes well and then pass
them through a mouli or mash using a
potato masher. Strain the stock, return to
the saucepan, add the olive oil and reheat
gently. Add the stock to the potato in a
thin steady stream, stirring continuously
with a flat wooden spoon. Season with
salt and pepper, then beat well until the
purée is smooth.

chicken with forty
cloves of garlic

☀ ☀

Preparation time: 20 minutes
Cooking time: 1 hour 45 minutes
Serves 4

10 g (¼ oz) butter
1 tablespoon olive oil
2kg (4 lb 8 oz) whole free-range chicken
40 garlic cloves, unpeeled
2 tablespoons chopped rosemary
2 thyme sprigs
275 ml (9½ fl oz) dry white wine
150 ml (5 fl oz) chicken stock
225 g (8 oz) plain (all-purpose) flour

chicken with forty cloves of garlic

1   Preheat the oven to 180°C (350°F/
Gas 4). Melt the butter and oil in a
4.5 litre (157 fl oz/18 cup) flameproof
casserole with a lid and brown the
chicken until golden all over. Remove.
2   Add the garlic, rosemary and thyme to
the dish and cook for 1 minute. Add the
chicken, wine and stock and bring to a
simmer, basting the chicken often.
3   Put the flour in a bowl and add up to
150 ml (5 fl oz) water to form a pliable

dough. Divide into four portions, then roll
each into a log and lay them around the
rim of the dish. Put the lid on, pressing
down firmly to seal. Bake for 1¼ hours.
Remove the lid by cracking the dough.
Bake for 15 minutes more, then transfer
the chicken to a plate. Reduce the juices
to 250 ml (9 fl oz/1 cup) over medium
heat. Carve the chicken, pierce the garlic
skins and squeeze the flesh onto the
chicken. Serve with the sauce.

lentils in red wine

☀

Preparation time: 20 minutes
Cooking time: 1 hour 15 minutes
Serves 4–6

2 tablespoons olive oil
1 celery stalk, finely diced
1 large carrot, finely diced
1 large onion, finely diced
2 garlic cloves, crushed
2 tablespoons tomato paste (concentrated
    purée)
280 g (10 oz/1½ cups) puy lentils or tiny
    blue-green lentils
250 ml (9 fl oz/1 cup) red wine
250 ml (9 fl oz/1 cup) beef stock
1 fresh bay leaf, crushed
5 thyme sprigs
3 tablespoons chopped parsley

1   Heat the oil in a large, heavy-based
saucepan. Add the celery, carrot and
onion and cook over low–medium heat
for 10 minutes. Add the garlic and cook
for another 2 minutes.

2   Add the tomato paste and cook over
low heat for 5 minutes. Stir in the lentils
and wine and cook over medium heat
for 3–5 minutes to reduce slightly. Add
the stock and 375 ml (13 fl oz/1½ cups)
water, bring to the boil, then reduce
the heat and add the herbs. Season and
simmer for 45–50 minutes, until the liquid
is absorbed and the lentils are cooked.

puy lentils

These tiny blue-green lentils
are highly prized and were
the first vegetable to be
awarded an AOC (Appellation
of Controlled Origin). As such,
only lentils grown near Le
Puy-en-Velay in the Auvergne
region of France can bear this
name. Their great advantage is
that they hold their shape and
texture when cooked, and they
have a deeper, richer flavour
than other lentils. Unlike other
pulses, it is not necessary to
soak puy lentils before cooking.
In fact, it is advisable not to
do so as they can ferment and
start to sprout.

sage

Once believed to enhance longevity and give wisdom, this strongly flavoured, fragrant herb is commonly paired with pork, chicken and veal in southern French cuisine as it was traditionally used to counteract rich, oily meats. Use sage, especially in its dried form, with discretion, as a heavy hand will cause its pungent flavour to overpower rather than complement the food with which it is being cooked.

pork with sage and capers

☀ ☀

Preparation time: 25 minutes
Cooking time: 1 hour 15 minutes
Serves 4

25 g (1 oz) butter
60 ml (2 fl oz/¼ cup) extra virgin olive oil
1 onion, finely chopped
105 g (3½ oz/1⅓ cups) fresh white breadcrumbs
2 teaspoons chopped sage
1 tablespoon chopped flat-leaf (Italian) parsley
2 teaspoons grated lemon zest
2½ tablespoons salted baby capers, rinsed and drained
1 egg
2 pork fillets (about 500 g/1 lb 2 oz each)
8 large, thin bacon or prosciutto slices
2 teaspoons plain (all-purpose) flour
100 ml (3½ fl oz) dry vermouth

310 ml (10¾ fl oz/1¼ cups) chicken or vegetable stock
8 whole sage leaves, to garnish

1 Preheat the oven to 170°C (325°F/ Gas 3). Heat the butter and 1 tablespoon of oil in a frying pan and cook the onion for 5 minutes, or until lightly golden. Mix with the breadcrumbs, chopped sage, parsley, lemon zest, 2 teaspoons of the capers and the egg and season well.
2 Split each pork fillet in half lengthways and open out. Spread the stuffing down the length of one fillet and cover with the other fillet. Stretch the bacon with the back of a knife and wrap, slightly overlapping, around the pork to form a neat parcel. Tie with kitchen string. Put in a roasting tin and drizzle with 1 tablespoon of the oil. Bake for 1 hour, or until the juices run clear. Transfer to a carving plate and cover with foil.
3 Place the roasting tin on the stovetop and stir in the flour. Add the vermouth and allow to bubble for 1 minute. Add

the stock and stir to remove any lumps. Simmer for 5 minutes, then add the remaining capers. Heat the remaining oil in a small saucepan and fry the whole sage leaves until crisp. Drain on crumpled paper towels. Carve the pork into 1 cm (½ inch) slices and serve with the sauce and crisp sage leaves.

vegetable tian

Preparation time: 40 minutes
Cooking time: 1 hour 20 minutes
Serves 6–8

1 kg (2 lb 4 oz) red capsicums (peppers)
125 ml (4 fl oz/½ cup) olive oil
800 g (1 lb 12 oz) silverbeet (Swiss chard), stalks removed and coarsely shredded
2 tablespoons pine nuts
freshly ground nutmeg, to taste
1 onion, chopped
2 garlic cloves
2 teaspoons chopped thyme
750 g (1 lb 10 oz) ripe tomatoes, peeled, seeded and diced
1 large eggplant (aubergine), cut into 1 cm (½ inch) thick rounds
5 small zucchini (courgettes) (about 500 g/ 1 lb 2 oz), thinly sliced on the diagonal
3 ripe tomatoes, extra, cut into 1 cm (½ inch) thick slices
1 tablespoon fresh breadcrumbs
30 g (1 oz) parmesan cheese, grated
30 g (1 oz) butter

1 Preheat the grill (broiler) to high. Remove the seeds and membrane from the capsicums and grill until black and blistered. Cool in a plastic bag, then peel and cut into long, thick slices. Place in a lightly greased 20 x 25 cm (8 x 10 inch) ovenproof dish and season lightly.
2 Heat 2 tablespoons of the olive oil in a heavy-based frying pan over medium heat and cook the silverbeet for 8–10 minutes, or until softened. Add the pine nuts and season, to taste, with salt, pepper and nutmeg. Place the silverbeet over the capsicum slices.

3 Heat another tablespoon of the olive oil in the frying pan. Add the onion and cook over medium heat for 7–8 minutes, or until soft and golden. Add the garlic and thyme, cook for 1 minute, then add the diced tomato and bring to the boil. Reduce the heat and simmer for 10 minutes. Spread the sauce evenly over the silverbeet. Wipe out the pan.
4 Preheat the oven to 200°C (400°F/ Gas 6). Heat the remaining olive oil in the frying pan and fry the eggplant rounds over high heat for 8–10 minutes, or until golden on both sides. Drain on paper towels and place in a single layer over the tomato sauce. Season lightly.
5 Arrange the zucchini and tomato slices in alternating layers over the eggplant. Sprinkle the breadcrumbs and parmesan over the top and then dot with the butter. Bake for 25–30 minutes or until golden. Serve warm or at room temperature.

tian

Tian is the name for a glazed earthenware dish that is used for baking. Now, tian has also come to mean the recipe itself.

poulpe provençal (octopus braised in tomato and wine)

✳ ✳

Preparation time: **25 minutes**
Cooking time: **1 hour 30 minutes**
Serves **6**

500 g (1 lb 2 oz) ripe tomatoes
1 kg (2 lb 4 oz) baby octopus
60 ml (2 fl oz/¼ cup) olive oil
1 large brown onion, chopped
2 garlic cloves
330 ml (11¼ fl oz/1⅓ cups) dry white wine
¼ teaspoon saffron threads
2 thyme sprigs
2 tablespoons roughly chopped flat-leaf (Italian) parsley

1 Score a cross in the base of each tomato. Place the tomatoes in a bowl of boiling water for 30 seconds, then plunge into cold water and peel the skin away from the cross. Cut each tomato in half and scoop out the seeds. Chop the flesh.
2 To clean each octopus, use a small sharp knife to cut each head from the tentacles. Remove the eyes by cutting a round of flesh from the base of each head. To clean the heads, carefully slit them open and remove the guts. Rinse thoroughly. Cut the heads in half. Push out the beaks from the centre of the tentacles from the cut side. Cut the tentacles into sets of four or two, depending on the size of the octopus.
3 Blanch all the octopus in boiling water for 2 minutes, then drain and allow to cool slightly. Pat dry with paper towels.
4 Heat the olive oil in a heavy-based frying pan over medium heat and cook the onion for 7–8 minutes until lightly golden. Add the octopus and garlic and cook for another 2–3 minutes. Add the tomato, wine, saffron and thyme. Add just enough water to cover the octopus.
5 Simmer, covered, for 1 hour. Uncover and cook for another 15 minutes, or until the octopus is tender and the sauce has thickened a little. The cooking time will

Grasp the body of the octopus and push the beak out and up through the centre of the tentacles with your finger.

To clean the octopus head, carefully slit through one side, avoiding the ink sac, and scrape out any guts from inside.

When you have slit the head open, rinse under running water to remove any remaining guts.

vary quite a bit depending on the size of the octopus. Season, to taste. Serve hot or at room temperature, sprinkled with the chopped parsley.

grilled fish with fennel and lemon

☀

Preparation time: 10 minutes
Cooking time: 10 minutes
Serves 4

4 whole red mullet or bream,
    scaled and gutted
1 lemon, thinly sliced
1 baby fennel bulb, thinly sliced
1½ tablespoons fennel seeds
60 ml (2 fl oz/¼ cup) lemon juice
80 ml (2½ fl oz/⅓ cup) olive oil

1 Cut three diagonal slashes on both sides of each fish. Place two or three slices of lemon and some slices of fennel bulb in the cavity of each fish. Place the fennel seeds in a mortar and pestle and bruise roughly. Sprinkle both sides of each fish with the bruised fennel seeds and some salt, making sure you rub them well into the flesh.
2 Mix the lemon juice and olive oil in a bowl. Heat a chargrill or hotplate and when very hot, add the fish. Drizzle a little of the lemon and oil over each fish. After 5 minutes, turn carefully with tongs, ensuring the filling doesn't fall out, and drizzle with the lemon and oil. Cook for a further 3–4 minutes. Flake gently with a fork to test whether it is cooked, then serve with a salad.

zucchini omelette

☀ ☀

Preparation time: 5 minutes
Cooking time: 15 minutes
Serves 4

80 g (2¾ oz) butter
400 g (14 oz) zucchini (courgettes), sliced

1 tablespoon finely chopped basil
pinch of freshly ground nutmeg
8 eggs, lightly beaten

1 Melt half the butter in a non-stick 23 cm (9 inch) frying pan. Add the zucchini and cook over medium heat for about 8 minutes, until lightly golden. Stir in the basil and nutmeg, season with salt and pepper and cook for 30 seconds. Transfer to a bowl and keep warm.
2 Wipe out the pan, return it to the heat and melt the remaining butter. Lightly season the egg and pour into the pan. Stir gently over high heat. Stop stirring when the mixture begins to set in uniform, fluffy small clumps. Reduce the heat and lift the edges with a fork to prevent it catching. Shake the pan from side to side to prevent the omelette sticking. When it is almost set but still runny on the surface, spread the zucchini down the centre. Using a spatula, fold the omelette over and slide onto a serving plate.

omelettes

Omelettes are a triumph of simple French country cooking. Using the freshest possible eggs, quality butter and uncomplicated flavourings, it is possible to have a satisfying meal in minutes if you follow these tips. Don't overbeat the eggs, but stir until just combined. Use simple fillings with flavours and quantities that don't overpower the subtle egg flavour. Don't overcook the omelette or it will be rubbery.

zucchini omelette

fougasse

☀ ☀

Preparation time: 30 minutes
  + 1 hour 20 minutes proving time
Cooking time: 35 minutes
Makes 4 small loaves

2 teaspoons dried yeast
1 teaspoon sugar
500 g (1 lb 2 oz/4 cups) strong white flour
60 ml (2 fl oz/¼ cup) olive oil
185 g (6½ oz/1 cup) pitted black olives,
  chopped (optional)
1 handful chopped mixed herbs (such as
  parsley, oregano and basil) (optional)

1 Put the yeast, sugar and 125 ml
(4 fl oz/½ cup) warm water in a bowl
and stir until dissolved. Leave in a warm,
draught-free place for 10 minutes, or
until bubbles appear on the surface. The
mixture should be frothy and slightly
increased in volume. If your yeast doesn't
foam, it is dead so you need to start again.
2 Sift the flour and 2 teaspoons salt into
a bowl and make a well in the centre. Add
the yeast mixture, olive oil and 185 ml
(6 fl oz/¾ cup) warm water. Mix to a soft

dough and gather into a ball. Turn out
onto a floured surface and knead for
10 minutes, or until smooth.
3 Place the dough in a large, lightly oiled
bowl, cover loosely with plastic wrap or a
damp tea towel (dish towel) and leave in
a warm, draught-free place for 1 hour, or
until it is doubled in size.
4 Punch down the dough and add the
olives and herbs, if desired. Knead for
1 minute. Divide the mixture into four
equal portions. Press each portion into
a large, oval shape about 1 cm (½ inch)
thick and make several cuts on either side
of each. Lay the dough on large, floured
baking trays, cover with plastic wrap and
leave to rise for 20 minutes.
5 Preheat the oven to 210°C (415°F/
Gas 6–7). Bake the bread for 35 minutes,
or until crisp. To make the crust of your
fougasse crispy, simply spray the inside of
the oven with water after the bread has
been cooking for 15 minutes.

NOTE: Although fougasse is traditionally
made as a plain bread, these days
bakeries often incorporate ingredients
such as fresh herbs, olives, chopped ham
and anchovies into the dough.

fougasse

garlic soup

☀

Preparation time: 15 minutes
Cooking time: 30 minutes
Serves 4

1 garlic bulb
2 large thyme sprigs
1 litre (35 fl oz/4 cups) chicken stock
80 ml (2½ fl oz/⅓ cup) pouring (whipping)
  cream
4 thick slices white bread, crusts removed
thyme, extra, to garnish

1 Preheat the oven to 180°C (350°F/
Gas 4). Crush the cloves (about 20) from
the garlic bulb using the side of a knife.
Discard the skins and put the garlic in a
large saucepan with the thyme, stock and
250 ml (9 fl oz/1 cup) water. Bring to the
boil, then reduce the heat and simmer,
uncovered, for 20 minutes. Strain through
a fine sieve into a clean saucepan. Add the
cream and reheat gently without allowing
to boil. Season to taste.
2 Meanwhile, cut the slices of bread into
bite-sized cubes. Spread on a baking tray
and bake for 5–10 minutes, or until lightly
golden. Divide among four bowls, then
pour the soup over the top. Garnish with
the extra thyme and serve immediately.

walnut bread

☀ ☀

Preparation time: 45 minutes
  + 2 hours 30 minutes proving time
Cooking time: 50 minutes
Makes 1 loaf

2½ teaspoons dried yeast
90 g (3¼ oz/¼ cup) liquid malt
2 tablespoons olive oil
300 g (10½ oz/3 cups) walnut halves,
  lightly toasted
540 g (1 lb 3 oz/4⅓ cups) strong white flour
1 egg, lightly beaten

1 Grease a baking tray. Put the yeast,
malt and 330 ml (11¼ fl oz/1⅓ cups)

warm water in a small bowl and stir well. Leave in a warm, draught-free place for 10 minutes, or until bubbles appear on the surface. The mixture should be frothy and slightly increased in volume. If your yeast doesn't foam, it is dead, and you will need to discard it and start again. Stir in the oil.

2 Process 200 g (7 oz/2 cups) of the walnuts in a food processor until they resemble coarse meal. Combine 500 g (1 lb 2 oz/4 cups) of the flour with 1½ teaspoons salt in a large bowl and stir in the walnut meal. Make a well in the centre and add the yeast mixture. Mix with a large metal spoon until just combined. Turn out onto a lightly floured surface and knead for 10 minutes, or until smooth, incorporating enough of the remaining flour to keep the dough from sticking — it should be soft and moist, but it won't become very springy. Shape the dough into a ball. Place in a lightly oiled bowl, cover with plastic wrap or a damp tea towel (dish towel) and leave in a warm place for up to 1½ hours, or until doubled in size.

3 Punch down the dough and turn out onto a lightly floured surface. With very little kneading, shape the dough into a flattened 20 x 25 cm (8 x 10 inch) rectangle. Spread with the remaining walnuts and roll up firmly from a long end. Place the loaf on the baking tray, cover with plastic wrap or a damp tea towel and leave to rise for 1 hour, or until doubled in size.

4 Preheat the oven to 190°C (375°F/ Gas 5). Glaze the loaf with the egg and bake for 45–50 minutes, or until golden and hollow sounding when tapped. Transfer to a wire rack to cool.

NOTE: It is worthwhile using good-quality, pale, plump walnuts even though they are a little more expensive, as cheaper varieties can often taste bitter.

walnuts

Walnuts are thought to have originated in ancient China or Persia (present-day Iran). In many countries of the Mediterranean, the word for walnut is also the word for nut. Fresh walnuts in the shell are far superior in taste to those shelled and packaged. When buying walnuts in the shell, choose those free of cracks and holes. Store in a cool, dry place for up to three months. Shelled walnuts should be plump and crisp when you buy them. They can be stored in an airtight container in the refrigerator for up to six months.

— do not boil. Pour the mixture into a chilled baking dish and set aside to cool slightly. Cover and refrigerate until cold.

2 Transfer to an ice-cream machine and freeze according to the manufacturer's instructions. Alternatively, transfer to a shallow metal tray and freeze, whisking every couple of hours until frozen and creamy. Freeze for 5 hours or overnight. Transfer to the fridge for 30 minutes before serving to soften slightly.

apricot compote

Preparation time: **30 minutes**
Cooking time: **30 minutes**
Serves **4–6**

1 orange
1 lemon
1 small vanilla bean, halved lengthways
125 g (4½ oz/½ cup) sugar, plus extra (optional)
1 kg (2 lb 4 oz) ripe, firm apricots, halved and stones removed

1 Peel two strips of zest, about 5 cm (2 inches) long, from both the orange and lemon. Squeeze all the juice from the orange (about 4 tablespoons) and 1 tablespoon from the lemon.

2 Place 750 ml (26 fl oz/3 cups) water in a saucepan, add the zest, vanilla bean and sugar and bring to the boil. Boil rapidly for 5 minutes.

3 Place the apricots in a wide saucepan and pour the hot syrup over the top. Gently bring to the boil and simmer until the apricots are tender. This can take from 2–10 minutes, depending on the fruit. Do not damage the apricots by over-cooking. Transfer the apricots to a bowl, using a slotted spoon, and then boil the syrup for 10 minutes, or until it thickens. Remove from the heat, allow to cool for 15 minutes, then stir in the orange and lemon juices. Taste for sweetness and add extra sugar if necessary. Strain the sauce over the apricots. Serve warm or at room temperature.

lavender ice cream

Preparation time: **15 minutes + freezing time**
Cooking time: **15 minutes**
Serves **6–8**

8 stems English lavender (or 4–6 if the lavender is in full flower, as it will have a stronger flavour)
625 ml (21½ fl oz/2½ cups) thick (double/heavy) cream
1 small piece lemon zest
165 g (5¾ oz/¾ cup) sugar
4 egg yolks, lightly whisked

1 Wash and dry the lavender, then put it in a medium saucepan with the cream and lemon zest. Heat until almost boiling, then stir in the sugar until dissolved. Strain through a fine sieve, then gradually whisk into the egg yolk in a bowl. Return to a clean pan and stir over low heat until thick enough to coat the back of a spoon

beignets de fruits

✦

Preparation time: 25 minutes + 3 hours
    marinating time
Cooking time: 10 minutes
Serves 4

3 granny smith or golden delicious apples,
    peeled and cored
70 g (2½ oz) raisins
60 ml (2 fl oz/¼ cup) Calvados or rum
1½ tablespoons caster (superfine) sugar
vegetable oil, for frying
2 tablespoons plain (all-purpose) flour,
    to coat
icing (confectioners') sugar, to dust

BATTER
1 egg, separated
70 ml (2¼ fl oz) warm beer
60 g (2¼ oz/½ cup) plain (all-purpose) flour
1 teaspoon vegetable oil

1 Cut the apples into 1 cm (½ inch)
cubes. Place the apple in a bowl with the
raisins, Calvados and sugar and set aside
for 3 hours to marinate.

2 When the fruit has been marinating
for 2 hours, make the batter. Beat the egg
yolk and beer together in a large bowl.
Blend in the flour, oil and a pinch of salt.
Stir until smooth. The batter will be very
thick at this stage. Cover and leave in a
warm place for 1 hour.

3 Pour the oil into a large saucepan to
a depth of 10 cm (4 inches) and heat
to 170°C (325°F), or until a cube of
bread dropped into the oil browns in
20 seconds. Add 1½ tablespoons of the
Calvados marinade to the batter and stir
until smooth. Whisk the egg white until
stiff and gently fold into the batter. Drain
the apples and raisins, toss with the flour
to coat, then lightly fold them through
the batter. Carefully lower heaped
tablespoons of batter into the oil in
batches and fry for 1–2 minutes, until the
fritters are golden on both sides. Remove
with a slotted spoon and drain on paper
towels. Keep them warm. Dust with the
icing sugar and serve.

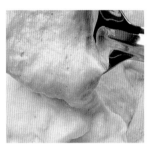

Gently fold the whisked egg white
into the batter.

When golden, remove the fritters
from the oil with a slotted spoon.

tarte au citron

☀ ☀

Preparation time: **30 minutes**
  + 30 minutes chilling time
Cooking time: **1 hour**
Serves 6–8

3 eggs
2 egg yolks
175 g (6 oz/¾ cup) caster (superfine) sugar
125 ml (4 fl oz/½ cup) pouring (whipping)
  cream
185 ml (6 fl oz/¾ cup) lemon juice
1½ tablespoons finely grated lemon zest
2 small lemons
140 g (5 oz/⅔ cup) sugar

PASTRY
125 g (4½ oz/1 cup) plain (all-purpose) flour
80 g (2¾ oz) unsalted butter, softened
1 egg yolk
2 tablespoons icing (confectioners') sugar,
  sifted

1 To make the pastry, sift the flour and
a pinch of salt into a large bowl. Make
a well in the centre and add the butter,
egg yolk and icing sugar. Work together
the butter, yolk and sugar with your
fingertips, then slowly incorporate the
flour. Bring together into a ball — you
may need to add a few drops of cold
water. Flatten the ball slightly, cover
with plastic wrap and refrigerate for
20 minutes.
2 Preheat the oven to 200°C (400°F/
Gas 6). Lightly grease a 21 cm (8¼ inch)
loose-based flan (tart) tin.
3 Roll out the pastry between two sheets
of baking paper until it is 3 mm (⅛ inch)
thick, to fit the base and side of the tin.
Gently place in the tin and trim the edge.
Refrigerate for 10 minutes. Line the pastry
with baking paper, fill with baking beads
or uncooked rice and bake for 10 minutes.
Remove the paper and beads and bake for
another 6–8 minutes, or until the pastry
looks dry all over. Allow to cool. Reduce
the temperature to 150°C (300°F/Gas 2).
4 Whisk the eggs, egg yolks and caster
sugar together, add the cream and lemon

juice and mix well. Strain and then add
the lemon zest. Place the tin on a baking
tray on the middle shelf of the oven and
carefully pour in the filling right up to
the top. Bake for 40 minutes, or until it is
just set — it should wobble in the middle
when the tin is firmly tapped. Cool the
tart before removing from the tin.
5 Meanwhile, wash and scrub the lemons
well to remove the wax from the skin.
Slice very thinly (2 mm/¹⁄₁₆ inch thick).
Combine the sugar and 200 ml (7 fl oz)

water in a small frying pan and stir over
low heat until the sugar has dissolved.
Add the lemon slices and simmer over
low heat for 40 minutes, or until the
peel is very tender and the pith looks
transparent. Lift out of the syrup and
drain on baking paper. If serving the
tart immediately, cover the surface with
the lemon slices. If not, keep the slices
covered and decorate the tart when ready
to serve. You can serve the tart warm or
chilled, with a little cream if desired.

tourte de blettes (apple, silverbeet and pine nut pie)

✹ ✹

Preparation time: 30 minutes
+ 30 minutes chilling time
Cooking time: 50 minutes
Serves 6–8

60 g (2¼ oz/½ cup) sultanas (golden raisins)
2 tablespoons brandy
400 g (14 oz) plain (all-purpose) flour
100 g (3½ oz) icing (confectioners') sugar
250 g (9 oz) unsalted butter, chilled and
　　chopped
3 eggs
800 g (1 lb 12 oz) silverbeet (Swiss chard),
　　stalks removed
100 g (3½ oz/⅔ cup) pine nuts, toasted
　　(see Note)
3 green cooking apples, peeled, cored and
　　thinly sliced
1 teaspoon grated lemon zest
115 g (4 oz) mild goat's cheese
1 egg yolk, to glaze
icing (confectioners') sugar, extra, to dust

1 Soak the sultanas in the brandy. To make the pastry, sift the flour and 1 tablespoon of the icing sugar into a large bowl. Using your fingertips, rub in the butter until the mixture resembles fine breadcrumbs. Make a well in the centre, add 1 egg and mix with a flat-bladed knife, using a cutting action, until the mixture comes together in beads. Add 1 tablespoon water if the mixture is too dry. Gather together and lift onto a lightly floured work surface. Press into a ball and flatten to a disc. Wrap in plastic wrap and refrigerate for 30 minutes.
2 Preheat the oven to 180°C (350°F/ Gas 4). Heat a baking tray in the oven.
3 Wash the silverbeet and pat dry. Place in a food processor with the remaining eggs and the remaining icing sugar. Process to chop the silverbeet and combine, but don't overprocess. Transfer to a bowl. Drain the sultanas and add to the bowl with the pine nuts, then season.

4 Bring the pastry to room temperature, then break into two portions. Roll out one portion and use to line a 26 cm (10½ inch) loose-based flan (tart) tin.
5 Toss the apples with the lemon zest. Put the silverbeet mixture on the pastry and top with the crumbled goat's cheese. Spiral the apple slices on top, making one or two layers.
6 Roll out the remaining pastry and cover the pie. Trim off the excess pastry and seal the edges with a little water. Crimp the edges.

7 Brush the pie with the egg yolk and bake for 45–50 minutes, or until golden. Cool slightly. Dust with the icing sugar. Serve warm or cold.

NOTE: To toast pine nuts, dry-fry them in a frying pan over medium heat until golden and aromatic, stirring and watching constantly so they don't burn.

tourte de blettes

This is one of Nice's most traditional and favoured desserts. The marriage of silverbeet with pine nuts and sultanas harks back to the arrival of the Arab spice traders in the Mediterranean region.

Although the combination may seem strange at first, you will be pleasantly surprised at how complementary the flavours actually are. It makes a perfect picnic option and can be eaten either warm or cold.

pears poached in wine

pears poached in wine

✹

Preparation time: 20 minutes
Cooking time: 45 minutes
Serves 4

4 firm ripe pears
750 ml (26 fl oz/3 cups) good-quality
    red wine
175 g (6 oz/¾ cup) caster (superfine) sugar
1 cinnamon stick
60 ml (2 fl oz/¼ cup) orange juice
5 cm (2 inch) piece orange zest
200 g (7 oz) mascarpone cheese, to serve

1 Peel the pears, being careful to keep
them whole with the stalks still attached.
2 Put the wine, sugar, cinnamon stick,
orange juice and zest in a saucepan that
is large enough for the pears to stand
upright. Stir over medium heat until the
sugar has dissolved. Add the pears to
the saucepan and stir gently to coat. The
pears should be almost covered with the
wine mixture. Cover the pan and simmer
for 20–25 minutes, or until the pears are
cooked. Allow to cool in the syrup.
3 Remove the pears with a slotted spoon.
Bring the liquid to the boil and boil
rapidly until about 185 ml (6 fl oz/¾ cup)
of liquid remains. Serve the pears with a
little syrup and the mascarpone.

amandine

✹ ✹

Preparation time: 25 minutes
Cooking time: 30 minutes
Serves 4–6

100 g (3½ oz) hazelnuts
120 g (4¼ oz) blanched almonds
185 g (6½ oz/1 cup) soft brown sugar
360 g (12¾ oz/1⅔ cups) sugar
175 g (6 oz/½ cup) honey
1 lemon, halved
115 g (4 oz) unsalted butter

1 Preheat the oven to 170°C (325°F/
Gas 3). Spread the hazelnuts on a baking

Carefully place the pears in the
saucepan and stir to gently coat
with the wine mixture.

Allow the pears to cool in the pan,
then remove using a slotted spoon.

tray and roast for about 5 minutes, or until their skins crack. Remove from the oven and reduce the temperature to 150°C (300°F/Gas 2). Wrap the nuts in a tea towel (dish towel), rub together to dislodge their skins and allow to cool. Put the skinned nuts in a food processor. Place the almonds on the baking tray and bake for 6 minutes, or until browned. Allow to cool, then transfer the almonds to the processor. Chop the nuts until they look like little pebbles.

2 Grease a large baking tray. Put 125 ml (4 fl oz/½ cup) water in a heavy-based saucepan with the sugars and honey. Bring to the boil, stirring only until the sugars have melted. Remove any visible seeds in the lemon halves and squeeze 2–3 drops of juice into the boiling syrup. Reserve the lemon. Simmer the syrup for 8–10 minutes, or until it reaches 150°C (300°F) on a sugar thermometer. Stir in the butter and, when melted, the nuts. Pour onto the greased baking tray and use the lemon halves to spread and smooth the toffee out to a 5 mm (¼ inch) thick sheet. Leave to cool and set hard. Crack into pieces to serve.

cherry clafoutis (french batter pudding)

❋ ❋

Preparation time: **15 minutes**
Cooking time: **40 minutes**
Serves **6–8**

500 g (1 lb 2 oz) fresh cherries (see Note)
90 g (3¼ oz/¾ cup) plain (all-purpose) flour
90 g (3 oz/⅓ cup) caster (superfine) sugar
2 eggs, lightly beaten
250 ml (9 fl oz/1 cup) milk
60 ml (2 fl oz/¼ cup) thick (double/heavy) cream
60 g (2¼ oz) unsalted butter, melted
icing (confectioners') sugar, for dusting

1 Preheat the oven to 180°C (350°F/ Gas 4). Grease a 1.5 litre (52 fl oz/6 cup)

ovenproof dish with melted butter.
2 Remove the stones from the cherries and spread in the dish in a single layer.
3 Sift the flour into a bowl and stir in the sugar. Add the egg, milk, cream and butter, and whisk until just combined. Do not overbeat.
4 Pour the batter over the cherries and bake for 30–40 minutes, or until a skewer comes out clean when inserted into the centre of the pudding. Serve warm, straight from the oven, and dust generously with the icing sugar.

NOTE: Use a 720 g (1 lb 9½ oz) jar of cherries if fresh ones aren't available. Make sure you drain the cherries thoroughly before using.

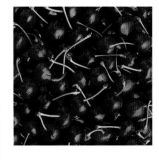

clafoutis

A clafoutis (pronounced 'clafootee') is a classic French batter pudding traditionally made with cherries. However, berries such as blueberries, blackberries, raspberries, or small strawberries can be used instead. A delicious version can also be made using slices of peach or pear.

cherry clafoutis

figs poached in red wine and thyme

Soak 375 g (13 oz) dried whole figs in boiling water for 10 minutes, then drain. Put 250 ml (9 fl oz/1 cup) good-quality red wine and 235 g (8½ oz/⅔ cup) honey in a saucepan and warm slightly over low heat, then add the figs and 4 thyme sprigs, tied with kitchen string. Cover and simmer for 10 minutes. Uncover and cook for another 10 minutes. Use a slotted spoon to transfer the figs to a bowl. Discard the thyme. Bring the syrup to the boil, then boil rapidly for 5–8 minutes, until the syrup is reduced and just coats the back of a spoon. Return the figs to the pan, stir to warm through, then allow to cool slightly. Serve warm or at room temperature, with cream. Garnish with extra thyme. Serves 4.

hot fruit soufflé

hot fruit soufflé

✹ ✹

Preparation time: **15 minutes**
Cooking time: **30 minutes**
Serves **4**

unsalted butter, melted, for greasing
caster (superfine) sugar, for sprinkling
60 g (2¼ oz) unsalted butter, extra
60 g (2¼ oz/½ cup) plain (all-purpose) flour
375 ml (13 fl oz/1½ cups) puréed fruit (see Note)
¼ cup (60 g/2 oz) caster (superfine) sugar, extra
4 egg whites
icing (confectioners') sugar, to dust

1 Prepare a 1.25 litre (44 fl oz/5 cup) soufflé dish by brushing melted butter evenly and generously over the dish, especially at the rim. Sprinkle with caster sugar, shake to coat evenly, then tip out any excess. Preheat the oven to 200°C

(400°F/Gas 6) and put a baking tray on the top shelf to heat.
2 Melt the extra butter in a saucepan, add the flour and mix well. Remove from the heat, stir until smooth, then stir in the puréed fruit. Return the pan to the heat, bring the mixture to the boil and simmer for 2 minutes. Add the extra sugar a little at a time, tasting as you go. Add a little more sugar if necessary. Leave to cool.
3 Whisk the egg whites in a clean, dry large bowl until soft peaks form. Add 1 tablespoon to the fruit mixture and mix well. Fold in the remaining whites, being careful not to lose too much volume. Fill the soufflé dish to three-quarters full.
4 Put the soufflé dish on the hot baking tray and bake for 20–25 minutes, until well risen and golden. Serve immediately, dusted with the icing sugar.

NOTE: Use fruits that purée well, such as raspberries, strawberries, mangoes, peaches, apricots and passionfruit. Bananas are a little too heavy.

nougat

✹ ✹

Preparation time: **30 minutes**
  + 4 hours chilling time
Cooking time: **15 minutes**
Makes **1 kg (2 lb 4 oz)**

440 g (15½ oz/2 cups) sugar
250 ml (9 fl oz/1 cup) liquid glucose
175 g (6 oz/½ cup) honey
2 egg whites
1 teaspoon natural vanilla extract
125 g (4½ oz) unsalted butter, softened
60 g (2¼ oz) almonds, unblanched and toasted
100 g (3½ oz) glacé cherries

1 Grease an 18 x 28 cm (7 x 11 inch) baking dish and line with baking paper. Put the sugar, glucose, honey, 60 ml (2 fl oz/¼ cup) water and ¼ teaspoon salt in a heavy-based saucepan and stir over low heat until dissolved. Bring to the boil and cook at a rolling boil for

8 minutes, or until the mixture reaches 122°C (252°F) on a sugar thermometer. (The correct temperature is very important, otherwise the mixture will not set properly.)

2 Beat the egg whites in a bowl using electric beaters until stiff peaks form. Slowly pour one-quarter of the sugar mixture onto the egg whites in a thin stream and beat for up to 5 minutes, or until the mixture holds its shape. Put the remaining syrup over the heat and cook for 2 minutes (watch that it doesn't burn), or until a small amount forms brittle threads when dropped into cold water, or it reaches 157°C (315°F) on a sugar thermometer. Pour the syrup slowly onto the meringue mixture with the beaters running and beat until the mixture is very thick.

3 Add the vanilla and butter and beat for a further 5 minutes. Stir in the almonds and cherries with a metal spoon. Turn the mixture into the prepared dish and smooth the top with a palette knife. Refrigerate for at least 4 hours, or until firm. Turn out onto a large chopping board and cut the nougat into 2 x 4 cm (¾ x 1½ inch) pieces. Wrap each piece in cellophane and store in the refrigerator.

nougat

Said to come from 'nux gatum', which is Latin for nut cake, the ancient ingredients of nougat are a key to its Mediterranean origins. Honey, almonds and other nuts were originally beaten with egg whites, then sun-dried. Today, the process is much quicker, although the flavourings remain the same.

spain

Nothing evokes visions of Spain more than the idea of sitting at a small table at a tapas bar, perhaps out in the warm sunshine, eating delicious, small snacks and sipping a thirst-quenching glass of chilled wine or sherry. In these bars, the Spaniards are able to indulge their passion for seafood as they choose from dishes such as Stuffed mussels, Salt cod fritters or Barbecued prawns. Spanish food embraces a world of brilliant colour that typifies all aspects of the lifestyle. Above all, Spanish food is simple and makes the most of the freshest of ingredients. Chillies, chickpeas, rice, eggs and garlic all feature prominently. Many flavours have been borrowed from South America, but Spanish food is not quite as hot and spicy.

empanadas (spanish turnovers)

✹ ✹

Preparation time: **30 minutes**
Cooking time: **25 minutes**
Makes **about 15**

2 eggs
40 g (1½ oz) stuffed green olives, chopped
95 g (3¼ oz) ham, finely chopped

30 g (1 oz/¼ cup) grated cheddar cheese
3 sheets ready-rolled puff pastry, thawed
1 egg yolk, lightly beaten

1 Place the eggs in a saucepan, cover with water and bring to the boil. Boil for 10 minutes, then drain and cool for 5 minutes in cold water. Peel and chop.
2 Preheat the oven to 220°C (425°F/ Gas 7). Lightly grease two baking trays. Combine the egg, olives, ham and cheese in a large bowl.

3 Cut about five 10 cm (4 inch) rounds from each pastry sheet. Spoon a tablespoon of the filling into the centre of each round, fold the pastry over and crimp the edges to seal.
4 Place the pastries on the trays, about 2 cm (¾ inch) apart. Brush with the egg yolk and bake in the centre or top half of the oven for 15 minutes, or until well browned and puffed. Swap the trays around after 10 minutes and cover loosely with foil if the empanadas start to brown too much. Serve hot.

empanadas

empanadas

Empanadas are traditional Spanish and Central American individual pastry turnovers. They usually have a savoury meat and vegetable filling, although they can also be filled with fruit and served as a dessert. They range from canapé size to those large enough to feed a family.

gambas al pil pil (chilli garlic prawns)

✹

Preparation time: **30 minutes**
 + 30 minutes chilling time
Cooking time: **10 minutes**
Serves **4–6**

1 kg (2 lb 4 oz) medium raw prawns (shrimp)
60 g (2¼ oz) butter
80 ml (2½ fl oz/⅓ cup) olive oil
3 garlic cloves, roughly chopped
¼ teaspoon chilli flakes
½ teaspoon paprika

1 Peel the prawns, leaving the tails intact. Gently pull out the dark vein from each prawn back, starting at the head end. Mix the prawns with ½ teaspoon salt in a large bowl, cover and refrigerate for about 30 minutes.
2 Heat the butter and oil in a frying pan over medium heat. When foaming, add the garlic and chilli and stir for 1 minute, or until golden. Add the prawns, cook for 3–6 minutes, or until they change colour, then sprinkle with paprika. Serve hot with bread for dipping.

NOTE: Traditionally, Gambas al pil pil is made and served in small earthenware dishes, with one small dish serving two people. You can make this recipe in two small earthenware dishes if you like.

calamares a la plancha (barbecued squid)

✳ ✳

Preparation time: 40 minutes
  + 30 minutes chilling time
Cooking time: 10 minutes
Serves 6

500 g (1 lb 2 oz) small squid
  (see Note)

PICADA DRESSING
2 tablespoons extra virgin olive oil
2 tablespoons finely chopped flat-leaf
  (Italian) parsley
1 garlic clove, crushed

1 To prepare the squid, gently pull the tentacles away from the tubes; the intestines should come away at the same time. Cut under the eyes to remove the intestines from the tentacles, then remove the beak (if it remains in the centre of the tentacles) by using your fingers to push up the centre. Pull away the soft bone.
2 Rub the tubes under cold running water and the skin should come away easily. Wash the tubes and tentacles and drain well. Place in a bowl, add ¼ teaspoon salt and mix well. Cover and refrigerate for 30 minutes.
3 To make the picada dressing, whisk together the oil, parsley, garlic, salt and ¼ teaspoon freshly ground black pepper.
4 Heat a lightly oiled barbecue hotplate or preheat a grill (broiler) to its highest setting. Cook the squid tubes in small batches for 2–3 minutes, or until white and tender. Cook the tentacles, turning to brown all over, for 1 minute, or until they curl. Serve hot, with the picada dressing.

NOTE: Use the smallest squid you can find for this recipe. Alternatively, you can use cuttlefish, octopus, prawns (shrimp) or even chunks of firm white fish fillet instead of the squid. Make the picada dressing as close to serving time as possible so the parsley doesn't discolour.

Gently pull the tentacles away from the squid tubes.

Remove the beak if it remains in the centre of the tentacles.

Pull away the soft bone, rinse the tubes and remove the skin.

tuna skewers with caperberries

Soak eight wooden skewers in cold water for 30 minutes to prevent them burning during cooking. Cut 250 g (9 oz) raw tuna into 24 even-sized cubes. Use a peeler to remove the zest from a lemon, avoiding the bitter white pith, and cut it into thin strips. Combine the tuna, zest and 1 tablespoon each of lemon juice and olive oil in a bowl. Thread 3 pieces of tuna, 2 caperberries and a green olive stuffed with anchovy fillet onto each skewer, alternating each ingredient. Place in a non-metallic dish and pour the marinade over. Grill under a hot grill (broiler) for 4 minutes, turning to cook each side, or until done to your liking. Makes 8.

marinated red capsicum

☀ ☀

Preparation time: **20 minutes**
  + overnight chilling time
Cooking time: **5 minutes**
Serves **6**

3 red capsicums (peppers)
3 thyme sprigs
1 garlic clove, thinly sliced
2 teaspoons roughly chopped flat-leaf (Italian) parsley
1 bay leaf
1 spring onion (scallion), sliced
1 teaspoon paprika
60 ml (2 fl oz/¼ cup) extra virgin olive oil
2 tablespoons red wine vinegar

1 Preheat the grill (broiler) to high. Cut the capsicums into quarters and discard the seeds and membrane. Grill, skin side up, until the skin is black and blistered. Cool in a plastic bag, then peel and slice thinly. Combine with the thyme, garlic, parsley, bay leaf and spring onion in a jar.
2 Whisk together the paprika, oil, vinegar and some salt and pepper. Pour over the capsicum mixture and stir to combine. Cover and refrigerate for at least 3 hours, or preferably overnight. Remove from the refrigerator about 30 minutes before serving.

NOTE: The capsicum can be refrigerated for up to 3 days.

chickpeas with chorizo sausage

✻ ✻

Preparation time: 15 minutes
   + overnight soaking time
Cooking time: 1 hour 10 minutes
Serves 6

165 g (5¾ oz/¾ cup) dried chickpeas
1 bay leaf
4 whole cloves
1 cinnamon stick
1 litre (35 fl oz/4 cups) chicken stock
2 tablespoons olive oil
1 onion, finely chopped
1 garlic clove, crushed
pinch of dried thyme
375 g (13 oz) chorizo sausages, chopped
1 tablespoon chopped flat-leaf (Italian)
   parsley

1 Put the chickpeas in a large bowl, cover well with water and soak overnight. Drain, then put in a large saucepan with the bay leaf, cloves, cinnamon stick and stock. Top up with a little water so the chickpeas are well covered in liquid, bring to the boil, then reduce the heat and simmer for 1 hour, or until the chickpeas are tender. If they need more time, add a little more water. There should be just a little liquid left in the saucepan. Drain and remove the bay leaf, cloves and cinnamon.
2 Heat the olive oil in a large frying pan, add the onion and cook over medium heat for 3 minutes, or until translucent. Add the garlic and thyme and cook, stirring, for 1 minute. Increase the heat to medium–high, add the chorizo and cook for a further 3 minutes.
3 Add the chickpeas to the frying pan, mix well, then stir over medium heat until they are heated through. Remove from the heat and stir in the parsley. Taste before seasoning with salt and freshly ground black pepper. This dish is equally delicious served hot or at room temperature.

cinnamon sticks

Cinnamon sticks are the curled, thin pieces of bark of a tropical evergreen tree. The bark is removed during the rainy season when it is pliable and easy to work with. When it dries, it curls into quills that are then cut to size or ground to a powder. It is a much-prized spice in Spanish cooking, widely used in both sweet and savoury dishes. Cinnamon keeps its flavour best when whole, however if the recipe calls for ground cinnamon, buy a small quantity.

166

barbecued prawns with romesco sauce

✺ ✺

Preparation time: **30 minutes**
 + 30 minutes chilling time
Cooking time: **20 minutes**
Serves **6–8**

30 raw large prawns (shrimp)

ROMESCO SAUCE
4 garlic cloves, unpeeled
1 roma (plum) tomato, halved and seeded
2 long red chillies
35 g (1¼ oz/¼ cup) blanched almonds
60 g (2¼ oz) roasted capsicums
 (peppers) in oil
1 tablespoon olive oil
1 tablespoon red wine vinegar

1 Peel the prawns, leaving the tails intact. Gently pull out the dark vein from each prawn back, starting at the head end. Mix with ¼ teaspoon salt and refrigerate for 30 minutes.

2 To make the romesco sauce, preheat the oven to 200°C (400°F/Gas 6). Wrap the garlic cloves in foil, put on a baking tray with the tomato and chillies and bake for 12 minutes. Spread the almonds on the tray and bake for 3–5 minutes more. Leave to cool for 15 minutes.

3 Transfer the almonds to a small blender or food processor and blend until finely ground. Squeeze the garlic and scrape the tomato flesh into the blender, discarding the skins. Split the chillies and remove the seeds. Scrape the flesh into the blender, discarding the skins. Pat the capsicums dry with paper towel, then chop them and add to the blender with the olive oil, vinegar, some salt and 2 tablespoons water. Blend until smooth, adding more water if necessary to form a soft dipping consistency.

4 Brush the prawns with a little oil and cook on a hot barbecue grill plate for 3 minutes, or until curled up and changed in colour. Serve with the sauce.

Squeeze the garlic and scrape the tomato flesh from the skins.

Blend the mixture together to form a soft dipping consistency.

stuffed mussels

✳ ✳

Preparation time: 40 minutes
Cooking time: 20 minutes
Makes 18

18 black mussels
2 teaspoons olive oil
2 spring onions (scallions), finely chopped
1 garlic clove, crushed
1 tablespoon tomato paste (concentrated purée)
2 teaspoons lemon juice
3 tablespoons chopped flat-leaf (Italian) parsley
35 g (1¼ oz/⅓ cup) dry breadcrumbs
2 eggs, beaten
vegetable oil, for deep-frying
lemon wedges, to serve

WHITE SAUCE
40 g (1½ oz) butter
30 g (1 oz/¼ cup) plain (all-purpose) flour
80 ml (2½ fl oz/⅓ cup) milk

1 Scrub the mussels with a stiff brush and pull out the hairy beards. Discard any open or damaged mussels. Bring 250 ml (9 fl oz/1 cup) water to the boil in a saucepan, add the mussels, cover and cook for 3–4 minutes, shaking the pan occasionally, until the mussels have just opened. Remove them as soon as they open or they will be tough. Strain the liquid into a bowl until you have 80 ml (2½ fl oz/⅓ cup). Discard any unopened mussels. Remove the opened mussels from their shells and discard one half-shell from each. Finely chop the mussel meat and set aside.

2 Heat the olive oil in a large frying pan over medium heat, add the spring onion and cook for 1 minute. Add the garlic and cook for 1 minute. Stir in the mussel meat, tomato paste, lemon juice, 2 tablespoons of the parsley and season with salt and pepper. Set aside to cool.

3 To make the white sauce, melt the butter in a saucepan over low heat. Stir in the flour and cook for 1 minute, or until pale and foaming. Remove the pan from the heat and gradually whisk in the reserved mussel liquid, milk and some pepper. Return to the heat and boil, stirring, for 1 minute, or until the sauce thickens. Reduce the heat and simmer for 2 minutes. Set aside to cool.

4 Spoon the mussel mixture into the reserved half-shells. Top each with some of the white sauce and smooth the surface, making the mixture heaped. Combine the breadcrumbs and remaining parsley. Dip the mussels in the egg, then press in the crumbs to cover the top.

5 Fill a deep heavy-based saucepan about one-third full of oil and heat to 180°C (350°F), or until a cube of bread dropped into the oil browns in 15 seconds. Cook the mussels in batches for 2 minutes each batch. Remove with a slotted spoon, drain well and keep warm. Serve the mussels hot with the lemon wedges.

pan con tomate

Slice a baguette diagonally and toast the slices very lightly. Rub them on one side with a cut garlic clove, then with half a tomato, squeezing the juice onto the bread. Season with a little salt and drizzle with extra virgin olive oil. Serve as part of a tapas, or as a simple snack.

chorizo

Chorizo is a popular sausage in Spanish cuisine and most regions have their own special variety. They are a pork sausage with a coarse texture, highly seasoned with paprika and garlic, and are either mild or made spicy with the addition of chillies. In Spain they are generally sold cured or smoked, and are indispensable in many traditional recipes. They can also be grilled, then cut into chunks and served as part of a tapas spread.

albondigas en picant salsa de tomate (meatballs in spicy tomato sauce)

☼ ☼

Preparation time: 40 minutes
   + 30 minutes chilling time
Cooking time: 35 minutes
Serves 6

175 g (6 oz) minced (ground) pork
175 g (6 oz) minced (ground) veal
3 garlic cloves, crushed
35 g (1¼ oz/⅓ cup) dry breadcrumbs
1 teaspoon ground coriander
1 teaspoon freshly ground nutmeg
1 teaspoon ground cumin
pinch of ground cinnamon
1 egg
2 tablespoons olive oil

SPICY TOMATO SAUCE
1 tablespoon olive oil
1 onion, chopped
2 garlic cloves, crushed
125 ml (4 fl oz/½ cup) dry white wine
400 g (14 oz) tin chopped tomatoes
1 tablespoon tomato paste (concentrated
   purée)
125 ml (4 fl oz/½ cup) chicken stock
½ teaspoon cayenne pepper
80 g (2¾ oz/½ cup) frozen peas

1 Combine the pork, veal, garlic, breadcrumbs, spices, egg and some salt and pepper in a bowl. Mix by hand until smooth and leaving the side of the bowl. Refrigerate, covered, for 30 minutes.
2 Roll tablespoons of the mixture into balls. Heat 1 tablespoon of the oil in a frying pan over medium–high heat and cook half the meatballs for 2–3 minutes, turning frequently, until browned. Remove and drain on paper towels. Add the remaining oil, if necessary, and brown the rest of the meatballs, then drain.
3 To make the spicy tomato sauce, heat the oil in a frying pan over medium heat and cook the onion, stirring occasionally,

for 3 minutes, or until translucent. Add the garlic and cook for 1 minute, then increase the heat to high, add the wine and boil for 1 minute. Add the tomatoes, tomato paste and stock and simmer for 10 minutes. Add the cayenne, peas and meatballs. Simmer for 5–10 minutes, or until the sauce is thick and the meatballs are cooked. Serve with crusty bread.

chorizo en sidra (chorizo in cider)

✽ ✽

Preparation time: **5 minutes**
Cooking time: **15 minutes**
Serves **4**

3 teaspoons olive oil
1 small onion, finely chopped
1½ teaspoons paprika
125 ml (4 fl oz/½ cup) alcoholic dry
  apple cider
60 ml (2 fl oz/¼ cup) chicken stock
1 bay leaf
280 g (10 oz) chorizo sausages,
  sliced on the diagonal
2 teaspoons sherry vinegar, or to taste
2 teaspoons chopped flat-leaf (Italian)
  parsley

1 Heat the oil in a saucepan over low heat and cook the onion, stirring occasionally, for 3 minutes or until soft. Add the paprika and cook for 1 minute.
2 Increase the heat to medium, add the apple cider, stock and bay leaf to the pan and bring to the boil. Reduce the heat and simmer for 5 minutes. Add the chorizo and simmer for 5 minutes, or until the sauce has reduced slightly. Stir in the vinegar and parsley. Serve hot.

salted almonds

Preheat the oven to 120°C (235°F/Gas ½). In a large bowl, lightly whisk an egg white and ¼ teaspoon sweet paprika with a fork until the mixture starts to froth. Add 500 g (1 lb 2 oz) blanched almonds and toss to coat evenly. Divide the nuts between two non-stick baking trays. Sprinkle with 1½ tablespoons coarse sea salt grains (not flakes), turning the nuts several times so that the salt adheres to them. Spread over the trays. Bake for 30 minutes, turning the nuts over occasionally to prevent them sticking. Turn off the heat and leave the almonds in the oven for 30 minutes. When completely cooled, store in an airtight jar. Serves 6–8.

bunuelos de bacalao (salt cod fritters)

Preparation time: 20 minutes
+ 24 hours soaking time
Cooking time: 1 hour
Makes 35

500 g (1 lb 2 oz) salt cod
1 all-purpose potato (about 200 g/7 oz)
2 tablespoons milk
60 ml (2 fl oz/¼ cup) olive oil
1 small onion, finely chopped
2 garlic cloves, crushed
30 g (1 oz/¼ cup) self-raising flour
2 eggs, separated
1 tablespoon chopped flat-leaf (Italian) parsley
olive oil, extra, for deep-frying
lemon wedges, to serve

1 Soak the salt cod in cold water for 24 hours, changing the water regularly to remove as much salt as possible. Cook the potato in boiling water for 20 minutes, or until soft. When cool, peel and mash with the milk and 2 tablespoons of olive oil.
2 Drain the cod, cut into large pieces and place in a saucepan. Cover with water, bring to the boil over high heat, then reduce the heat to medium and cook for 10 minutes, or until soft. Drain. When cool enough to handle, remove the skin and any bones, then mash with a fork.
3 Heat the remaining oil in a small frying pan over medium heat and cook the onion for 5 minutes, or until softened. Add the garlic and cook for 1 minute. Set aside.
4 Combine the mashed potato, cod, onion and garlic, flour, egg yolks and parsley in a bowl and season with salt and pepper. Whisk the egg whites until stiff, then fold into the potato and cod mixture.
5 Fill a large heavy-based saucepan about one-third full of olive oil and heat to 190°C (375°F), or until a cube of bread browns in 10 seconds. Drop heaped tablespoons of mixture in the oil and cook for 2 minutes, or until puffed and golden. Drain and serve with lemon wedges.

rinones al jerez (kidneys in sherry)

Preparation time: 15 minutes
Cooking time: 20 minutes
Serves 4

2 tablespoons olive oil
1 large onion, finely chopped
2 garlic cloves, crushed

1 tablespoon plain (all-purpose) flour
310 ml (10¾ fl oz/1¼ cups) chicken stock
1 tablespoon tomato paste (concentrated purée)
1 bay leaf
1 kg (2 lb 4 oz) lambs' kidneys, halved
40 g (1½ oz) butter
150 ml (5 fl oz) dry sherry
1 tablespoon chopped flat-leaf (Italian) parsley

1 Heat the oil in a frying pan and cook the onion and garlic over medium heat

bunuelos de bacalao

Remove the skin and any bones from the cooked salt cod.

Fold the whisked egg white into the potato and cod mixture.

Deep-fry the fritters in hot oil until puffed and golden.

for about 5 minutes, until the onion softens. Add the flour and cook, stirring, for 1 minute. Add the stock, tomato paste and bay leaf. Bring to the boil and cook, stirring, until thickened. Season with salt and ground black pepper and simmer for 3–4 minutes. Keep warm.

2 Cut out the white cores from the kidneys. Slice each half into three. Melt the butter in a large frying pan and add half the kidneys. Cook over high heat, stirring often, until browned on all sides. Remove from the pan and cook the rest. Remove, pour the sherry into the pan and cook over high heat, stirring to deglaze, until reduced by half. Return the kidneys to the pan, add the sauce and stir the parsley through. Taste for seasoning and simmer for another 2 minutes before serving. Delicious with rice.

patatas bravas (crisp potatoes in spicy tomato sauce)

☀ ☀

Preparation time: **15 minutes**
Cooking time: **1 hour**
Serves **6**

1 kg (2 lb 4 oz) all-purpose potatoes
 (such as desiree)
vegetable oil, for deep-frying
500 g (1 lb 2 oz) ripe roma (plum)
 tomatoes
2 tablespoons olive oil
¼ red onion, finely chopped
2 garlic cloves, crushed
3 teaspoons paprika
¼ teaspoon cayenne pepper
1 bay leaf
1 teaspoon sugar
1 tablespoon chopped flat-leaf (Italian)
 parsley, to garnish

patatas bravas

1 Cut the potatoes into 2 cm (¾ inch) cubes. Rinse, then drain well and pat completely dry.

2 Fill a large heavy-based saucepan or deep-fryer one-third full of oil and heat to 180°C (350°F), or until a cube of bread dropped into the oil browns in 15 seconds. Cook the potato in batches for 10 minutes, or until golden. Drain well on paper towels. Do not discard the oil.

3 Score a cross in the base of each tomato. Put the tomatoes in a heatproof bowl and cover with boiling water. Leave for 30 seconds, then transfer to cold water, drain and peel the skin away from the cross. Cut the tomatoes in half and roughly chop the flesh.

4 Heat the olive oil in a saucepan over medium heat and cook the onion for 3 minutes, or until softened. Add the garlic, paprika and cayenne pepper and cook for 1–2 minutes, until aromatic.

5 Add the tomato, bay leaf, sugar and 90 ml (3 fl oz) water and cook, stirring occasionally, for 20 minutes, or until thick and pulpy. Cool slightly and remove the bay leaf. Transfer to a food processor and blend until smooth, adding a little water if necessary. Before you are ready to serve, return the sauce to the pan and simmer over low heat for 2 minutes. Season well.

6 Reheat the oil to 180°C (350°F) and cook the potato again, in batches, for 2 minutes, or until very crisp and golden. Drain on paper towels. This second frying makes the potato extra crispy and stops the sauce soaking in immediately. Place on a platter and spoon over the tomato sauce. Sprinkle with parsley and serve.

Roll 2 tablespoons of the mixture into croquette shapes.

Use two forks to dip each floured croquette in the egg.

croquetas del jamon y de la seta (ham and mushroom croquettes)

✹ ✹

Preparation time: 35 minutes + 2 hours cooling and 30 minutes chilling time
Cooking time: 20 minutes
Makes 18

90 g (3¼ oz) butter
1 small onion, finely chopped
110 g (3¾ oz) mushroom caps, finely chopped
90 g (3¼ oz/¾ cup) plain (all-purpose) flour
250 ml (9 fl oz/1 cup) milk
185 ml (6 fl oz/¾ cup) chicken stock
110 g (3¾ oz) ham, finely chopped
60 g (2¼ oz/½ cup) plain (all-purpose) flour, extra
2 eggs, lightly beaten
50 g (1¾ oz/½ cup) dry breadcrumbs
vegetable oil, for deep-frying

1 Melt the butter in a saucepan over low heat, add the onion and cook for 5 minutes, or until translucent. Add the mushroom and cook over low heat, stirring occasionally, for 5 minutes. Add the flour and stir over low–medium heat for 1 minute, or until the mixture is dry and crumbly and begins to change colour. Remove from the heat and gradually add the milk, stirring until smooth. Stir in the stock and return to the heat, stirring until the mixture boils and thickens. Stir in the ham and some black pepper, then transfer to a bowl to cool for about 2 hours.

2 Roll 2 tablespoons of mixture at a time into croquette shapes, 6 cm (2½ inches) long. Put the extra flour, egg and breadcrumbs in three shallow bowls. Toss the croquettes in flour, dip in egg, then roll in breadcrumbs. Place on a baking tray and refrigerate for about 30 minutes.

3 Fill a deep-fryer or heavy-based saucepan one-third full of oil and heat to 180°C (350°F), or until a cube of bread browns in 15 seconds. Deep-fry the croquettes, in batches, for 3 minutes, turning, until brown. Drain well.

NOTE: You can replace the ham with finely chopped chicken or flaked cooked fish and add finely chopped herbs.

champinones al ajillo (garlic mushrooms)

✳

Preparation time: **10 minutes**
Cooking time: **10 minutes**
Serves **4**

6 garlic cloves
1½ tablespoons lemon juice
650 g (1 lb 7 oz) button mushrooms, sliced
   (see Note)
60 ml (2 fl oz/¼ cup) olive oil
¼ small red chilli, finely chopped
2 teaspoons chopped flat-leaf (Italian)
   parsley

1 Crush four of the garlic cloves and thinly slice the rest. Sprinkle the lemon juice over the sliced mushrooms.
2 Heat the olive oil in a large frying pan and add the crushed garlic and chilli. Stir over medium–high heat for 10 seconds, then add the mushrooms. Season with salt and pepper and cook, stirring often, for 8–10 minutes. Stir in the sliced garlic and parsley and cook for 1 minute. Serve hot.

NOTE: You can also use field, Swiss brown or any wild mushrooms, but the more fragile wild mushrooms will cook faster.

gambas al ajillo (garlic prawns)

✳

Preparation time: **20 minutes**
Cooking time: **15 minutes**
Serves **4**

1.25 kg (2 lb 12 oz) medium raw prawns
   (shrimp)
80 g (2¾ oz) butter, melted
185 ml (6 fl oz/¾ cup) olive oil
8 garlic cloves, crushed
2 spring onions (scallions), thinly sliced

1 Preheat the oven to 250°C (500°F/ Gas 9). Peel the prawns, leaving the tails intact. Pull out the dark vein from each prawn back, starting at the head end. Cut a slit down the back of each prawn.
2 Divide the combined butter and oil among four 500 ml (17 fl oz/2 cup) cast-iron pots. Add half the garlic.
3 Place the pots on a baking tray and heat in the oven for 10 minutes, or until the mixture is bubbling. Remove and divide the prawns and remaining garlic among the pots. Return to the oven for 5 minutes, or until the prawns are cooked. Stir in the spring onion. Season, to taste. Serve with bread to mop up the juices.

NOTE: Garlic prawns can also be made in a cast-iron frying pan in the oven or on the stovetop.

champinones al ajillo

clams

When buying clams, look for tightly closed shells. Before cooking, they need to be soaked in salted water for at least an hour as this helps them to purge any grit. Clams only require gentle cooking, otherwise they will be tough and chewy. Like other molluscs such as mussels, once cooked, any that haven't opened must be discarded as they were dead before being cooked.

almejas a la marinera (clams in white wine)

Preparation time: 10 minutes
    + 1 hour soaking time
Cooking time: 20 minutes
Serves 4

1 kg (2 lb 4 oz) clams (vongole) (see Note)
2 large tomatoes
2 tablespoons olive oil
1 small onion, finely chopped
2 garlic cloves, crushed
1 tablespoon chopped flat-leaf (Italian)
    parsley
pinch of freshly grated nutmeg
80 ml (2½ fl oz/⅓ cup) dry white wine
flat-leaf (Italian) parsley, extra, to garnish

1   Soak the clams in salted water for 1 hour to release any grit. Rinse under cold running water and discard any open clams. Score a cross in the base of each tomato. Put in a heatproof bowl and cover with boiling water. Leave for 30 seconds, then transfer to cold water and peel the skin from the cross. Cut the tomatoes in half, scoop out the seeds and finely chop.

2   Heat the oil in a large flameproof casserole and cook the onion over low heat for 5 minutes. Add the garlic and tomato and cook for 5 minutes. Stir in the parsley, nutmeg and salt and pepper. Add 80 ml (2½ fl oz/⅓ cup) water.

3   Add the clams and cook over low heat until they open. Discard any that don't open. Add the wine and cook over low heat for 3–4 minutes, or until the sauce thickens, gently moving the dish back and forth a few times, rather than stirring the clams, so the clams stay in the shells. Serve garnished with the extra parsley and with bread to mop up the juices.

NOTE: You can use mussels instead of clams in this recipe.

alcachofas en aromatico vinaigrette (artichokes in aromatic vinaigrette)

Preparation time: **20 minutes**
Cooking time: **20 minutes**
Serves **4**

2 tablespoons lemon juice
4 large globe artichokes
2 garlic cloves, crushed
1 teaspoon finely chopped oregano
½ teaspoon ground cumin
½ teaspoon ground coriander
pinch of dried chilli flakes
3 teaspoons sherry vinegar
60 ml (2 fl oz/¼ cup) olive oil

1 Add the lemon juice to a bowl of cold water to make acidulated water. Trim an artichoke, cutting off the stalk to within 5 cm (2 inches) of the base and removing the tough outer leaves. Cut off the top quarter of the leaves. Slice the artichoke in half from top to base, or into quarters if large. Use a teaspoon to remove the hairy choke, then put the artichoke in the acidulated water to prevent it discolouring while you prepare the rest.
2 Bring a large non-reactive saucepan of water to the boil, add the artichokes and a teaspoon of salt and simmer for 20 minutes, or until tender. The cooking time will depend on the artichoke size. Test by pressing a skewer into the base — the artichoke should be soft and give little resistance. Strain, then put the artichokes on their cut side to drain while cooling.
3 To make the vinaigrette, combine the garlic, oregano, cumin, coriander and chilli flakes in a bowl. Season with salt and ground black pepper, and blend in the vinegar. Beating constantly, slowly pour in the olive oil to form an emulsion.
4 Arrange the artichokes in rows on a serving platter. Pour the vinaigrette over the top and allow to cool completely.

sherry vinegar

This intense, deeply flavoured vinegar began its life as a by-product of the process of making sherry. Any barrels of wine that weren't good enough for making sherry were given to friends and family as vinegar for cooking. It's now appreciated, and made, in its own right and a good-quality sherry vinegar can cost more than sherry itself. Use it to add flavour to sauces, dressings, casseroles and soups. Sherry vinegar is available in speciality food stores and delicatessens.

tortilla

✳ ✳

Preparation time: 25 minutes
Cooking time: 35 minutes
Serves 6–8

500 g (1 lb 2 oz) all-purpose potatoes,
    cut into 1 cm (½ inch) slices
60 ml (2 fl oz/¼ cup) olive oil
1 onion, thinly sliced
4 garlic cloves, thinly sliced
2 tablespoons finely chopped flat-leaf
    (Italian) parsley
6 eggs

1 Put the potato in a large saucepan, cover with cold water and bring to the boil. Boil for 5 minutes, drain, set aside.
2 Heat the olive oil in a deep non-stick frying pan over medium heat. Add the onion and garlic and cook for 5 minutes, or until the onion softens. Add the potato and parsley and stir to combine. Cook over medium heat for 5 minutes, gently pressing down into the pan.
3 Whisk the eggs with 1 teaspoon each of salt and pepper and pour evenly over the potato. Cover and cook over low–medium heat for 20 minutes, or until the eggs are just set. Cut into wedges to serve.

scallops ceviche

✳ ✳

Preparation time: 20 minutes
    + 2 hours marinating time
Cooking time: nil
Makes 15

15 scallops on the half shell
1 teaspoon finely grated lime zest
60 ml (2 fl oz/¼ cup) lime juice
2 garlic cloves, chopped
2 fresh red chillies, seeded and chopped
1 tablespoon chopped parsley
1 tablespoon olive oil

1 Take the scallops off their shells. If any need to be cut off the shell, use a small sharp knife to slice the attached part from the shell, being careful to leave as little scallop meat on the shell as possible. Remove the dark vein and white muscle from each scallop and wash the shells.
2 In a non-metallic bowl, mix the lime zest and juice, garlic, chilli, parsley and oil and season with salt and ground black pepper. Add the scallops and stir to coat. Cover with plastic wrap and refrigerate for 2 hours to 'cook' the scallop meat.
3 To serve, slide the scallops onto the half shells and spoon the dressing over them. Serve cold.

NOTE: These scallops will keep for up to 2 days in the dressing.

tortilla

octopus in garlic almond sauce

✳

Preparation time: 25 minutes
Cooking time: 40 minutes
Serves 4

1 kg (2 lb 4 oz) baby octopus
½ small red capsicum (pepper)
120 g (4¼ oz/1⅓ cups) flaked almonds
3 garlic cloves, crushed
80 ml (2½ fl oz/⅓ cup) red wine vinegar
185 ml (6 fl oz/¾ cup) olive oil
125 ml (4 fl oz/½ cup) boiling water
2 tablespoons chopped flat-leaf
   (Italian) parsley, plus parsley sprigs,
   to garnish

1   Using a small knife, carefully cut between the head and tentacles of the octopus and push the beak out and up through the centre of the tentacles with your finger. Cut the eyes from the head of the octopus by slicing off a small disc with a sharp knife. Discard the eye section.
2   To clean the octopus head, carefully slit through one side and rinse out the guts. Drop the octopus into a large saucepan of boiling water and simmer for 20–40 minutes, depending on size, until tender. After 15 minutes of cooking, start pricking them with a skewer to test for tenderness. When ready, remove from the heat and cool in the pan for 15 minutes.
3   To make the sauce, cut the capsicum into quarters, then remove the seeds and membrane. Put the capsicum quarters, skin side up, under a hot grill (broiler). Cook until the skin blackens and blisters. Remove from the grill and put in a plastic bag until cool, then peel off the skin. Put the capsicum flesh in a food processor with the almonds and garlic, then purée. With the motor running, gradually pour in the vinegar followed by the olive oil. Stir in the boiling water and parsley. Season to taste with salt and pepper.
4   Place the octopus in a serving bowl with the sauce and toss to coat. Serve warm, or chilled, garnished with parsley.

octopus in garlic almond sauce

almonds

Almonds are the kernel from the fruit of the almond tree, and although Mediterranean in origin, they are now also grown in California, Australia and South Africa. There are two varieties available: the sweet almond, which is readily available and should be used in recipes where no variety is specified, and the bitter almond, primarily used to flavour extracts and liqueurs.

huevos a la flamenca (spanish baked eggs)

✳

Preparation time: 20 minutes
Cooking time: 50 minutes
Serves 4

500 g (1 lb 2 oz) ripe tomatoes
60 ml (2 fl oz/¼ cup) olive oil
400 g (14 oz) all-purpose potatoes,
    cut into 2 cm (¾ inch) cubes
1 red capsicum (pepper), cut into strips
1 onion, chopped
100 g (3½ oz) serrano ham (or thickly sliced
    soft, pale prosciutto)
150 g (5½ oz) asparagus spears, trimmed
100 g (3½ oz/⅔ cup) fresh or frozen
    green peas
100 g (3½ oz) baby green beans,
    trimmed and halved
2 tablespoons tomato paste
    (concentrated purée)
4 eggs
100 g (3½ oz) chorizo sausage, thinly sliced
2 tablespoons chopped flat-leaf (Italian)
    parsley

1 Score a cross in the base of each tomato. Put the tomatoes in a heatproof bowl and cover with boiling water. Leave for 30 seconds, then transfer to cold water and peel the skin away from the cross. Roughly chop the flesh.

2 Heat the olive oil in a large frying pan and sauté the potato over medium heat for 8 minutes, or until golden. Remove with a slotted spoon. Lower the heat and add the capsicum and onion to the pan. Slice two of the ham slices into pieces similar in size to the capsicum and add to the pan. Fry for 6 minutes, or until the onion is soft.

3 Reserve four asparagus spears. Add the rest to the pan with the peas, beans, tomato and tomato paste. Stir in 125 ml (4 fl oz/½ cup) water and season well with salt and pepper. Return the potato to the pan. Cover and cook over low heat for 10 minutes, stirring occasionally.

4 Preheat the oven to 180°C (350°F/ Gas 4). Grease a large ovenproof dish. Transfer the vegetables to the dish, without any excess liquid. Using the back of a spoon, make four evenly spaced, deep indentations in the vegetables and carefully break an egg into each. Top with the reserved asparagus spears and the sliced chorizo. Slice the remaining ham into large pieces and distribute over the top. Sprinkle with the parsley. Bake for 20 minutes, or until the egg whites are just set. Serve warm.

huevos a la flamenca

earthenware dishes

The ideal dish to use for Huevos a la flamenca is an earthenware one with 2 cm (¾ inch) deep sides, although any shallow round dish will be acceptable. Four individual dishes can also be used. Earthenware dishes can be purchased from speciality food and homeware stores.

piquant potato salad

✳ ✳

Preparation time: 10 minutes
Cooking time: 10 minutes
Serves 4

500 g (1 lb 2 oz) baby chat potatoes
    (see Note)
2 teaspoons chopped dill
2 spring onions (scallions), chopped
1 tablespoon capers, coarsely chopped
2 tablespoons extra virgin olive oil
1½ tablespoons lemon juice
1 teaspoon finely grated orange zest

1 Place the potatoes in a large saucepan of salted water and bring to the boil. Cook for 10 minutes, or until tender when pierced with a knife. Drain well.
2 Place the potatoes in a bowl with the dill, spring onion and capers, and season. Mix well to combine. Whisk together the oil, lemon juice and orange zest in a small jug and pour over the hot potatoes. Toss to coat the potatoes and serve warm.

NOTE: Any small, waxy potato works well in this delicious salad. You can choose from those which are readily available such as pink fir, bintje or kipfler.

serrano ham

'Jamon serrano' is the name given to Spanish salt-cured and air-dried ham. The method of production is carefully controlled to ensure a quality product, and it is used in many dishes in all regions of Spain, as well as simply served in thick slices, topped with pimento, as a tapas dish. Serrano ham is left to dry for a minimum of 12 months, and the most deliciously flavoured serrano is matured for 18 months.

broad beans
with ham

Preparation time: **10 minutes**
Cooking time: **30 minutes**
Serves **4**

20 g (¾ oz) butter
1 onion, chopped
180 g (6¼ oz) serrano ham, roughly
    chopped (see Note)
2 garlic cloves, crushed
500 g (1 lb 2 oz) broad (fava) beans,
    fresh or frozen
125 ml (4 fl oz/½ cup) dry white wine
185 ml (6 fl oz/¾ cup) chicken stock

1 Melt the butter in a large saucepan and add the onion, ham and garlic. Cook over medium heat for 5 minutes, stirring often, until the onion softens.
2 Add the broad beans and wine and cook over high heat until reduced by half. Add the stock, reduce the heat, then cover and cook for 10 minutes. Uncover and simmer for another 10 minutes. Serve hot as a vegetable accompaniment to meat, or warm as a snack with crusty bread.

NOTE: Instead of serrano ham, you can use thickly sliced prosciutto.

broad beans with ham

escalivada

half and remove the seeds and membrane. Cut into thick slices.

5 Arrange all the vegetables on a large serving platter. Drizzle the olive oil over them and season. Scatter the parsley, garlic and capers over the top. Serve cold.

NOTE: Grilling the vegetables under a griller (broiler) or roasting them in a hot oven also works, although the dish will lack the characteristic smoky flavour.

esparrago de andalucia (andalucian asparagus)

Preparation time: **10 minutes**
Cooking time: **15 minutes**
Serves **4**

500 g (1 lb 2 oz) asparagus, ends trimmed
1 thick slice crusty bread
60 ml (2 fl oz/¼ cup) extra virgin olive oil
2–3 garlic cloves, peeled
12 blanched almonds
1 teaspoon paprika
1 teaspoon ground cumin
1 tablespoon red wine vinegar or sherry
     vinegar

1 Discard the crusts from the bread, then cut the bread into cubes. Heat the oil in a heavy-based frying pan and cook the bread cubes, garlic and almonds over medium heat for 2–3 minutes, or until all of the ingredients are golden brown. Using a slotted spoon, transfer to a food processor and then add the paprika, cumin, vinegar, some salt and pepper and 1 tablespoon water. Process until the mixture forms a coarse meal.

2 Return the pan to the heat and add the asparagus with a little extra oil if needed. Cook over medium heat for 3–5 minutes, then add the bread and almond mixture with 200 ml (7 fl oz) water. Simmer for 3–4 minutes, or until the asparagus is tender but firm to the bite and only a little liquid remains. Serve.

escalivada (grilled vegetable salad)

Preparation time: **20 minutes**
Cooking time: **10 minutes**
Serves **4**

1 red onion
6 small–medium eggplants (aubergines)
4 red capsicums (peppers)
4 orange capsicums (peppers)
1 tablespoon baby capers
80 ml (2½ fl oz/⅓ cup) quality olive oil
1 tablespoon chopped flat-leaf (Italian)
     parsley
2 garlic cloves, finely chopped

1 Without slicing through the base, cut the onion from top to base into six sections, leaving it attached at the base.
2 Put the onion on a barbecue, or over an open-flamed grill or gas stovetop, with the eggplants and capsicums. Cook the vegetables over medium heat for about 10 minutes, turning them occasionally, until the eggplants and capsicum skins are blackened and blistered. Cool the capsicums in a plastic bag for 10 minutes and set the onion and eggplant aside.
3 Dry-fry the capers with a pinch of salt until crisp. Cut the onion into its sections and discard the charred outer skins.
4 Peel the skins off the eggplants and remove the stalks. Cut from top to bottom into slices. Peel the capsicums, cut them in

insalata russa (russian salad)

✳

Preparation time: 40 minutes
Cooking time: 40 minutes
Serves 4–6

3 preserved globe artichoke hearts
3 waxy potatoes, unpeeled
100 g (3½ oz) baby green beans, trimmed
    and cut into 1 cm (½ inch) lengths
1 large carrot, cut into 1 cm (½ inch) cubes
125 g (4½ oz) fresh peas
30 g (1 oz) cornichons, chopped
2 tablespoons baby capers, rinsed, drained
4 anchovy fillets, finely chopped
10 black olives, each cut into 3 slices
black olives, to garnish

MAYONNAISE
2 egg yolks
1 teaspoon dijon mustard
125 ml (4 fl oz/½ cup) extra virgin olive oil
2 tablespoons lemon juice
2 small garlic cloves, crushed

1 To make the mayonnaise, beat the egg yolks with the mustard and ¼ teaspoon salt using electric beaters until creamy. Gradually add the oil in a thin stream, beating constantly until all the oil has been added. Add the lemon juice, garlic and 1 teaspoon boiling water and beat for 1 minute until well combined. Season, to taste, and set aside.

2 Cut each artichoke into quarters. Rinse the potatoes, cover with cold salted water and simmer gently for 15–20 minutes, or until tender. Drain and allow to cool slightly. Peel and set aside. When the potatoes are completely cool, cut into 1 cm (½ inch) cubes.

3 Blanch the beans in boiling salted water until tender but firm to the bite. Refresh in cold water, then drain. Repeat the process with the carrot and peas.

4 Set aside a small quantity of each vegetable, including the cornichons, for the garnish and season, to taste. Put the remainder in a bowl with the capers, anchovy and sliced olives. Add the mayonnaise, toss to combine and season. Arrange on a dish and garnish with the reserved vegetables and whole olives.

NOTE: This salad will keep in the refrigerator for up to 2 days. Bring to room temperature before serving.

insalata russa

Insalata Russa is served in tapas bars all over Spain and is said to date back to the time of the Napoleonic Wars, when many French were residing in Spain and brought with them the Russian 'trend' popular in Paris at the time.

tapas

The eating of tapas lies at the heart of Spanish tradition, where friends come together to share bowls of simple, yet delicious morsels washed down with a glass of chilled sherry or wine.

origins of tapas

The word 'tapa' literally means 'lid' in Spanish. This comes from the days when bar owners served their customers a drink with an edible lid placed over the glass to keep out the flies. Cheese and sausage were then added to make it more appealing and encourage trade. From here grew the extraordinary variety of tapas found today in bars all over Spain, ranging from a simple bowl of marinated olives or a plate of sliced serrano ham, to warm salt cod fritters or bubbling dishes of garlic prawns.

Like many countries in Europe, the food of Spain differs quite significantly from region to region, all responding to different climatic, geographical and historical influences. These regional variations are best characterised by the Spanish saying that refers to both climate and cooking technique: 'In the north you stew, in the central region, you roast, in the east you simmer, and in the south you fry.'

So while tapas bars in the south of Spain take full advantage of not only an abundance of fresh seafood but also the rich history of Arabic influences, further inland towards the north, heartier tapas dishes of pulses and meat provide comfort from often inhospitable weather while embracing the many influences from northern neighbours.

There are a few dishes, however, that do not have culinary borders and can be found in tapas bars all over Spain. The most simple of these 'national' favourites is the raw serrano ham or 'mountain ham'. Similar to prosciutto, although with its own distinct flavour, jamon serrano is very lean and depending on age, even a little tough due to the fact that the pigs are well exercised from roaming in the forest. It is also reputed to be the sweetest ham in the world. The ham is usually served very simply, just sliced and served on a plate with some country-style bread and a glass of wine.

The dishes we have shown opposite are popular tapas fare, but there are many others that are enjoyed in most parts of Spain. These include Escalivada (page 180), Patatas bravas (page 171), Tortilla (page 176) and Cocido madrileno (page 194), a one-pot dish of meats, sausages and vegetables, although each varies from region to region incorporating local flavours and fresh produce.

Like the Italian antipasti, tapas are perfect entertaining options because most of the food can be prepared in advance. Fried dishes are the exception as they should be served straight after cooking. Almost any of the dishes in this chapter can be served as tapas because it is really only the size of the portions that makes them appetisers. However, because tapas are intended to whet the appetite, they tend to be those dishes that are rich in spice, garlic, lemon or vinegar. All the recipes from pages 162 to 181 are classic tapas dishes. However, more substantial dishes such as Salt cod with red capsicums (page 188) or Rice with stuffed squid (page 186) also work well as part of a selection for a larger party.

The tiny oval dishes traditionally used in Spain are becoming more readily available from homeware stores. Regular small plates can also be used. As well as Spanish olives, chunks of rustic, country-style bread should also accompany every tapas meal. Keep in mind that nearly all the dishes in this chapter can be adapted to suit your needs, whether you are serving two people or as many as twenty.

ajo blanco (chilled garlic and almond soup)

✹ ✹

Preparation time: 20 minutes
+ 2 hours chilling time
Cooking time: 3 minutes
Serves 4–6

1 loaf (200 g/7 oz) day-old white Italian bread, crust removed, plus 75 g (2¾ oz), extra, crust removed and cut into 1 cm (½ inch) cubes

155 g (5½ oz/1 cup) blanched almonds
3–4 garlic cloves, chopped
125 ml (4 fl oz/½ cup) extra virgin olive oil
80 ml (2½ fl oz/⅓ cup) sherry vinegar or white wine vinegar
310–375 ml (10¾–13 oz/1¼–1½ cups) vegetable stock
2 tablespoons olive oil
200 g (7 oz) small seedless green grapes

1 Soak the loaf of bread in cold water for 5 minutes, then squeeze out any excess liquid. Chop the almonds and garlic in a food processor until well ground. Add the bread and process until smooth.

2 With the motor running, add the oil in a thin, steady stream until the mixture is the consistency of thick mayonnaise. Slowly add the vinegar and 310 ml (10¾ fl oz/1¼ cups) of the stock. Blend for 1 minute. Season with salt. Refrigerate for at least 2 hours. The soup thickens on refrigeration so you may need to add stock or water to thin it.

3 When ready to serve, heat the oil in a frying pan and toss the extra bread over medium heat for 3 minutes, until golden. Drain on paper towels. Serve the soup very cold, topped with grapes and bread.

red gazpacho (chilled tomato soup)

✹

Preparation time: 40 minutes
+ 2 hours chilling time
Cooking time: nil
Serves 4

1 kg (2 lb 4 oz) vine-ripened tomatoes
2 slices day-old white Italian bread, crust removed, broken into pieces
1 red capsicum (pepper), seeded, membrane removed and roughly chopped
2 garlic cloves, chopped
1 small green chilli, chopped (optional)
1 teaspoon sugar
2 tablespoons sherry vinegar or red wine vinegar
2 tablespoons extra virgin olive oil
8 ice cubes

GARNISH
½ Lebanese (short) cucumber, seeded and finely diced
½ red capsicum (pepper), seeded, membrane removed and finely diced
½ green capsicum (pepper), seeded, membrane removed and finely diced
½ red onion, finely diced
½ ripe tomato, finely diced

1 Score a cross in the base of each tomato. Put the tomatoes in a heatproof bowl and cover with boiling water. Leave

red gazpacho

for 30 seconds, then transfer to cold water and peel the skin away from the cross. Cut the tomatoes in half, scoop out the seeds and roughly chop.

2 Soak the bread in cold water for 5 minutes, then squeeze out any excess liquid. Put the bread in a food processor with the tomato, capsicum, garlic, chilli, sugar and vinegar, and process until combined and smooth.

3 With the motor running, add the oil to make a smooth creamy mixture. Season to taste. Refrigerate for at least 2 hours. Add a little extra vinegar, if desired.

4 To make the garnish, mix all the ingredients in a bowl. Put 2 ice cubes in each bowl of soup and serve the garnish in a separate bowl.

zarzuela de pescado (catalan fish stew)

✳ ✳ ✳

Preparation time: **30 minutes**
Cooking time: **35 minutes**
Serves **6–8**

300 g (10½ oz) red mullet fillets
400 g (14 oz) firm white fish fillets
300 g (10½ oz) cleaned calamari tubes
1.5 litres (52 fl oz/6 cups) fish stock
80 ml (2½ fl oz/⅓ cup) olive oil
1 onion, chopped
6 garlic cloves, chopped
1 small fresh red chilli, chopped
1 teaspoon paprika
pinch of saffron threads
150 ml (5 fl oz) white wine
400 g (14 oz) tin chopped tomatoes
16 raw medium prawns (shrimp), peeled
    and deveined, tails left intact
2 tablespoons brandy
24 black mussels, cleaned
1 tablespoon chopped flat-leaf (Italian)
    parsley, to garnish

PICADA
2 tablespoons olive oil
2 slices day-old bread, cubed
2 garlic cloves, peeled

zarzuela de pescado

5 blanched almonds, toasted
2 tablespoons chopped parsley

1 Cut the fish and calamari into 4 cm (1½ inch) pieces. Put the stock in a large saucepan, bring to the boil and boil for 15–20 minutes, or until reduced by half.

2 For the picada, heat the oil in a frying pan and cook the bread for 2–3 minutes, or until golden, adding the garlic for the last minute. Process with the almonds and parsley in a food processor and add enough stock to make a smooth paste.

3 Heat 2 tablespoons of the oil in a large saucepan, add the onion, garlic, chilli and paprika, and cook, stirring, for 1 minute.

Add the saffron, wine, tomatoes and stock. Bring to the boil, then reduce the heat and simmer.

4 Heat the remaining oil in a frying pan over medium heat and fry the fish and calamari for 3–5 minutes. Remove. Add the prawns, cook for 1 minute and then add the brandy. Ignite it and let the flames burn down. Remove from the pan.

5 Add the mussels to the stock and simmer, covered, for 2–3 minutes, or until opened. Discard any that do not open. Add all the seafood and the picada, stirring until the sauce has thickened and the seafood has cooked. Season, to taste. Serve garnished with parsley.

rice with stuffed squid

✹ ✹ ✹

Preparation time: 40 minutes
Cooking time: 1 hour 15 minutes
Serves 4

8 small squid
about 2 teaspoons plain (all-purpose)
    flour

STUFFING
1 small onion
2 tablespoons olive oil
2 tablespoons currants
2 tablespoons pine nuts
25 g (1 oz/⅓ cup) fresh breadcrumbs
1 tablespoon chopped mint
1 tablespoon chopped flat-leaf (Italian)
    parsley
1 egg, lightly beaten

SAUCE
1 tablespoon olive oil
1 small onion, finely chopped
1 garlic clove, crushed
60 ml (2 fl oz/¼ cup) dry white wine
400 g (14 oz) tin chopped tomatoes
½ teaspoon sugar
1 bay leaf

RICE
1.25 litres (44 fl oz/5 cups) fish stock
60 ml (2 fl oz/¼ cup) olive oil
1 onion, finely chopped
3 garlic cloves, crushed
275 g (9¾ oz/1¼ cups) calasparra
    or short-grain white rice
¼ teaspoon cayenne pepper
3 teaspoons squid ink or four 4 g sachets
60 ml (2 fl oz/¼ cup) dry white wine
60 g (2¼ oz/¼ cup) tomato paste
    (concentrated purée)

2 tablespoons chopped flat-leaf
    (Italian) parsley

1 To clean the squid, pull each body
from the tentacles. Cut off and keep the
tentacles as well as the wings from either
side of each tube. If using the ink sacs,
extract them and squeeze the ink into a
small bowl. Peel the skin from each tube
and dislodge and remove the quills. Rinse
under cold water.
2 To make the stuffing, finely chop the
tentacles, wings and onion in a food
processor. Heat the oil in a frying pan
and cook the currants and pine nuts
over low heat, stirring until the nuts are
lightly browned. Transfer to a bowl using
a slotted spoon. Add the onion mixture
to the pan and cook gently over low heat
for 5 minutes. Add to the bowl and add
the breadcrumbs, mint, parsley and egg.

After cutting away the tentacles,
peel the skin from each tube.

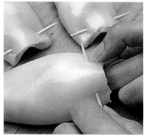

Close each opening and secure
with a toothpick.

Season and mix well. Stuff into the squid tubes. Close the openings and secure with toothpicks. Dust with the flour.

3 To make the sauce, wipe out the frying pan with paper towels. Heat the oil, add the onion and cook over low heat for 5 minutes, or until softened. Stir in the garlic, cook for 30 seconds, then add the wine. Cook over high heat for 1 minute, then add the tomatoes, sugar and bay leaf. Season, reduce the heat and simmer for 5 minutes. Stir in 125 ml (4 fl oz/ ½ cup) water. Place the squid in the pan in a single layer. Simmer, covered, for about 20 minutes, or until tender.

4 To make the rice, bring the stock to a simmer in a saucepan. Heat the oil in a large saucepan, add the onion and cook over low heat for 5 minutes, or until softened. Add the garlic and cook for 15 seconds, then stir in the rice and cayenne. Add the ink to 80 ml (2½ fl oz/ ⅓ cup) of hot stock. Stir into the rice, then add the wine and tomato paste. Stir until the liquid has almost evaporated, then add 250 ml (9 fl oz/1 cup) of hot stock. Simmer until it evaporates, then stir in more stock, 250 ml (9 fl oz/1 cup) at a time, until the rice is tender and creamy, about 15 minutes. Cover the pan and leave off the heat for 5 minutes. Season.

5 To serve, spread the rice on serving dishes and stir in the parsley. Arrange the squid on top and spoon over the sauce.

NOTE: Squid ink is available from larger seafood suppliers.

garlic chicken

✳ ✳

Preparation time: 20 minutes
Cooking time: 35 minutes
Serves 6

1 kg (2 lb 4 oz) boneless, skinless chicken
    thighs
1 tablespoon paprika
2 tablespoons olive oil
8 garlic cloves, unpeeled
60 ml (2 fl oz/¼ cup) brandy

125 ml (4 fl oz/½ cup) chicken stock
1 bay leaf
2 tablespoons chopped parsley

1 Trim any excess fat from the chicken and cut the thighs into thirds. Combine the paprika with some salt and pepper in a bowl, add the chicken and toss to coat.

2 Heat half of the olive oil in a large frying pan over medium heat and cook the garlic for 1–2 minutes, until browned. Remove from the pan. Increase the heat to high and cook the chicken thighs in batches for 5 minutes each batch, or until browned. Return all the chicken to the pan, add the brandy and boil for 30 seconds, then add the stock and bay leaf. Reduce the heat, cover and simmer over low heat for 10 minutes.

3 Meanwhile, peel the garlic and put it in a mortar or small bowl. Add the parsley and pound with the pestle or crush with a fork to form a paste. Stir into the chicken, then cover and cook for 10 minutes, or until tender. Serve hot.

rice

Rice was introduced into Spain by the Moors in the eighth century, and since then has become an important staple. Far from being considered an accompaniment, rice forms an important base for many traditional dishes, from the famous Paella, to the delicious Rice with stuffed squid. The variety of rice used in Spain is specially produced to absorb the flavours of the ingredients it is cooked with.

salt cod with red capsicums

Preparation time: **35 minutes**
  + **24 hours soaking time**
Cooking time: **25 minutes**
Serves **6**

400 g (14 oz) salt cod or bacalao
1 red capsicum (pepper)
1 tablespoon olive oil
1 small onion, chopped
1 garlic clove, crushed
¼ teaspoon dried chilli flakes
1 teaspoon paprika
60 ml (2 fl oz/¼ cup) dry white wine
2 ripe tomatoes, finely chopped
1 tablespoon tomato paste
  (concentrated purée)
1 tablespoon chopped flat-leaf (Italian)
  parsley

1 Soak the salt cod in plenty of water for 24 hours, changing the water five or six times to remove excess saltiness. Add the cod to a saucepan of boiling water and boil for 5 minutes. Drain and leave for 10 minutes, or until cool enough to handle. Remove the skin and flake the fish into large pieces, removing any bones. Place in a bowl.
2 Preheat the grill (broiler) to high. Cut the capsicum into quarters and grill, skin side up, until the skin blackens and blisters. Place in a plastic bag and leave to cool, then peel away the skin. Slice thinly.
3 Heat the oil in a pan over medium heat, add the onion and cook, stirring occasionally, for 3 minutes, or until translucent. Add the garlic, chilli flakes and paprika and cook for 1 minute. Increase the heat to high, add the wine and simmer for 30 seconds. Reduce the heat, add the tomato and tomato paste and cook, stirring occasionally, for 5 minutes, or until thick.
4 Add the cod, cover and simmer for about 5 minutes. Gently stir in the sliced capsicum and parsley and taste before seasoning with salt. Serve hot.

salt cod

Salt cod is widely used throughout Spain, and indeed the whole of the Mediterranean. Salting is a simple process in which the fish are gutted and packed flat in salt, later washed, and then dried. The fish are rehydrated in several changes of water and then used for cooking. Salting was one of the earliest forms of preservation and meant that the cod, which was plentiful in the North Atlantic, could be readily and also inexpensively transported. Salt cod has become an important ingredient in traditional cooking.

spinach with raisins and pine nuts

✷

Preparation time: **15 minutes**
Cooking time: **20 minutes**
Serves 6

500 g (1 lb 2 oz) English spinach (see Note)
1 small red onion
2 tablespoons pine nuts
1 tablespoon olive oil
1 garlic clove, thinly sliced
2 tablespoons raisins
pinch of ground cinnamon

1 Trim the stalks from the spinach and discard. Wash and shred the leaves. Slice the onion.

2 Put the pine nuts in a frying pan and stir over medium heat for 3 minutes, or until lightly brown. Remove from the pan.
3 Heat the oil in the pan, add the onion and cook over low heat, stirring occasionally, for 10 minutes, or until translucent. Increase the heat to medium, add the garlic and cook for 1 minute. Add the spinach with the water clinging to it, the raisins and cinnamon. Cover and cook for 2 minutes, or until the spinach wilts. Stir in the pine nuts, and season to taste.

NOTE: Silverbeet (Swiss chard) works equally well in this recipe, although it may take a little longer to cook.

sangria

This is a refreshing chilled drink. Place 1½ tablespoons caster (superfine) sugar and 1 tablespoon each of lemon juice and orange juice into a large jug or bowl and stir until the sugar has dissolved. Add 750 ml (26 fl oz/3 cups) red wine, 500 ml (17 fl oz/2 cups) lemonade and 2 tablespoons each of gin and vodka. Cut a lemon, an orange and a lime into halves, remove the seeds and slice all the fruit finely. Add the slices to the jug and fill with ice. Stir well. Serves 10.

raisins

Raisins are sun-dried grapes that are used in cooking and also eaten on their own as a snack. They add a sweet, caramel note to many savoury dishes and are often combined with pine nuts and English spinach or silverbeet.

baked fish with capsicums, chilli and potatoes

☀ ☀

Preparation time: 30 minutes
  + 2 hours marinating time
Cooking time: 1 hour 35 minutes
Serves 4–6

1.25 kg (2 lb 12 oz) whole red bream,
  or red snapper, cleaned
1 lemon
60 ml (2 fl oz/¼ cup) olive oil
800 g (1 lb 12 oz) potatoes,
  thinly sliced
3 garlic cloves, thinly sliced
3 tablespoons finely chopped parsley
1 small red onion, thinly sliced
1 small dried chilli (guindilla), seeded and
  finely chopped
1 red capsicum (pepper), seeded, membrane
  removed and sliced into thin rings
1 yellow capsicum (pepper), seeded,
  membrane removed and sliced into
  thin rings
2 bay leaves
3–4 thyme sprigs
60 ml (2 fl oz/¼ cup) dry sherry

1 Cut off and discard the fins from the fish and place it in a large non-metallic dish. Cut 2 thin slices from one end of the lemon and reserve. Squeeze the juice from the rest of the lemon inside the fish. Add 2 tablespoons of the oil. Refrigerate, covered, for 2 hours.

2 Preheat the oven to 190°C (375°F/Gas 5). Lightly oil a shallow earthenware baking dish large enough to hold the whole fish. Spread half the potato slices on the base and scatter the garlic, parsley, onion, chilli and capsicum over the top. Season with salt and pepper. Cover with the rest of the potato slices. Pour in 80 ml (2½ fl oz/⅓ cup) water and sprinkle the remaining olive oil over the top. Cover with foil and bake for 1 hour.

3 Increase the temperature to 220°C (425°F/Gas 7). Season the fish inside and out with salt and pepper and place the bay leaves and thyme inside the cavity. Make 3–4 diagonal slashes on each side of the fish. Cut the reserved lemon slices in half and fit these into the slashes on one side of the fish, to resemble fins. Nestle the fish into the potato with the lemon on top. Bake, uncovered, for 30 minutes, or until the fish is cooked through and the potato is tender.

4 Pour the sherry over the fish and return to the oven for 3 minutes. Serve straight from the dish for added effect.

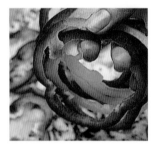

Scatter the garlic, parsley, onion, chilli and capsicum over the potato slices in the dish.

Make 3–4 diagonal slashes on each side of the fish.

tumbet (vegetable casserole)

Preparation time: 30 minutes
Cooking time: 1 hour 10 minutes
Serves 6–8

250 ml (9 fl oz/1 cup) olive oil
500 g (1 lb 2 oz) all-purpose potatoes,
    cut into 5-mm (¼-inch) thick rounds
500 g (1 lb 2 oz) eggplants (aubergines),
    cut into 5-mm (¼-inch) thick slices
500 g (1 lb 2 oz) green capsicum (pepper),
    seeded, membrane removed, and
    cut into 3 cm (1¼ inch) pieces
1 large handful flat-leaf (Italian) parsley,
    roughly chopped

TOMATO SAUCE
1 kg (2 lb 4 oz) tomatoes
2 tablespoons olive oil
3 garlic cloves, crushed
1 red onion, finely chopped
2 teaspoons thyme leaves, chopped

1 To make the tomato sauce, score a cross in the base of each tomato. Put in a heatproof bowl and cover with boiling water. Leave for 30 seconds, then transfer to cold water and peel the skin away from the cross. Cut each tomato in half, scoop out the seeds and finely chop the flesh. Heat the oil in a heavy-based frying pan and cook the garlic and onion over low heat for 5–6 minutes, or until softened. Add the tomato and thyme and cook for 20 minutes over medium heat, or until thickened. Season to taste.
2 While the sauce is cooking, heat the oil in a heavy-based frying pan over low heat and cook the potato rounds, in batches until they are tender but not browned. Transfer to a casserole dish measuring about 21 x 27 cm (8¼ x 10¾ inches) and lightly season with salt and pepper.
3 Increase the heat to high and pan-fry the eggplant slices for 15 minutes, or until golden, turning after about 7 minutes. Drain the eggplant slices on paper towels, then place on top of the potato slices and season lightly. Preheat the oven to 180°C (350°F/Gas 4).
4 Cook the capsicum in the same pan until tender but not browned, adding a little more olive oil if needed. Remove with a slotted spoon, drain on paper towels and arrange over the eggplant. Season lightly. Pour the tomato sauce over the top and bake for 20 minutes. Serve warm, sprinkled with parsley.

eggplants

Eggplants (aubergines) are renowned for their versatility in preparation and their natural affinity with the robust flavours of Mediterranean cuisine. Choose eggplants that are medium-sized, shiny and firm. The best eggplants have dense, firm and sweet flesh, with small seeds. Eggplants that are old, or simply over-mature, will be full of bitter seeds, and will therefore need to be salted for up to an hour before they are used, to ensure the unpleasant bitter flavour is removed.

preparing olives

Olives differ in colour at various stages of ripeness. All are inedible straight from the tree and need to be cured, then preserved. Each requires a different curing process and the resulting textures and flavours vary.

curing green olives

Crack or split the olives to the stone, either with a wooden mallet or paring knife. Cover the olives in cold water and soak for 2 weeks, replacing the water every day. If they're still bitter, continue soaking as before. This may take up to 4 weeks.

curing black olives

Completely cover the olives in cold water, cover and soak for 6 weeks, replacing the water every second day. Drain the olives, then cover with rock salt and set aside for 2 days. Rinse well.

preserving olives in oil

Spread the olives out on paper towels and leave overnight in a warm place to dry. Steep the olives in 2 parts olive oil to 1 part vinegar, seasoning with garlic, mint, peppercorns and salt, to taste. Cover, stirring occasionally, for 3 days. Transfer it all to sterilised glass jars and cover with olive oil. Refrigerate for up to 6 weeks. Serve at room temperature.

preserving olives in brine

Dry olives as above. Make a brine solution with 10 parts water to 1 part rock salt. Bring to the boil, then simmer for 5 minutes with bay leaves, citrus zest, peppercorns and herbs. Pack into sterilised glass jars, cover with brine, seal and store for a week before eating. Use within a month and refrigerate after opening.

roasted olives with fennel and orange

Sauté 1 finely shaved fennel bulb and 1 teaspoon fennel seeds in olive oil for 10 minutes. Place in a baking dish together with 350 g (12 oz/2 cups) olives, 2 sliced garlic cloves, 1 tablespoon finely grated orange zest and 60 ml (2 fl oz/¼ cup) each of orange juice and red wine vinegar. Bake in a 180°C (350°F/ Gas 4) oven for 20 minutes. Season, to taste, drizzle with olive oil and serve warm or at room temperature. These olives may be refrigerated for up to 2 weeks.

herbed olives

Put 250 g (9 oz) each of cracked green and cracked kalamata olives, 3 thyme sprigs, 1 tablespoon oregano leaves, 2 bay leaves, 1 teaspoon paprika and 2 teaspoons lemon zest in a bowl and toss. Spoon into a 1 litre (35 fl oz/4 cup) sterilised jar and pour in 500 ml (17 fl oz/2 cups) olive oil. Marinate for 1–2 weeks in the refrigerator. Will keep for up to a month.

preserved lemon and chilli olives

Drain 500 g (1 lb 2 oz) olives preserved in brine, cover with cold water and leave for 1 hour. Drain, add the thinly sliced zest from ¼ preserved lemon, 2 halved fresh red chillies, 2 bruised garlic cloves and 2 teaspoons dried oregano. Pack into sterilised jars, cover with olive oil, seal, then leave for a week to allow the flavours to infuse. Keep for up to 4 months in the refrigerator. NOTE: If the oil solidifies, return the olives to room temperature before use. When the olives are finished, use the oil in dressings, to dip bread in, or to drizzle over grilled fish or chicken.

sterilising jars

Rinse the jars and lids with boiling, soapy water, then place the jars in a 120°C (235°F/Gas ½) oven to dry completely.

cochifrito

habas verdes en salsa de tomate (green beans in tomato sauce)

✳

Preparation time: 10 minutes
Cooking time: 30 minutes
Serves 4

300 g (10½ oz) green beans, trimmed
1 tablespoon olive oil
1 onion, finely chopped
2 garlic cloves, finely chopped
1 tablespoon paprika
¼ teaspoon chilli flakes
1 fresh bay leaf, crushed
400 g (14 oz) tin chopped tomatoes
2 tablespoons chopped flat-leaf (Italian)
  parsley

1 Cook the beans in boiling water for
3–5 minutes or until tender. Drain well
and set aside.
2 Heat the oil in a frying pan. Add the
onion and cook over medium heat for
5 minutes, or until soft. Add the garlic
and cook for 1 minute. Add the paprika,
chilli flakes and bay leaf, cook for
1 minute, then add the tomatoes. Simmer
over medium heat for 15 minutes, or until
reduced and pulpy. Add the beans and
parsley and cook for 1 minute, or until
warmed through. Season, to taste. Serve
warm or at room temperature.

cocido madrileno (madrileno meat and vegetables)

✳✳

Preparation time: 25 minutes
  + overnight soaking time
Cooking time: 2 hours 45 minutes
Serves 6–8

220 g (7¾ oz/1 cup) dried chickpeas
1 kg (2 lb 4 oz) whole chicken, trussed
500 g (1 lb 2 oz) beef brisket, in one piece
250 g (9 oz) piece smoke-cured bacon

cochifrito (lamb braise)

✳

Preparation time: 15 minutes
Cooking time: 2 hours 20 minutes
Serves 4

80 ml (2½ fl oz/⅓ cup) olive oil
1 kg (2 lb 4 oz) lamb shoulder, diced
1 large onion, finely chopped
4 garlic cloves, crushed
2 teaspoons paprika
100 ml (3½ fl oz) lemon juice
2 tablespoons chopped flat-leaf
  (Italian) parsley

1 Heat the oil in a large, heavy-based
frying pan over high heat. Sauté the lamb
in two batches for 5 minutes each batch,
until well browned. Remove all the lamb
from the pan and set aside.
2 Add the onion to the pan and cook
for 5 minutes, or until soft and golden.
Add the garlic and paprika and stir for
1 minute. Return the meat to the pan,
add 80 ml (2½ fl oz/⅓ cup) of the lemon
juice and 1.75 litres (61 fl oz/7 cups)
water and simmer over low heat, stirring
occasionally, for 2 hours, until the liquid
has almost evaporated and the oil starts
to reappear. Stir in the remaining lemon
juice and the parsley. Season with salt and
pepper, to taste, and serve.

125 g (4½ oz) tocino, streaky bacon or
    speck
1 pig's trotter
200 g (7 oz) chorizo sausage
1 onion, studded with 2 cloves
1 bay leaf
1½ teaspoons salt
1 morcilla blood sausage (optional)
250 g (9 oz) green beans, sliced lengthways
250 g (9 oz) green cabbage, cut into
    sections through the heart
300 g (10½ oz) silverbeet (Swiss chard),
    rinsed, stalks removed
4 small potatoes
2 leeks, cut into 10 cm (4 inch) lengths
pinch of saffron threads
75 g (2¾ oz) dried rice vermicelli

1 Soak the chickpeas in cold water
overnight. Drain and rinse. Tie loosely in
a muslin (cheesecloth) bag.
2 Put 3 litres (105 fl oz/12 cups) cold
water in a large, deep saucepan. Add the
chicken, beef, bacon and tocino and bring
to the boil. Add the chickpeas, trotter
and chorizo, return to the boil, and add
the onion, bay leaf and ½ teaspoon salt.
Simmer, partially covered, for 2½ hours.
3 After 2 hours, bring a saucepan of
water to the boil, add the morcilla and
gently boil for 5 minutes. Drain and set
aside. Tie the beans loosely in a muslin
bag. Bring 1 litre (35 fl oz/4 cups) water
to the boil in a large saucepan. Add the
beans, cabbage, silverbeet, potatoes, leek,
saffron and remaining salt. Return to the
boil and simmer for 30 minutes.
4 Strain the stock from the meat and
vegetable pans and combine in a large
saucepan. Bring to the boil, adjust the
seasoning and add the vermicelli. Simmer
for 6–7 minutes. Release the chickpeas
and pile in the centre of a large warm
platter. Discard the trotter, then slice the
meats and sausages. Arrange in groups
around the chickpeas at one end of the
platter. Release the beans. Arrange the
vegetables around the other end. Spoon
a little of the simmering broth (minus the
vermicelli) over the meat, then pour the
rest into a tureen. Serve together, though
the broth is traditionally eaten first.

Slice the green beans lengthways.

Add the chickpeas, pig's trotter
and chorizo to the saucepan.

stuffed leg of lamb

✷ ✷

Preparation time: 25 minutes
Cooking time: 2 hours 15 minutes
Serves 6–8

1 large leg of lamb (3 kg/6 lb 12 oz),
    boned
1 teaspoon sweet paprika
1 tablespoon plain (all-purpose) flour
4 garlic cloves, peeled
2 tablespoons olive oil
375 ml (13 fl oz/1½ cups) dry white wine

1 tablespoon lard
125 ml (4 fl oz/½ cup) chicken stock

STUFFING
1 thick slice white bread, crusts removed
70 g (2½ oz) chicken livers, trimmed
60 g (2¼ oz) tocino or bacon
1 tablespoon dry sherry
1 garlic clove, crushed
1 tablespoon chopped flat-leaf (Italian)
    parsley
½ tablespoon snipped chives
1 teaspoon finely chopped rosemary
1 tablespoon capers, finely chopped

1 To make the stuffing, break the bread
into pieces and process with the chicken
livers and tocino in a food processor until
fine–medium. Put in a bowl with the
sherry, garlic, parsley, chives, rosemary
and capers. Season and mix well.
2 Preheat the oven to 210°C (415°F/
Gas 6–7). Lay the lamb out flat and put
the filling down the centre. Roll the meat
up to enclose the filling. Tie up firmly
with kitchen string. Combine the paprika
and flour with ¼ teaspoon salt and rub all
over the lamb. Put the garlic in a row in
the centre of a roasting tin and pour the

Lay the lamb out flat and spoon
the filling down the centre.

Spread the seasoned flour all over
the lamb.

oil over the top. Put the lamb on the garlic and pour the wine over the top. Spread the lard over the surface.

3 Bake for 20 minutes, then reduce the heat to 170°C (325°F/Gas 3). Baste, then bake for a further 1 hour 45 minutes, basting frequently, until the lamb is well cooked. Transfer to a carving tray and keep warm. Spoon off excess oil from the pan juices, then transfer the contents of the roasting tin to a saucepan; there will be about 125 ml (4 fl oz/½ cup). Add the stock and cook over high heat until slightly thickened. Slice the lamb and arrange on a serving platter. Pour the sauce over the lamb.

chicken and chorizo paella

✳ ✳

Preparation time: 30 minutes
Cooking time: 1 hour
Serves 6

60 ml (2 fl oz/¼ cup) olive oil
1 large red capsicum (pepper), cut into
    5 mm (¼ inch) strips
600 g (1 lb 5 oz) boneless, skinless
    chicken thighs, cut into 3 cm
    (1¼ inch) pieces
200 g (7 oz) chorizo, cut into 2-cm
    (¾-inch) thick slices
200 g (7 oz) mushrooms, such as button or
    caps, thinly sliced
3 garlic cloves, crushed
1 tablespoon finely grated lemon zest
700 g (1 lb 9 oz) ripe tomatoes,
    roughly chopped
200 g (7 oz) green beans, trimmed and
    cut into 3 cm (1¼ inch) lengths
1 tablespoon chopped rosemary
2 tablespoons chopped flat-leaf (Italian)
    parsley
¼ teaspoon saffron threads, soaked in
    60 ml (2 fl oz/¼ cup) hot water
440 g (15½ oz/2 cups) short-grain white
    rice (such as calasparra)
750 ml (26 fl oz/3 cups) hot chicken stock
6 lemon wedges, to serve

1 Heat the olive oil in a paella pan or in a large, heavy-based, deep frying pan over medium heat. Add the capsicum and cook, stirring, for about 6 minutes, or until softened, then remove from the pan.
2 Add the chicken to the pan and cook for 10 minutes, or until browned. Remove from the pan. Add the chorizo to the pan and cook for 5 minutes, or until golden. Remove from the pan. Add the mushroom, garlic and lemon zest to the pan, and cook over medium heat for 5 minutes or until the mushroom is soft.

3 Stir in the tomato and capsicum, and cook for a further 5 minutes, or until the tomato is soft.
4 Add the beans, rosemary, parsley, saffron mixture, rice, chicken and chorizo. Stir briefly and add the stock. Do not stir at this point. Reduce the heat and simmer for 30 minutes. Remove from the heat, cover and leave to stand for 10 minutes. Serve with lemon wedges.

NOTE: Paella pans are available from speciality kitchenware shops.

198

requesón cheese

Requesón is basically a
Hispanic version of ricotta
cheese. It is also made
from whey, a by-product of
cheesemaking, and is soft,
moist and slightly salty, slightly
sweet. It is used widely in
Spanish cooking, both fresh
and cooked in savoury and
sweet dishes.

torte de la almendra (almond torte)

Preparation time: **15 minutes**
Cooking time: **1 hour 20 minutes**
Serves 8

450 g (1 lb) blanched almonds, lightly
toasted
150 g (5½ oz) unsalted butter,
softened
400 g (14 oz) caster (superfine) sugar
6 eggs
150 g (5½ oz) plain (all-purpose) flour
2 teaspoons finely grated lemon zest
2 tablespoons lemon juice
icing (confectioners') sugar, for dusting

1 Preheat the oven to 170°C (325°F/
Gas 3). Lightly grease a 24 cm (9½ inch)
springform cake tin. Grind the almonds
finely in a food processor and set aside.
2 Cream the butter and caster sugar in a
bowl using electric beaters until light and
fluffy. Add the eggs one at a time, beating
well after each addition. Fold in the flour,
ground almonds and the lemon zest. Stir
until just combined and almost smooth.
3 Pour the batter into the tin and bake
for 1 hour 20 minutes, or until a skewer
inserted in the centre comes out clean.
Cool for 5 minutes, then brush the top
with lemon juice. Transfer to a wire rack
to cool completely. Just before serving,
dust the torte with icing sugar (over
two strips of baking paper to make a
decorative cross if you wish).

ricotta with honey and pine nuts

Preparation time: **5 minutes**
Cooking time: **Nil**
Serves 2

300 g (10½ oz) ricotta
2 tablespoons honey
pine nuts, toasted, to serve

1 Divide the ricotta between two bowls,
drizzle with honey and sprinkle with the
pine nuts. Serve.

NOTE: This simple dessert is traditionally
made with Requesón cheese.

higos rellenos (stuffed figs)

✳ ✳

Preparation time: 30 minutes
  + 3 hours soaking time
Cooking time: 30 minutes
Makes 18

175 g (6 oz/½ cup) honey
125 ml (4 fl oz/½ cup) sweet dark sherry
¼ teaspoon ground cinnamon
18 large dried figs
18 whole blanched almonds
100 g (3½ oz) dark (bittersweet) chocolate,
  cut into shards
thick (double/heavy) cream, to serve

1 Put the honey, sherry, cinnamon, figs
and 375 ml (13 fl oz/1½ cups) water in
a large saucepan over high heat. Bring to
the boil, then reduce the heat and simmer
for 10 minutes. Remove from the heat
and set aside for 3 hours. Remove the figs
with a slotted spoon, reserving the liquid.
Preheat the oven to 180°C (350°F/Gas 4).
2 Return the pan of liquid to the stovetop
and boil over high heat for 5 minutes, or
until syrupy, then set aside.
3 Cut the stems from the figs, then cut a
slit in the top of each fig. Push an almond
and a few shards of chocolate into each
slit. Put the figs in a lightly buttered
ovenproof dish and bake for 15 minutes,
or until the chocolate has melted. Serve
with a little of the syrup and the cream.

almond horchata

This drink is traditionally made with tiger nuts, but almonds make a perfect substitute. In a food processor, grind 500 g (1 lb 2 oz) blanched almonds into a coarse meal with 1 litre (35 fl oz/4 cups) warm water until you have a very thick paste. Spoon into a large bowl. Cut half a lemon into slices and add to the paste with 1 cinnamon stick and 500 ml (17 fl oz/2 cups) warm water. Stir well, cover and leave at room temperature for at least 2 hours. Strain through muslin (cheesecloth), add 2 tablespoons sugar, or to taste, and serve chilled. Serves 4.

Use a sharp knife to cut the dark chocolate into shards.

Push an almond and a few of the chocolate shards into each fig.

leche frita (fried custard squares)

✳

Preparation time: 20 minutes
   + 1 hour cooling time
Cooking time: 25 minutes
Serves 4–6

500 ml (17 fl oz/2 cups) milk
1 cinnamon stick
5 x 1 cm (2 x ½ inch) strip lemon zest
1 vanilla bean, split lengthways
140 g (5 oz) unsalted butter
250 g (9 oz/2 cups) plain (all-purpose) flour

160 g (5¾ oz/⅔ cup) caster (superfine)
   sugar
4 eggs, separated
125 g (4½ oz/1¼ cups) dry breadcrumbs
vegetable oil, for frying
4 tablespoons caster (superfine) sugar,
   extra, for dusting
1 teaspoon ground cinnamon, for dusting

1   Grease a 17 x 27 cm (7 x 11 inch) slice tin and line the base and two long sides with baking paper. Bring the milk, cinnamon stick, lemon zest and vanilla bean to the boil. Take off the heat.
2   Melt the butter in a large heavy-based saucepan. Stir in 185 g (6½ oz/1½ cups) of the flour. The mixture will form a loose clump around your spoon. Stir over low heat for 30 seconds. Stir in the sugar. Gradually strain the milk into the pan, stirring constantly. Beat until a smooth, glossy mass forms. Remove from the heat and stir in the egg yolks one at a time, beating well after each addition. Spread in the tin, smoothing the surface with your hand. Set aside for about 1 hour, to cool and set.
3   Lightly whisk the egg whites together with a fork. Lift the set custard from the tin and carefully cut into 5 cm (2 inch) squares. Dip in the remaining flour to coat all sides. Dip into the egg whites, then the breadcrumbs. Set aside.
4   Pour the oil into a large frying pan to a depth of 1 cm (½ inch). Heat the oil and cook a few custard squares at a time for about 1 minute each side, until browned. Drain on paper towels and dust all over with the combined sugar and cinnamon while still hot. Serve hot or cold.

helado de canela (cinnamon ice cream)

✳ ✳

Preparation time: 15 minutes + freezing time
Cooking time: 15 minutes
Serves 6

1 litre (35 fl oz/4 cups) milk
2 strips lemon zest
3 cinnamon sticks
375 g (13 oz/1½ cups) caster (superfine)
   sugar
6 egg yolks
1 teaspoon ground cinnamon

1   Put the milk, lemon zest, cinnamon sticks and half the sugar in a saucepan and heat to just below boiling. Set aside for 10 minutes. Remove the lemon zest and cinnamon sticks.
2   Using a wire whisk, combine the yolks, remaining sugar and ground cinnamon in a bowl until thick and pale. Add the milk in a steady stream, whisking constantly.

helado de canela

3 Wash the pan, pour in the mixture and stir over very low heat for 5–10 minutes, until thickened and your finger leaves a clear line when run through the mixture on the back of a wooden spoon. Strain into a bowl, cool to room temperature, then put in a 1.25 litre (44 fl oz/5 cup) shallow metal container. Freeze for 2 hours, or until the edges are half frozen.
4 Remove from the freezer, beat well and then freeze again. Repeat the beating and freezing process twice more.

crema catalana (catalan burnt cream)

✸ ✸

Preparation time: **15 minutes**
　+ **6 hours chilling time**
Cooking time: **20 minutes**
Serves **6**

1 litre (35 fl oz/4 cups) milk
1 vanilla bean, halved lengthways
1 cinnamon stick
zest of 1 small lemon, sliced into thin strips
2 strips, 4 x 2 cm (1½ x ¾ inch), orange zest
8 egg yolks
125 g (4½ oz/½ cup) caster (superfine) sugar
40g (1½ oz/⅓ cup) cornflour (cornstarch)
3 tablespoons soft brown sugar

1 Place the milk, scraped vanilla bean, cinnamon and all the zest in a saucepan and bring to the boil. Simmer for 5 minutes, then strain and set aside.
2 Whisk the egg yolks and caster sugar in a bowl for about 5 minutes, until pale and creamy. Add the cornflour and mix well. Slowly add the warm milk mixture and whisk continuously. Return to the pan and cook over low–medium heat, stirring constantly, for 5–10 minutes, or until thick and creamy. Do not boil. Pour into six 250 ml (9 fl oz/1-cup) ramekins and refrigerate for 6 hours, or overnight.
3 When ready to serve, sprinkle evenly with the brown sugar and grill (broil) for 3 minutes, or until caramelised.

membrillo (quince paste)

Wash 3 large quinces, place in a saucepan, cover with water and simmer for 30 minutes, or until tender. Drain. Peel and core the quinces, then push them through a sieve or potato ricer. Weigh the fruit pulp, place in a heavy-based saucepan and add the same weight of sugar. Cook over low heat, stirring occasionally with a wooden spoon, for 3½–4½ hours, or until very thick. Pour into a shallow 18 x 28 cm (7 x 11¼ inch) rectangular tin lined with plastic wrap. Allow to cool. Quince paste can be kept for several months in a tightly sealed container. Serve with cheese, or with game such as pheasant.

churros

☀ ☀

Preparation time: **10 minutes**
Cooking time: **25 minutes**
Serves **4**

125 g (4½ oz/½ cup) sugar
1 teaspoon freshly ground nutmeg
30 g (1 oz) butter
150 g (5½ oz) plain (all-purpose) flour
½ teaspoon finely grated orange zest
¼ teaspoon caster (superfine) sugar
2 eggs
1 litre (35 fl oz/4 cups) vegetable oil,
    for deep-frying

1 Combine the sugar and nutmeg and spread out on a plate.
2 Place the butter, flour, orange zest, caster sugar, 170 ml (5½ fl oz/⅔ cup) water and a pinch of salt in a heavy-based saucepan. Stir over low heat until the butter softens and forms a dough with the other ingredients. Keep cooking for 2–3 minutes, stirring constantly, until the dough forms a ball around the spoon and leaves a coating on the base of the pan.
3 Transfer the dough to a food processor and, with the motor running, add the eggs. Do not overprocess. If the dough is too soft to snip with scissors, return it to the pan and stir over low heat until firmer. Spoon it into a piping (icing) bag fitted with a 5 mm (¼ inch) star nozzle.
4 Heat the oil in a wide saucepan to 180°C (350°F), or until a cube of bread dropped into the oil browns in 15 seconds. Pipe lengths of batter 6–8 cm (2½–3¼ inches) long into the oil, a few at a time. An easy technique is to pipe with one hand and cut the batter off using kitchen scissors in the other hand. Fry for about 3 minutes, until puffed and golden, turning once or twice. Transfer each batch to paper towels to drain. While the churros are still hot, toss them in the sugar and nutmeg mixture and serve.

NOTE: Churros is a popular breakfast snack in Spain and is usually eaten with hot chocolate (see opposite page).

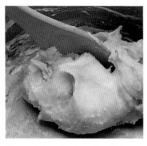

Keep stirring the dough until it forms a ball around the spoon and leaves a coating on the pan.

Fry the lengths of dough until puffed and golden.

aniseed biscuits

✳ ✳

Preparation time: **15 minutes**
Cooking time: **35 minutes**
Makes **16**

375 g (13 oz/3 cups) plain (all-purpose) flour
125 ml (4 fl oz/½ cup) olive oil
125 ml (4 fl oz/½ cup) beer
60 ml (2 fl oz/¼ cup) anisette liqueur
115 g (4 oz/½ cup) caster (superfine) sugar
40 g (1½ oz/¼ cup) sesame seeds
2 tablespoons aniseeds

1 Preheat the oven to 200°C (400°F/ Gas 6). Lightly grease a baking tray and line with baking paper. Sift the flour and 1 teaspoon salt into a large bowl and make a well in the centre. Add the oil, beer and anisette and mix with a large metal spoon until the dough comes together. Knead on a lightly floured surface for 3–4 minutes, or until smooth. Divide into 16 equal portions. Combine the sugar, sesame seeds and aniseeds.

2 Make a small pile of the seed mix on a work surface and roll out a portion of dough over the mix to a 15 cm (6 inch) round with the seeds embedded underneath. Place on the baking tray with the seeds on top and repeat with the remaining dough and seed mix. Bake batches for 5–6 minutes, or until the bases are crisp. Place 10 cm (4 inches) below a hot grill (broiler) for about 40 seconds, or until the sugar is caramelised and biscuits are golden. Transfer to a wire rack to cool.

aniseeds

Aniseeds are from a bush related to hemlock and are of Middle Eastern origin. They have an intense liquorice flavour, but used in moderation they add sweet, interesting undertones to stuffings for fish, as well as breads, cakes and biscuits such as these.

spanish hot chocolate

Chocolate a la taza is traditionally used for making this drink because it contains a starch that thickens as it cooks. However, since this is not readily available, you can use cornflour (cornstarch) as the thickening agent. Mix 2 tablespoons cornflour with 2 tablespoons milk to a smooth paste. Place 1 litre (35 fl oz/4 cups) milk and 200 g (7 oz) chopped good-quality dark (bittersweet) chocolate in a saucepan and whisk constantly over low heat until just warm. Add 2 tablespoons of the milk to the cornflour paste, then return all the paste to the milk. Whisking constantly, cook the mixture until it just begins to boil. Remove from the heat, add sugar, to taste, and whisk for another minute. Serves 4–6.

north africa

North Africa encompasses perhaps the most exotic parts of the Mediterranean region, covering Morocco, Algeria and Tunisia. Moroccan food is among the most exciting in the world. Great pride is taken in meal preparation. And it's all quite easy thanks to the way Moroccan meals are planned, usually involving one or two tagines, long-simmering stews of meat, chicken or vegetables. Cloves, nutmeg, paprika, saffron, cayenne pepper, cumin, ginger and cinnamon are major features in North African cuisine. Also prominent are couscous, citrus, pomegranates, dates, almonds, apricots and chickpeas.

fish fillets with harissa and olives

Preparation time: **15 minutes**
Cooking time: **25 minutes**
Serves **4**

80 ml (2½ fl oz/⅓ cup) olive oil
4 white fish fillets (such as cod, snapper or perch)
seasoned flour, for dusting
1 brown onion, chopped
2 garlic cloves, crushed
400 g (14 oz) tin chopped tomatoes
2 teaspoons harissa
2 bay leaves
1 cinnamon stick
185 g (6½ oz/1 cup) kalamata olives
1 tablespoon lemon juice
2 tablespoons chopped flat-leaf (Italian) parsley

1 Heat half the olive oil in a heavy-based frying pan. Dust the fish with flour and cook over medium heat for 2 minutes each side, or until golden. Transfer to a plate.
2 Add the remaining olive oil to the pan and cook the onion and garlic for 3–4 minutes, or until softened. Add the tomatoes, harissa, bay leaves and cinnamon. Cook for 10 minutes, or until the sauce has thickened. Season with salt and freshly ground black pepper, to taste.
3 Return the fish to the pan, add the olives and cover the fish with the sauce. Remove the bay leaves and cinnamon stick and continue cooking for 2 minutes, or until the fish is tender. Add the lemon juice and parsley and serve.

fish fillets with harissa and olives

harissa

Preparation time: **30 minutes**
  + 1 hour soaking time
Cooking time: **nil**
Fills a 600 ml (21 fl oz) jar

125 g (4½ oz) dried red chillies, stems removed
1 tablespoon dried mint
1 tablespoon ground coriander
1 tablespoon ground cumin
1 teaspoon ground caraway seeds
10 garlic cloves, chopped
125 ml (4 fl oz/½ cup) olive oil

1 Roughly chop the chillies, cover with boiling water and soak for 1 hour. Drain and place in a food processor with the mint, spices, garlic, 1 tablespoon of the oil and ½ teaspoon salt. Process for 20 seconds, scrape down the bowl, then process for another 30 seconds. Add 2 tablespoons oil and process again. Repeat and process until a thick paste.

harissa

This spicy paste blend is a popular accompaniment for many North African dishes. It is traditionally served with couscous, but is also used as a flavouring in soups, casseroles, tagines and dried bean salads. It can also be mixed with a little olive oil and served with flatbread. Commercial harissa can be purchased from delicatessens.

2 Spoon the paste into a clean jar (see Note), cover with a thin layer of olive oil and seal. Label and date.

NOTE: To prepare a storage jar, preheat the oven to 120°C (235°F/Gas ½). Wash the jar and lid in hot soapy water and rinse with hot water. Put the jar in the oven for 20 minutes, or until fully dry. Do not dry with a tea towel (dish towel).

This hot pepper sauce will keep in the fridge for up to 6 months. It is delicious with tagines and couscous, or can be added to salad dressings, marinades and pasta sauces for extra flavour.

hamad m'rakad (preserved lemons)

Preparation time: **1 hour**
  + 6 weeks standing time
Cooking time: **nil**
Fills **a 2 litre (70 fl oz/8 cup) jar**

8–12 small thin-skinned lemons
315 g (11 oz/1 cup) rock salt
500 ml (17 fl oz/2 cups) lemon juice
  (8–10 lemons)
½ teaspoon black peppercorns
1 bay leaf
olive oil

1 Scrub the lemons under warm running water with a soft-bristle brush to remove the wax coating. Cut into quarters, leaving the base attached at the stem end. Gently open each lemon, remove any visible seeds and pack 1 tablespoon of the salt against the cut edges of each lemon. Push the lemons back into shape and pack tightly into a 2 litre (70 fl oz/ 8 cup) jar that has a clip or tight-fitting lid. Depending on the size of the lemons, you may not need all 12. They should be firmly packed and fill the jar.
2 Add 250 ml (9 fl oz/1 cup) of the lemon juice, the peppercorns, bay leaf and remaining rock salt to the jar. Fill the jar to the top with the remaining lemon juice. Seal and shake to combine all the ingredients. Leave in a cool, dark place for 6 weeks, inverting the jar each week. (In warm weather, store the jar in the refrigerator.) The liquid will be cloudy initially, but will clear by the fourth week.
3 To test if the lemons are preserved, cut through the centre of one of the lemon quarters. If the pith is still white, the lemons aren't ready. If this is the case, re-seal and leave for another week before testing again. The lemons should be soft-skinned and the pith should be the same colour as the skin.

4 Once the lemons are preserved, cover the brine with a layer of olive oil. Replace the oil each time you remove some of the lemon pieces. Refrigerate after opening.

NOTE: Preserved lemons can be stored for up to 6 months in a cool, dark place. Use preserved lemons to flavour couscous, stuffings, tagines and casseroles. Only the zest is used in cooking. Discard the flesh and bitter pith, rinse and finely slice or chop the zest before adding to the dish.

flatbread

Unleavened flatbread is commonly used for wrapping kebabs and other popular sandwich fillings. It can also be toasted until crisp, with a variety of seasonings, and served as an accompaniment for dips. Flatbread freezes well, so it is perfect to have on hand to serve to unexpected guests.

broad bean dip

Preparation time: 10 minutes
    + overnight soaking time
Cooking time: 6 hours
Serves 6

200 g (7 oz/1 cup) dried broad (fava)
    beans (see Note)
2 garlic cloves, crushed
¼ teaspoon ground cumin
1½ tablespoons lemon juice
up to 75 ml (2½ fl oz) olive oil
2 tablespoons chopped flat-leaf (Italian)
    parsley
flatbread, to serve

1 Rinse the beans well, place in a large bowl and cover with 500 ml (17 fl oz/ 2 cups) water and soak overnight.
2 If using peeled beans, transfer with their soaking water to a large heavy-based saucepan. If using unpeeled brown beans, drain, then add to the pan with 500 ml (17 fl oz/2 cups) fresh water. Bring to the boil, cover, and simmer over low heat for 5–6 hours. Check the water level from time to time and add a little boiling water, as necessary, to keep the beans moist. Do not stir, but shake the pan occasionally to prevent sticking. Set aside to cool slightly.
3 Purée the contents of the pan in a food processor, then transfer to a bowl and stir in the garlic, cumin and lemon juice. Gradually stir in enough olive oil to give a dipping consistency, starting with about 50 ml (1½ fl oz). As the mixture cools it may become thick, in which case you can stir through a little warm water to return the mixture to dipping consistency.
4 Spread over a large dish and sprinkle the parsley over the top. Serve with the flatbread, cut into triangles.

NOTE: The dried broad beans can be the ready-peeled white ones or the small, unpeeled brown ones.

pickled fried fish

✵✵

Preparation time: 15 minutes
+ 24 hours marinating time
Cooking time: 15 minutes
Serves 4–6

60 g (2¼ oz/½ cup) plain (all-purpose) flour
pinch of cayenne pepper
500 g (1 lb 2 oz) firm white fish (such as ling or blue eye), cut into 24 strips
125 ml (4 fl oz/½ cup) olive oil
250 g (9 oz) brown onions, thinly sliced
250 g (9 oz) carrots, thinly sliced
8 spring onions (scallions), sliced on the diagonal
12 garlic cloves, chopped
1 tablespoon chopped thyme
2 bay leaves
2 whole cloves
8 juniper berries
1 teaspoon black peppercorns
250 ml (9 fl oz/1 cup) white wine vinegar
250 ml (9 fl oz/1 cup) white wine
2 tablespoons chopped flat-leaf (Italian) parsley

1 Season the flour with the cayenne pepper and salt. Pat the fish dry with paper towels, coat each piece in the flour and shake off any excess.
2 Heat 2 tablespoons of the oil in a large frying pan and cook the fish in batches until golden brown. Don't overcook the fish or it will break up when the marinade is poured over it. Place the fish in a non-metallic dish.
3 Clean the frying pan and then heat 60 ml (2 fl oz/¼ cup) oil and sauté the onion, carrot and spring onion for 5 minutes, or until soft but not brown. Add the garlic, herbs and spices, vinegar, wine and 250 ml (9 fl oz/1 cup) water. Simmer for 2 minutes, then season with 1 teaspoon salt.
4 Pour the hot mixture over the fish and leave to cool. Cover and refrigerate for at least 24 hours.
5 Return the dish to room temperature, then remove the fish and vegetables from the liquid using a slotted spoon. Place on a serving dish. Combine the parsley with 2 tablespoons of the liquid and pour over the fish. Serve at room temperature.

algerian eggplant jam

algerian eggplant jam

✵✵

Preparation time: 10 minutes
+ 30 minutes standing time
Cooking time: 20 minutes
Serves 6–8

2 eggplants (aubergines), about 400 g (14 oz)
olive oil, for pan-frying
2 garlic cloves, crushed
1 teaspoon sweet paprika
1½ teaspoons ground cumin
½ teaspoon sugar
1 tablespoon lemon juice

1 Cut the eggplant into 1 cm (½ inch) slices. Sprinkle with some salt and drain in a colander for 30 minutes. Rinse well, squeeze gently and pat dry.
2 Heat 5 mm (¼ inch) of oil in a large frying pan and fry the eggplant in batches over medium heat until golden brown on both sides. Drain on paper towels, then chop finely. Place in a colander until most of the oil has drained off, then transfer to a bowl and add the garlic, sweet paprika, cumin and sugar.
3 Wipe out the pan, add the eggplant mixture and stir constantly over medium heat for 2 minutes. Transfer to a bowl, stir in the lemon juice and season. Serve at room temperature.

dill

The wispy, green, fern-like leaves of the herb dill are similar in appearance to fennel fronds, only smaller. Both the leaves and seeds from the plant are used in cooking. Dill's unique flavour marries particularly well with seafood and it is a key ingredient in tartare sauce and gravlax.

tunisian carrot salad

Preparation time: **10 minutes**
Cooking time: **5 minutes**
Serves **6**

500 g (1 lb 2 oz) carrots
3 tablespoons finely chopped flat-leaf
   (Italian) parsley
1 teaspoon ground cumin

80 ml (2½ fl oz/⅓ cup) olive oil
60 ml (2 fl oz/¼ cup) red wine vinegar
2 garlic cloves, crushed
¼–½ teaspoon harissa
12 black olives
2 hard-boiled eggs, quartered

1 Thinly slice the carrots. Bring 500 ml (17 fl oz/2 cups) water to the boil in a saucepan. Add the carrot and cook until tender. Drain and transfer to a bowl. Add the parsley, cumin, olive oil, vinegar and garlic. Season with the harissa and some salt and pepper. Stir well.
2 Transfer the carrots to a serving dish and garnish with the black olives and hard-boiled egg.

cucumber, feta, mint and dill salad

Preparation time: **15 minutes**
Cooking time: **nil**
Serves **4**

120 g (4¼ oz) feta cheese
4 Lebanese (short) cucumbers
1 small red onion, thinly sliced
1½ tablespoons finely chopped dill
1 tablespoon dried mint
60 ml (2 fl oz/¼ cup) olive oil
1½ tablespoons lemon juice

1 Crumble the feta into 1 cm (½ inch) pieces and put in a large bowl. Peel and seed the cucumbers and cut into 1 cm (½ inch) cubes. Add to the bowl along with the onion and dill.
2 Grind the mint using a mortar and pestle, or force through a sieve, until powdered. Combine with the oil and lemon juice, then season. Pour over the salad and toss well.

tunisian carrot salad

tunisian brik

✳ ✳

Preparation time: 30 minutes
Cooking time: 20 minutes
Serves 2

30 g (1 oz) butter
1 small onion, finely chopped
185 g (6½ oz) tin tuna in oil, drained
1 tablespoon tiny capers, rinsed and
  chopped
2 tablespoons finely chopped flat-leaf
  (Italian) parsley
2 tablespoons grated parmesan cheese
6 sheets filo pastry
30 g (1 oz) butter, extra, melted
2 small eggs

1 Preheat the oven to 200°C (400°F/
Gas 6). Melt the butter in a small frying
pan and cook the onion over low heat for
5 minutes, or until soft but not brown.
Combine the onion, tuna, capers, parsley
and parmesan in a bowl and season.

2 Cut the filo pastry sheets in half
widthways. Layer four of the half-sheets
together, brushing each with melted
butter. Keep the remaining pastry covered
with a damp tea towel (dish towel).
Spoon half the tuna mixture along one
short end of the buttered pastry, leaving
a border. Make a well in the centre of the
mixture and break an egg into the well,
being careful to leave it whole.

3 Layer two more sheets of filo together,
brushing with melted butter, and place on
top of the tuna and egg. Fold in the pastry
sides, then roll into a firm parcel, keeping
the egg whole. Place on a lightly greased
baking tray and brush with melted butter.
Repeat with the remaining pastry, filling
and egg. Bake for 15 minutes, or until the
pastry is golden brown. Serve warm or at
room temperature.

NOTE: The yolk is soft after 15 minutes.
If you prefer a firmer egg, bake for a little
longer. In Tunisia, almost anything goes
inside a brik. Instead of filo pastry, you
can use large spring roll wrappers, then
deep-fry the briks in hot oil.

Crack an egg into the centre of the
tuna mixture.

Lay two sheets of filo over the
tuna and egg and fold in the sides.

Gently roll up the pastry into a firm
package, keeping the egg intact.

salatet ads

salatet ads (lentil salad)

✳ ✳

Preparation time: 15 minutes
+ 30 minutes standing time
Cooking time: 30 minutes
Serves 4–6

1 small onion
2 whole cloves
300 g (10½ oz/1½ cups) puy lentils or tiny blue-green lentils
1 strip lemon zest
2 garlic cloves, peeled
1 bay leaf
2 teaspoons ground cumin
2 tablespoons red wine vinegar
60 ml (2 fl oz/¼ cup) olive oil
1 tablespoon lemon juice
2 tablespoons finely chopped mint
3 spring onions (scallions), thinly sliced

1 Stud the onion with the cloves and put in a saucepan with the lentils, lemon zest, garlic, bay leaf, 1 teaspoon of cumin and 875 ml (30 fl oz/3½ cups) water. Bring to the boil and simmer gently over medium heat for 25–30 minutes, or until the lentils

are tender. Drain off any excess liquid and discard the onion, zest and bay leaf. Reserve the garlic and finely chop.
2 Whisk together the vinegar, oil, lemon juice, garlic and remaining cumin. Stir the dressing through the lentils with the mint and spring onion. Season well, then leave for 30 minutes to allow the flavours to develop. Serve at room temperature.

chorba bil hout (fish soup)

✳

Preparation time: 30 minutes
Cooking time: 30 minutes
Serves 6

2 red capsicums (peppers), quartered, seeded and membrane removed
1 long fresh red chilli, seeded
2 tablespoons extra virgin olive oil
1 brown onion, finely chopped
1 tablespoon tomato paste (concentrated purée)
2–3 teaspoons harissa (see page 206)
4 garlic cloves, finely chopped
2 teaspoons ground cumin
750 ml (26 fl oz/3 cups) fish stock
400 g (14 oz) tin chopped tomatoes
750 g (1 lb 10 oz) skinless, firm white fish fillets (such as blue eye or ling), cut into 2 cm (¾ inch) pieces
2 bay leaves
2 tablespoons chopped coriander (cilantro) leaves
6 thick baguette slices
1 garlic clove, extra, halved

1 Grill (broil) the capsicum and chilli until the skin is blackened and blistered. Cool in a plastic bag, then peel and cut into thin strips.
2 Heat the oil in a large saucepan and cook the onion for 5 minutes, or until softened. Add the tomato paste, harissa, garlic, cumin and 125 ml (4 fl oz/ ½ cup) water and stir to combine. Add the fish stock, tomatoes and 500 ml (17 fl oz/2 cups) water. Bring to the boil,

then reduce the heat and add the fish and bay leaves. Simmer for 7–8 minutes, or until the fish is just cooked. Remove the fish with a slotted spoon and place on a plate. Discard the bay leaves. Cool the soup slightly, then add half the chopped coriander and purée in a food processor, in batches, until smooth. Season, to taste.

3 Return the soup to the pan. Add the fish, capsicum and chilli and simmer gently. Toast the bread and, while still warm, rub with the cut garlic. Place one slice of bread in each soup bowl and top with the fish pieces. Ladle the soup over and garnish with the remaining coriander.

orange and date salad

Preparation time: 30 minutes + chilling time
Cooking time: nil
Serves 4–6

6 navel oranges
2 teaspoons orange flower water
8 dates, stoned and thinly sliced lengthways
90 g (3¼ oz) slivered almonds,
   lightly toasted
1 tablespoon shredded mint
¼ teaspoon ras-el-hanout or ground
   cinnamon

1 Peel the oranges, removing all the pith. Section them by cutting away all the membranes from the flesh. Place the segments in a bowl and squeeze the juice from the remainder of the orange over them. Add the orange flower water and stir gently to combine. Cover with plastic wrap and refrigerate until chilled.

2 Place the segments and the juice on a large flat dish and scatter the dates and almonds over the top. Sprinkle the mint and ras el hanout over the orange segments. Serve chilled.

Remove the stones from the dates and slice the dates thinly.

Separate the oranges into sections and remove all the membranes.

harira (chickpea, lamb and coriander soup)

✳

Preparation time: **15 minutes**
Cooking time: **2 hours 25 minutes**
Serves **4**

2 tablespoons olive oil
2 small brown onions, chopped
2 large garlic cloves, crushed
500 g (1 lb 2 oz) lamb shoulder steaks,
    trimmed of excess fat and sinew,
    and cut into small chunks
1½ teaspoons ground cumin
2 teaspoons paprika
½ teaspoon ground cloves
1 bay leaf
2 tablespoons tomato paste (concentrated
    purée)
1 litre (35 fl oz/4 cups) beef stock
2 x 400 g (14 oz) tins chickpeas, rinsed and
    drained
800 g (1 lb 12 oz) tin chopped tomatoes
30 g (1 oz) finely chopped coriander
    (cilantro) leaves, plus extra, to garnish
small black olives, to serve

1 Heat the oil in a large heavy-based saucepan or stockpot, add the onion and garlic and cook for 5 minutes, or until softened. Add the meat, in batches, and cook over high heat until browned on all sides. Return all the meat to the pan.
2 Add the spices and bay leaf to the pan and cook until aromatic. Add the tomato paste and cook for 2 minutes, stirring constantly. Stir in the stock and bring to the boil. Add the chickpeas, tomatoes and chopped coriander to the pan. Stir, then bring to the boil. Reduce the heat and simmer for 2 hours, or until the meat is tender. Stir occasionally. Season, to taste.
3 Serve garnished with coriander leaves and small black olives. This dish can also be served with toasted pitta bread drizzled with a little extra virgin olive oil.

molokhia soup

✳

Preparation time: **20 minutes**
Cooking time: **35 minutes**
Serves **4**

1.25 litres (44 fl oz/5 cups) chicken stock
1 onion, halved
6 cardamom pods, lightly crushed
2 silverbeet (Swiss chard) leaves, finely
    chopped, stalks discarded
400 g (14 oz) packet frozen shredded
    molokhia leaves (see Note) or
    30 g (1 oz) dried leaves, crumbled
2 tablespoons ghee
4 garlic cloves, crushed
1 teaspoon ground coriander
pinch of chilli powder

DRESSING
1 small onion, finely chopped
2 tablespoons lemon juice

1 Put the stock, onion and cardamom pods in a large saucepan, bring to the boil and boil for 12–15 minutes, or until the

harira

stock reduces to about 1 litre (35 fl oz/ 4 cups). Remove the onion and cardamom with a slotted spoon. Add the silverbeet and molokhia leaves to the pan. Bring to the boil, reduce the heat and simmer, uncovered, for 10 minutes.

2 Meanwhile, heat the ghee in a small saucepan, add the garlic and ¼ teaspoon salt and cook over low heat, stirring, until the garlic is golden. Remove from the heat and stir in the coriander and chilli.

3 To make the dressing, combine the ingredients in a small serving bowl.

4 Stir the garlic mixture into the soup and simmer for 2 minutes. Serve with the dressing on the side.

NOTE: Molokhia is an Egyptian plant similar to spinach. If you are using frozen cooked melokhia leaves, you will notice they appear to be mixed with egg white — don't try to rinse this off. The cooked leaves have a viscous consistency similar to okra and this is what gives the soup its characteristic texture. It is available from Middle Eastern speciality food stores.

tuna skewers with moroccan spices and chermoula

Preparation time: **20 minutes**
Cooking time: **10 minutes**
Serves 4

800 g (1 lb 12 oz) tuna steaks
2 tablespoons olive oil
½ teaspoon ground cumin
2 teaspoons finely grated lemon zest

CHERMOULA
½ teaspoon ground coriander
3 teaspoons ground cumin
2 teaspoons paprika
pinch of cayenne pepper
15 g (½ oz/½ cup) chopped flat-leaf (Italian) parsley
25 g (1 oz/½ cup) chopped coriander (cilantro) leaves

4 garlic cloves, crushed
80 ml (2½ fl oz/⅓ cup) lemon juice
125 ml (4 fl oz/½ cup) olive oil

1 If using wooden skewers, soak them for about 30 minutes to prevent them from burning during cooking.

2 Cut the tuna into 3 cm (1¼ inch) cubes and put in a shallow non-metallic dish. Combine the oil, cumin and zest and pour over the tuna. Toss to coat, cover and place in the refrigerator for 10 minutes.

3 Meanwhile, to make the chermoula, cook the spices in a small frying pan over medium heat for 30 seconds, until aromatic. Combine with the remaining chermoula ingredients and set aside.

4 Thread the tuna onto the skewers. Lightly oil a chargrill pan or barbecue and cook the skewers for 1 minute each side for rare or 2 minutes for medium. Serve the tuna skewers with chermoula drizzled over. Garnish with spring onion (scallion) and serve with couscous, if desired.

Add the pumpkin, cauliflower and zucchini to the pan and cook for 10 minutes.

Add the remaining oil and butter to the couscous and fluff it up with a fork.

vegetable couscous

Preparation time: 40 minutes
Cooking time: 30 minutes
Serves 4–6

60 ml (2 fl oz/¼ cup) olive oil
2 small onions, thinly sliced
1 teaspoon turmeric
½ teaspoon chilli powder
2 teaspoons grated fresh ginger
1 cinnamon stick
2 carrots, thickly sliced

2 parsnips, thickly sliced
375 ml (13 fl oz/1½ cups) vegetable stock
315 g (11 oz) pumpkin (winter squash), cut into small cubes
250 g (9 oz) cauliflower, cut into florets
2 zucchini (courgettes), cut into thick slices
400g (14 oz) tin chickpeas, drained
pinch of saffron threads
2 tablespoons chopped coriander (cilantro) leaves
2 tablespoons chopped parsley
230 g (8 oz/1¼ cups) instant couscous
250 ml (9 fl oz/1 cup) boiling water
30 g (1 oz) butter

1 Heat 2 tablespoons of the oil in a large saucepan. Add the onion and cook over medium heat for 5 minutes, or until the onion is soft, stirring occasionally. Add the turmeric, chilli powder and ginger and cook, stirring, for another minute.
2 Add the cinnamon stick, carrot, parsnip and stock to the pan and stir to combine. Cover and bring to the boil. Reduce the heat and simmer for 5 minutes, or until the vegetables are almost tender.
3 Add the pumpkin, cauliflower and zucchini to the pan and simmer for 10 minutes more. Stir in the chickpeas,

saffron, coriander and parsley and simmer, uncovered, for 5 minutes or until all the vegetables are tender.

4 Place the couscous in a heatproof bowl and add the boiling water. Cover, allow to stand for 5 minutes, then add the remaining oil and butter and fluff it up with a fork. Serve the vegetable mixture with the couscous.

NOTE: Almost any seasonal vegetables can be used in this recipe. Potato, orange sweet potato, green beans, baby onions, or red or green capsicums (peppers) are all suitable.

lamb tagine with quince

Preparation time: 20 minutes
Cooking time: 1 hour 40 minutes
Serves 4–6

1.5 kg (3 lb 5 oz) lamb shoulder,
    cut into 3 cm (1¼ inch) pieces
2 large onions, diced
½ teaspoon ground ginger
½ teaspoon cayenne pepper
¼ teaspoon crushed saffron threads
1 teaspoon ground coriander
1 cinnamon stick
25 g (1 oz/½ cup) roughly chopped
    coriander (cilantro) leaves
40 g (1½ oz) butter
500 g (1 lb 2 oz) quinces, peeled, cored
    and quartered
100 g (3½ oz) dried apricots
coriander (cilantro) sprigs, extra, to garnish

1 Place the lamb in a heavy-based, flameproof casserole dish and add half the onion, the ginger, cayenne pepper, saffron, ground coriander, cinnamon stick, coriander leaves and some salt and pepper. Cover with cold water and bring to the boil over medium heat. Reduce the heat and simmer, partly covered, for 1½ hours, or until the lamb is tender.

2 While the lamb is cooking, melt the butter in a heavy-based frying pan and cook the remaining onion and the quince over medium heat, stirring often, for 15 minutes or until lightly golden.

3 When the lamb has been cooking for 1 hour, add the quince mixture and apricots and continue cooking.

4 Taste the sauce and adjust the seasoning if necessary. Transfer to a warm serving dish and sprinkle with coriander sprigs. Serve with couscous or rice.

afelia (cypriot pork and coriander stew)

✳ ✳

Preparation time: 15 minutes
  + overnight chilling time
Cooking time: 1 hour 20 minutes
Serves 4–6

800 g (1 lb 12 oz) pork fillet,
  cut into 2 cm (¾ inch) cubes

1½ tablespoons coriander seeds
1 tablespoon plain (all-purpose) flour
60 ml (2 fl oz/¼ cup) olive oil
1 large onion, thinly sliced
375 ml (13 fl oz/1½ cups) red wine
250 ml (9 fl oz/1 cup) chicken stock
1 teaspoon sugar
coriander (cilantro) sprigs, to garnish

1 Place the pork in a bowl. Crush the coriander seeds using a mortar and pestle, add ½ teaspoon cracked black pepper and toss through the pork to coat. Cover and refrigerate overnight.

2 Add the flour to the pork and toss. Heat 2 tablespoons of the oil in a frying pan and cook the pork in batches over high heat for 1–2 minutes, or until brown. Remove from the pan.

3 Heat the remaining oil in the pan, add the onion and cook over medium heat for 2–3 minutes, or until just golden. Return the meat to the pan and add the wine, stock and sugar. Season, bring to the boil, then reduce the heat and simmer, covered, for 1 hour.

4 Remove the meat. Return the pan to the heat and boil over high heat for 3–5 minutes, or until the sauce is reduced and slightly thickened. Pour over the meat and garnish with the coriander sprigs.

bisteeya (moroccan chicken pie)

✳ ✳ ✳

Preparation time: 30 minutes
Cooking time: 1 hour 30 minutes
Serves 6–8

200 g (7 oz) butter
1.5 kg (3 lb 5 oz) chicken, cut into
  4 portions
1 large onion, finely chopped
3 teaspoons ground cinnamon
1 teaspoon ground ginger
2 teaspoons ground cumin
¼ teaspoon cayenne pepper
½ teaspoon ground turmeric
½ teaspoon saffron threads, soaked in
  2 tablespoons warm water
125 ml (4 fl oz/½ cup) chicken stock
4 eggs, lightly beaten
25 g (1 oz/½ cup) chopped coriander
  (cilantro) leaves
3 tablespoons chopped flat-leaf (Italian)
  parsley
50 g (1¾ oz/⅓ cup) chopped almonds
30 g (1 oz/¼ cup) icing (confectioners')
  sugar
375 g (13 oz) filo pastry
icing (confectioners') sugar, extra, to dust

afelia

1 Preheat oven to 180°C (350°F/Gas 4). Grease a 30 cm (12 inch) pizza tray.

2 Melt 40 g (1½ oz) of the butter in a large frying pan. Add the chicken, onion, 2 teaspoons of the cinnamon, all the other spices, including the saffron soaking liquid, and the stock. Season, cover and simmer for 30 minutes, or until the chicken is cooked through.

3 Remove the chicken from the sauce. When cool enough to handle, remove the meat from the bones, discard the skin and bones and shred the meat into thin strips.

4 Bring the liquid in the pan to a simmer and add the egg. Cook the mixture, stirring constantly, until the egg is cooked and the mixture is quite dry. Add the chicken, chopped coriander and parsley, season well with salt and pepper and mix. Remove from the heat.

5 Bake the almonds on a baking tray until golden brown. Cool slightly, then blend in a food processor or spice grinder with the icing sugar and remaining cinnamon until the mixture resembles coarse crumbs.

6 Melt the remaining butter. Place a sheet of filo on the pizza tray and brush with melted butter. Place another sheet on top in a pinwheel effect and brush with butter. Continue brushing and layering until you have used eight sheets. Put the chicken mixture on top and sprinkle with the almond mixture.

7 Fold the overlapping filo pastry over the top of the filling. Place a sheet of filo over the top and brush with butter. Continue to layer buttered filo sheets over the top in the same pinwheel effect until you have used another eight sheets. Tuck the overhanging edges over the pie to form a neat round parcel. Brush well with the remaining butter. Bake the pie for 40–45 minutes, or until cooked through and golden. Dust with the icing sugar before cutting into wedges to serve.

Sprinkle the almond mixture all over the chicken.

Fold the overlapping sheets of filo over the top of the filling.

mechoui

1 teaspoon paprika
1 tablespoon ground cumin, extra,
   for dipping

1 Preheat the oven to 220°C (425°F/
Gas 7). With a small sharp knife, cut small
deep slits in the top and sides of the lamb.
2 Mix the butter, garlic, spices and
¼ teaspoon salt in a small bowl until a
smooth paste forms.
3 With the back of a spoon, rub the paste
all over the lamb, then use your fingers to
spread the paste and make sure all of the
lamb is covered.
4 Put the lamb, bone side down, in a
deep roasting tin and place on the top
shelf of the oven. Bake for 10 minutes,
then baste and return to the oven.
Reduce the temperature to 160°C (315°F/
Gas 2–3). Bake for 3 hours 20 minutes,
basting every 20–30 minutes. Basting
makes the lamb tender and flavoursome.
Carve the lamb into chunky slices. Mix the
extra cumin with 1½ teaspoons salt and
serve on the side for dipping.

chicken with almonds

Preparation time: **15 minutes**
Cooking time: **1 hour 5 minutes**
Serves **6**

1.5 kg (3 lb 5 oz) whole chicken, quartered
60 g (2¼ oz) butter
1 onion, chopped
½ teaspoon ground ginger
½ teaspoon saffron powder or 2 pinches
   of saffron threads
½ teaspoon ground cinnamon
1 tablespoon finely chopped coriander
   (cilantro) leaves
2 tablespoons olive oil
125 g (4½ oz) blanched almonds
30 g (1 oz/1 cup) finely chopped flat-leaf
   (Italian) parsley

1 Put the chicken in a large saucepan or
stockpot. Add the butter, onion, spices,
coriander and 1 teaspoon each of salt and
pepper. Add 310 ml (10¾ fl oz/1¼ cups)

mechoui

Traditionally, mechoui was a
dish consisting of an entire
lamb roasted in a mud oven
that was dug deep in the
ground. In many parts of North
Africa it is still prepared in this
way for family celebrations and
on special holy days. Regarded
as a national dish, it is often
served as the centrepiece
of mechoui parties and is
also an integral part of the
region's street food, where it
is accompanied by a mixture of
salt and ground cumin.

mechoui (slow-roasted lamb with cumin and paprika)

Preparation time: **15 minutes**
Cooking time: **3 hours 30 minutes**
Serves **6**

2.25 kg (5 lb) leg of lamb
80 g (2¾ oz) butter, softened
3 garlic cloves, crushed
2 teaspoons ground cumin
3 teaspoons ground coriander

water, cover and cook over low heat for 1 hour. Turn the chicken over occasionally and add more water if necessary.

2 Heat the oil in a frying pan over low heat, add the almonds and cook until golden. Remove.

3 Add the parsley to the chicken and cook for 2–3 minutes. Serve sprinkled with the almonds.

okra with coriander and tomato sauce

❋

Preparation time: **5 minutes**
Cooking time: **15 minutes**
Serves **4–6**

60 ml (2 fl oz/¼ cup) olive oil
1 onion, chopped
2 garlic cloves, crushed
500 g (1 lb 2 oz) fresh okra (see Note)
400 g (14 oz) tin chopped tomatoes
2 teaspoons sugar
60 ml (2 fl oz/¼ cup) lemon juice
60 g (2¼ oz) coriander (cilantro) leaves,
    finely chopped

1 Heat the oil in a large frying pan, add the onion and cook over medium heat for 5 minutes, or until translucent and golden. Add the garlic and cook for another minute.

2 Add the okra to the pan and cook, stirring, for 4–5 minutes. Add the tomatoes, sugar and lemon juice and simmer, stirring occasionally, for 3–4 minutes, or until softened.

3 Stir in the coriander, remove from the heat and serve.

NOTE: If fresh okra is not available, you can use 800 g (1 lb 12 oz) of tinned okra instead. Rinse and drain the okra before adding with the coriander.

okra

Okra is a vegetable native to Africa that was introduced to Middle Eastern and Arabian countries by slave traders. When sliced and cooked slowly, the texture becomes sticky and is perfect for thickening and adding body to stews. Okra has become an integral ingredient in many North African and Middle Eastern dishes, the texture melding with tomatoes, garlic, onions and spices. The sticky texture is minimal if the okra is left whole and cooked simply and quickly.

okra with coriander and tomato sauce

semit (egyptian sesame bread rings)

✹ ✹

Preparation time: 45 minutes
+ 1 hour 30 minutes proving time
Cooking time: 15 minutes
Makes 20

2 teaspoons dried yeast
1 teaspoon sugar
375 g (13 oz/3 cups) plain (all-purpose) flour
125 ml (4 fl oz/½ cup) milk
125 g (4½ oz/1 cup) plain (all-purpose) flour, extra
1 egg, lightly beaten
80 g (2¾ oz/½ cup) sesame seeds

1 Place the yeast, sugar and 60 ml (2 fl oz/¼ cup) warm water in a small bowl and stir until dissolved. Leave in a warm, draught-free place for 10 minutes, or until bubbles appear on the surface. The mixture should be frothy and slightly increased in volume. If your yeast doesn't foam, it is dead and you must start again.
2 Sift the flour into a bowl and season with 1 teaspoon salt. Heat the milk and 125 ml (4 fl oz/½ cup) water together until lukewarm. Make a well in the flour and pour in the liquid and the yeast mixture. Mix with a wooden spoon, adding the extra flour, a little at a time (you may not need all of it), until a soft dough forms. Turn onto a lightly floured surface and knead for 10 minutes, or until smooth and elastic. Place in an oiled bowl, cover and leave in a warm, draught-free place for 1 hour, or until doubled in size.
3 Turn the dough onto a floured surface and punch it down. Break off pieces the size of an egg and roll each into a rope 1 cm (½ inch) thick and 20 cm (8 inches) long. Form the rope into a ring. Moisten the edges to seal. Continue until you have used all the dough.
4 Preheat the oven to 200°C (400°F/ Gas 6). Place an ovenproof dish filled with hot water on the bottom of the oven to create steam while cooking the rings.
5 Grease two baking trays and dust with flour. Place the rings on the trays. Brush with the egg and sprinkle with the sesame seeds. Cover the rings with a damp tea towel (dish towel) and leave to rise in a warm place for 30 minutes. Bake the rings for 15 minutes, or until cooked and golden. While still hot, brush the rings with hot water to help create crisp crusts while they are cooling.

semit

chicken with preserved lemon and olives

✹

Preparation time: 10 minutes
Cooking time: 1 hour
Serves 4

60 ml (2 fl oz/¼ cup) olive oil
1.6 kg (3 lb 8 oz) whole free-range chicken
1 onion, chopped
2 garlic cloves, chopped
625 ml (21½ fl oz/2½ cups) chicken stock
½ teaspoon ground ginger
1½ teaspoons ground cinnamon
pinch of saffron threads

100 g (3½ oz) green olives
¼ preserved lemon (see page 207),
   pulp removed, zest washed and
   cut into slivers
2 bay leaves
2 chicken livers
3 tablespoons chopped coriander (cilantro)

1 Preheat the oven to 180°C (350°F/ Gas 4). Heat 2 tablespoons oil in a large frying pan, add the chicken and brown on all sides. Place in a deep baking dish.
2 Heat the remaining oil, add the onion and garlic and cook over medium heat for 3–4 minutes, or until softened. Add the stock, ginger, cinnamon, saffron, olives, lemon and bay leaves, then pour around the chicken. Bake for 45 minutes, adding a little more water or stock if needed.
3 Remove the chicken from the dish, cover with foil and leave to rest. Pour the contents of the baking dish into a frying pan, add the chicken livers and mash into the sauce as they cook. Cook for 5–6 minutes, or until the sauce has reduced and thickened. Stir in the coriander. Cut the chicken into four equal pieces and serve with the sauce spooned over the top.

moroccan mint tea

moroccan mint tea

Preparation time: **5 minutes**
Cooking time: **nil**
Serves **1**

1 tablespoon green tea leaves
30 g (1 oz) sugar
1 large handful of spearmint leaves and stalks
boiling water

1 Heat the teapot and add the tea leaves, sugar and spearmint. Fill with boiling water and brew for at least 5 minutes. Adjust the sweetness if necessary.

NOTE: In Morocco, this light sweet tea is often served before, and always after every meal. Traditionally, it is served from a silver teapot into ornate glasses.

moroccan flatbread

Preparation time: **45 minutes**
   + 30 minutes proving time
Cooking time: **12 minutes**
Makes **16**

375 g (13 oz/2½ cups) wholemeal
   (whole-wheat) flour
1 teaspoon caster (superfine) sugar
2 teaspoons dried yeast
½ teaspoon sweet paprika
50 g (1¾ oz/⅓ cup) cornmeal
1 tablespoon olive oil
1 egg, lightly beaten
2 tablespoons sesame seeds

1 Preheat the oven to 180°C (350°F/ Gas 4). Lightly grease a baking tray. Put 75 g (2¾ oz/½ cup) of the flour, the sugar, yeast, 1 teaspoon salt and 310 ml (10¾ fl oz/1¼ cups) lukewarm water in a bowl and stir until dissolved. Cover and leave in a warm, draught-free place for 10 minutes, or until the mixture is frothy and slightly increased in volume.
2 Sift the paprika, cornmeal and remaining flour into a bowl. Add the oil, then stir in the yeast mixture. Mix to a firm dough and knead until smooth. Cover and leave in a warm, draught-free place for 20 minutes.
3 Divide the dough into 16 portions, roll each into a ball then flatten into 8 cm (3¼ inch) rounds. Place on the baking tray, brush with the egg and sprinkle with the sesame seeds. Cover and set aside for 10 minutes, or until puffed up. Bake for 12 minutes, or until golden.

sweet couscous

Preparation time: **20 minutes**
Cooking time: **5 minutes**
Serves **4–6**

80 g (2¾ oz) combined pistachio nuts, pine nuts and blanched almonds
45 g (1¾ oz/¼ cup) dried apricots
90 g (3¼ oz/½ cup) stoned dried dates
250 g (9 oz) instant couscous
55 g (2 oz/¼ cup) caster (superfine) sugar
250 ml (9 fl oz/1 cup) boiling water
90 g (3¼ oz) unsalted butter, softened

TO SERVE
2 tablespoons caster (superfine) sugar
½ teaspoon ground cinnamon
375 ml (13 fl oz/1½ cups) hot milk

1 Preheat the oven to 160°C (315°F/ Gas 2–3). Spread the nuts on a baking tray and bake for 5 minutes, until light golden. Cool, then roughly chop and place in a bowl. Slice the apricots into matchstick-sized pieces and quarter the dates lengthways. Add to the bowl and toss to combine.
2 Put the couscous and sugar in a large bowl and cover with the boiling water.
Stir, then add the butter and a pinch of salt. Stir until the butter melts. Cover with a tea towel (dish towel) and set aside for 10 minutes. Fluff with a fork, then toss half the fruit and nut mixture through.
3 To serve, pile the warm couscous in the centre of a platter. Arrange the remaining nut mixture around the base. Combine the sugar and cinnamon in a small bowl and serve separately for sprinkling. Pass around the hot milk for guests to pour over the couscous, if desired.

om ali (nut and filo pudding)

Preparation time: **20 minutes**
Cooking time: **35 minutes**
Serves **6**

6 sheets filo pastry
3 tablespoons butter, melted
60 g (2¼ oz) raisins
140 g (5 oz) mixed nuts, such as pistachios, flaked almonds and chopped hazelnuts
1 litre (35 fl oz/4 cups) milk
310 ml (10¾ fl oz/1¼ cups) thick (double/heavy) cream
90 g (3¼ oz/⅓ cup) sugar
1 teaspoon ground cinnamon

1 Preheat the oven to 200°C (400°F/ Gas 6). Lightly grease a baking tray.
2 Remove a sheet of filo and cover the rest with a damp tea towel (dish towel). Brush the filo sheet with melted butter and place on the tray. Cover loosely with two more buttered sheets. Repeat with the other three sheets on another tray. Bake for 5 minutes, or until the pastry is crisp and golden. Reduce the temperature to 180°C (350°F/Gas 4). Crumble the filo into a 2 litre (70 fl oz/8 cup) baking dish, sprinkling some of the raisins and nuts over each sheet as you go.
3 Heat the milk, cream and sugar over low heat until just below boiling point. Pour over the pastry and bake for 25–30 minutes, or until golden brown. Sprinkle with the cinnamon. Serve warm or cold.

sweet couscous

Roll each portion of almond mixture into a log shape.

Add the cinnamon to the egg yolk and brush over the snake.

m'hanncha (almond filo snake)

✹ ✹

Preparation time: 30 minutes
Cooking time: 40 minutes
Serves 8

70 g (2½ oz/⅔ cup) ground almonds
30 g (1 oz/⅓ cup) flaked almonds
175 g (6 oz) icing (confectioners') sugar
1 egg, separated
1 teaspoon finely grated lemon zest
¼ teaspoon natural almond extract
1 tablespoon rosewater
2 tablespoons olive oil
2 tablespoons almond oil
9 sheets filo pastry

pinch of ground cinnamon
icing (confectioners') sugar, extra, to dust

1 Preheat the oven to 180°C (350°F/ Gas 4). Lightly grease a 20 cm (8 inch) round springform cake tin.
2 Put all of the almonds in a bowl with the icing sugar. Put the egg white in a bowl and lightly beat with a fork. Add to the almonds with the lemon zest, almond extract and rosewater. Mix to a paste.
3 Divide the mixture into three portions and roll each portion into a log 45 cm (17¾ inches) long and 1 cm (½ inch) thick. If the paste is too sticky to roll, dust the work surface with icing sugar.
4 Mix the oils in a bowl. Remove one sheet of filo and cover the rest with a damp tea towel (dish towel) to prevent

them from drying out. Brush the filo sheet with the oils, then cover with two more oiled sheets. Place one almond log along the length of the oiled pastry and roll up to enclose the filling. Form into a coil and sit the coil in the centre of the tin. Use oil to join the other logs and continue shaping to make a large coil.
5 Add the cinnamon to the egg yolk and brush over the snake. Bake for 30 minutes, then remove the side of the tin and turn the snake over. Bake for another 10 minutes to crisp the base. Dust with icing sugar and serve warm.

NOTE: The snake will keep for up to 3 days but should not be refrigerated.

fried honey cakes

✹ ✹

Preparation time: 20 minutes
    + 1 hour standing time
Cooking time: 20 minutes
Serves 4–6

3 eggs
60 ml (2 fl oz/¼ cup) orange juice
60 ml (2 fl oz/¼ cup) vegetable oil
1 tablespoon grated orange zest

60 g (2¼ oz/¼ cup) caster (superfine)
    sugar
300 g (10½ oz) plain (all-purpose) flour
1 teaspoon baking powder
about 4 tablespoons flour, extra, for rolling

SYRUP
2 tablespoons lemon juice
275 g (9 ½ oz) sugar
115 g (4 oz/⅓ cup) honey
1 tablespoon finely grated orange zest
vegetable oil, for deep-frying

fried honey cakes

1 Whisk the eggs, orange juice and oil together in a large bowl. Add the orange zest and sugar and whisk until frothy. Sift in the flour and baking powder and mix with a wooden spoon until smooth, but a bit sticky. Cover and set aside for 1 hour.
2 For the syrup, heat the lemon juice, sugar and 310 ml (10¾ fl oz/1¼ cups) cold water in a saucepan, stirring until the sugar dissolves. Bring to the boil, reduce the heat and simmer for 5 minutes. Add the honey and orange zest and simmer for another 5 minutes. Keep warm.
3 Sprinkle a little of the extra flour onto the dough and transfer it to a lightly floured surface. Work in just enough extra flour to give a dough that doesn't stick to your hands. Roll it out to a thickness of 5 mm (¼ inch). It will be very elastic, so keep rolling and resting it until it stops shrinking. Using a 5 cm (2 inch) pastry cutter, cut out round cakes.
4 Heat the oil in a large, deep-sided frying pan to 170°C (325°F), or until a cube of bread dropped into the oil browns in 20 seconds. Fry 3 or 4 cakes at a time until puffed and golden, about 1 minute on each side. Remove with tongs and drain on paper towels.
5 Using tongs, dip each cake into the warm syrup long enough for it to soak in. Transfer to a platter. Serve warm or cold.

date candies

✹

Preparation time: 10 minutes
Cooking time: 20 minutes
Serves 6–8

150 g (5½ oz/1½ cups) walnut halves
2 tablespoons sesame seeds
100 g (3½ oz) ghee
600 g (1 lb 5 oz) stoned dried dates,
    coarsely chopped

1 Preheat the oven to 180°C (350°F/ Gas 4) and line the base and two opposite sides of an 18 cm (7 inch) square baking tin with baking paper. Spread the walnuts on a baking tray and bake for 5 minutes,

Mix with a wooden spoon until smooth, but still a bit sticky.

Use a pastry cutter to cut out round cakes.

or until lightly toasted. Chop coarsely. Bake the sesame seeds until golden.

2 Melt the ghee in a large heavy-based saucepan and cook the dates, covered, over low heat for about 10 minutes, stirring often, until they soften. Using the back of a spoon dipped in cold water, spread half the date mixture into the tin. Scatter the walnuts on top and press into the dates. Spread the remaining date mixture over the walnuts. Smooth the surface with wet fingers and press down firmly. Sprinkle with the sesame seeds and press lightly into the dates. When cool, cut the date slice into small diamonds and serve with tea or coffee.

baked spiced quince

✳

Preparation time: 25 minutes
Cooking time: 1 hour
Serves 4–6

4 quinces (see Note)
40 g (1½ oz) unsalted butter
1 tablespoon rosewater
310 g (11 oz/1¼ cups) sugar
½ teaspoon ground cinnamon
¼ teaspoon ground cloves
Greek-style yoghurt, to serve
honey, to serve
roasted pistachio nuts, to serve

1 Preheat the oven to 150°C (300°F Gas 2). Lightly grease an ovenproof dish.

2 Peel the quinces, then cut them into quarters, removing the cores.

3 Place the pieces of quince in the dish, cut side up, then distribute the butter among them and sprinkle with rosewater, sugar and spices. Cover the dish tightly with foil and bake for 1 hour, or until the quince is tender. Serve with a spoonful of yoghurt, drizzled with honey and sprinkled with roasted pistachios.

NOTE: The cooking time will vary depending on the size of the quinces, so be sure to test if they are tender.

baked spiced quince

quinces

When cooked slowly, quinces become a glorious, deep reddish pink. They are meltingly tender, sweet and perfumed, and it is easy to understand why they became the symbol of love, happiness and fertility in ancient times. They can be used in the making of desserts, for adding a sweetness to savoury dishes, in pastes to serve with cheeses, and jellies to spread on your breakfast brioche.

middle east

A history dating back thousands of years has led to an interesting variety in Middle Eastern cuisine developed by a diverse group of people. Ingredients commonly used elsewhere along the Mediterranean, such as parsley, mint, citrus, olive oil and cinnamon, are used far more subtly here. Allspice, yoghurt, dried beans, rice and burghul (bulgur), artichokes, fish, lamb and chicken all come into play. The cooking may seem elaborate but is surprisingly easy. The unique dishes tabouleh, baba ghanoush and kibbeh are popular in many places besides this area. Some dishes require lengthy cooking but involve little preparation, and many can be cooked ahead. Meals don't usually include sweets or puddings but these are enjoyed with visitors and on festive occasions.

split broad beans

Legumes, such as split broad (fava) beans, are a key feature of Middle Eastern cuisine, due in part to the dietary laws of the region's predominant religion, Islam, as they can be eaten during times of fasting. Split (broad) fava beans are available from specialist food stores and health food stores.

falafel (deep-fried chickpea balls)

Preparation time: 20 minutes + 48 hours
    soaking and 50 minutes standing time
Cooking time: 10 minutes
Makes 30

150 g (5½ oz/1 cup) dried split broad (fava)
    beans (see Note)
220 g (7¾ oz/1 cup) dried chickpeas
1 onion, roughly chopped
6 garlic cloves, roughly chopped
2 teaspoons ground coriander
1 tablespoon ground cumin
15 g (½ oz/½ cup) chopped flat-leaf (Italian)
    parsley
¼ teaspoon chilli powder
½ teaspoon bicarbonate of soda
    (baking soda)
3 tablespoons chopped coriander (cilantro)
    leaves
light olive oil, for deep-frying

1 Place the broad beans in a large bowl, cover well with cold water and soak for 48 hours. Drain, then rinse several times in fresh water.
2 Meanwhile, place the chickpeas in a large bowl, cover well with water and soak for 12 hours.
3 Drain the broad beans and chickpeas well, then process in a food processor with the onion and garlic until smooth.
4 Add the ground coriander, cumin, parsley, chilli powder, bicarbonate of soda and chopped coriander. Season, to taste, and mix until well combined. Transfer to a large bowl and set aside for 30 minutes.
5 Shape tablespoons of the mixture into balls, flatten to 4 cm (1½ inch) rounds, place on a tray and refrigerate for 20 minutes.
6 Fill a deep, heavy-based saucepan one-third full of oil and heat to 180°C (350°F), or until a cube of bread dropped into the oil browns in 15 seconds. Cook the falafel in batches for 1–2 minutes, or until golden. Drain on paper towels. Serve hot or cold with hummus or baba ghanoush and pitta bread.

NOTE: If whole broad beans are used, they need to be skinned after soaking. To do this, squeeze each broad bean to allow the skin to pop off, or pierce each skin with your fingernail and then peel it off.

tabouleh

tabouleh

Preparation time: 20 minutes + 1½ hours
 soaking and 30 minutes standing time
Cooking time: nil
Serves 6

130 g (4½ oz/¾ cup) burghul (bulgur)
3 ripe tomatoes
1 telegraph (long) cucumber
4 spring onions (scallions), sliced
120 g (4¼ oz) chopped flat-leaf (Italian)
 parsley
2 large handfuls mint leaves, chopped

DRESSING
80 ml (2½ fl oz/⅓ cup) lemon juice
60 ml (2 fl oz/¼ cup) olive oil
1 tablespoon extra virgin olive oil

1 Put the burghul in a bowl, cover with
500 ml (17 fl oz/2 cups) water and leave
for 1½ hours to soak.
2 Cut the tomatoes in half, squeeze to
remove any excess seeds and cut into
1 cm (½ inch) cubes. Cut the cucumber
in half lengthways, remove the seeds with
a teaspoon and cut the flesh into 1 cm
(½ inch) cubes.
3 To make the dressing, put the lemon
juice and 1½ teaspoons salt in a bowl
and whisk until well combined. Season
with freshly ground black pepper and
slowly whisk in the olive oil and extra
virgin olive oil.
4 Drain the burghul and squeeze out any
excess water. Spread the burghul out on
a tea towel (dish towel) or paper towels
and leave to dry for about 30 minutes.
Put the burghul in a large salad bowl,
add the tomato, cucumber, spring onion,
parsley and mint, and toss well to
combine. Pour the dressing over the salad
and toss until evenly coated.

red capsicum, walnut and pomegranate dip

Preparation time: 10 minutes
 + overnight chilling time
Cooking time: 15 minutes
Serves 4–6

450 g (1 lb) red capsicums (peppers)
50 g (1¾ oz/½ cup) walnuts
2 garlic cloves, crushed
40 g (1½ oz/½ cup) fresh white
 breadcrumbs
2 small fresh red chillies, seeded and
 finely chopped
2 tablespoons olive oil
1 teaspoon pomegranate syrup
2 tablespoons lemon juice
1 teaspoon cumin seeds, roughly ground
½ teaspoon crushed red chilli flakes

1 Preheat the grill (broiler) to hot. Cut
the capsicums into large, flat pieces and
remove the seeds and membrane. Put
the capsicum pieces, skin side up, under
the grill until they are blackened and
blistered. Cool in a plastic bag, then peel
and process until fine.
2 Chop the walnuts, garlic and
breadcrumbs in a food processor until
finely ground. Add the capsicum, chilli,
olive oil, pomegranate syrup and lemon
juice and process in short bursts to
combine. Transfer to a bowl and stir in the
cumin and chilli flakes. Season with salt,
then chill overnight to allow the flavours
to mellow. Serve at room temperature
with pide (Turkish/flat bread).

marinated yoghurt cheese balls

✺ ✺ ✺

Preparation time: 10 minutes
  + 4 days chilling time
Cooking time: nil
Makes 12

500 g (1 lb 2 oz/2 cups) Greek-style
  yoghurt
2 teaspoons sea salt
1 tablespoon dried oregano
2 teaspoons dried thyme
330 ml (11¼ fl oz/1⅓ cups) olive oil,
  or enough to cover
1 bay leaf
crusty bread, to serve

1 Fold a 30 x 60 cm (12 x 24 inch) piece of muslin (cheesecloth) in half to make a 30 cm (12 inch) square.
2 Combine the yoghurt, salt and 1 teaspoon black pepper in a bowl. Line another bowl with the muslin and spoon the mixture into the centre. Bring the corners together and, using a piece of kitchen string, tie as closely as possible to the yoghurt, leaving a loop at the end. Thread the loop through the handle of a wooden spoon and hang over a bowl to drain in the refrigerator for 3 days.
3 Combine the oregano and thyme in a dish. Pour half the oil into a 500 ml (17 fl oz/2 cup) jar. Add the bay leaf.
4 Roll level tablespoons of the yoghurt into balls. Toss in the combined herbs and put in the jar of oil. Pour in the remaining oil to cover the balls completely. Seal and refrigerate for at least 1 day. Serve at room temperature, with crusty bread.

marinated yoghurt cheese balls

fatayer sabanikh (spinach pies)

✺ ✺

Preparation time: 25 minutes
  + 2 hours proving time
Cooking time: 20 minutes
Makes about 20

1 teaspoon dried yeast
1 teaspoon sugar
375 g (13 oz/3 cups) plain
  (all-purpose) flour
125 ml (4 fl oz/½ cup) olive oil
750 g (1 lb 10 oz) English spinach,
  trimmed
1 large onion, finely chopped
1 garlic clove, crushed
80 g (2¾ oz/½ cup) pine nuts, toasted
2 tablespoons lemon juice
1 teaspoon finely grated lemon zest
¼ teaspoon freshly ground nutmeg
1 egg, lightly beaten, to glaze

1 Place the yeast and sugar in a bowl with 60 ml (2 fl oz/¼ cup) warm water. Set aside for 10 minutes until frothy.

bay leaves

A feature of Middle Eastern food is the use of aromatics such as bay leaves. Available either fresh or dried, bay leaves come from the native Mediterranean evergreen bay laurel tree. A historical symbol of triumph, honour and celebration, they are an essential ingredient in a bouquet garni and are used to impart their aroma to vegetable and meat dishes, soups and stews. Be careful not to overuse them, as they can make a dish taste bitter.

Sift the flour into a bowl, add the yeast mixture, 2 tablespoons olive oil and 185 ml (6 fl oz/¾ cup) warm water. Mix to form a dough, then turn onto a lightly floured surface and knead for 10 minutes until smooth and elastic. Place in an oiled bowl and leave in a warm, draught-free place for up to 2 hours, until the dough has doubled in size.

2 Preheat the oven to 190°C (375°F/ Gas 5). Grease two large baking trays. Wash the spinach, leaving a generous amount of water on the leaves. Place in a saucepan, cover and cook over high heat until wilted. Transfer to a colander and squeeze against the sides to remove the excess water. Chop roughly.

3 Heat 1 tablespoon of the oil in a frying pan and cook the onion and garlic until softened. Place in a bowl with the spinach, pine nuts, lemon juice and zest. Season with the nutmeg and some salt and pepper. Set aside to cool.

4 Turn the dough onto a floured surface and punch it down. Divide into balls the size of an egg and roll each into a 10 cm (4 inch) round. Place 1 tablespoon of the filling in the centre of each round. Brush the edges of the rounds with water, then bring up the sides at three points to form a triangle, pressing the edges together to seal. Place on the trays, leaving room for the pies to rise as they cook. Brush them with beaten egg and bake for 15 minutes until golden. Serve hot.

baba ghanoush (eggplant dip)

※

Preparation time: **20 minutes** + 30 minutes cooling time
Cooking time: **50 minutes**
Makes **1¾ cups**

2 large eggplants (aubergines)
3 garlic cloves, crushed
½ teaspoon ground cumin
80 ml (2½ fl oz/⅓ cup) lemon juice
2 tablespoons tahini

pinch of cayenne pepper
1½ tablespoons olive oil
1 tablespoon chopped flat-leaf (Italian) parsley

1 Preheat the oven to 200°C (400°F/ Gas 6). Prick the eggplants several times with a fork, then cook over an open flame for about 5 minutes, until the skin is blackened and blistered. Transfer to a baking dish and bake for 40–45 minutes, or until the eggplants are very soft and wrinkled. Place in a colander over a bowl to drain off any bitter juices, leaving them for 30 minutes, or until cool.

2 Carefully peel the skin from the eggplants, chop the flesh and put in a food processor with the garlic, cumin, lemon juice, tahini, cayenne pepper and olive oil. Process until smooth and creamy. Alternatively, use a potato masher or fork. Season with salt and stir in the parsley. Spread over a shallow bowl or onto a plate and serve with pide (Turkish/flat bread) for dipping.

NOTE: You can bake the eggplant on a baking tray in a 200°C (400°F/Gas 6) oven for 1 hour, or until it is very soft, instead of cooking over a flame first.

fish and cumin kebabs

☀ ☀

Preparation time: 10 minutes
  + overnight marinating time
Cooking time: 10 minutes
Serves 4

750 g (1 lb 10 oz) skinless, firm
    white fish fillets (such as blue-eye,
    snapper or perch)
2 tablespoons olive oil
1 garlic clove, crushed
3 tablespoons chopped coriander (cilantro)
    leaves
2 teaspoons ground cumin

1 Cut the fish fillets into 3 cm (1¼ inch) cubes. Thread onto skewers and place in a non-metallic dish.
2 To make the marinade, combine the oil, garlic, coriander, cumin and 1 teaspoon ground black pepper in a small bowl. Brush the marinade over the fish, cover with plastic wrap and refrigerate for several hours or overnight, turning occasionally. Drain, reserving the marinade. Season just before cooking.
3 Put the skewers on a hot, lightly oiled barbecue flatplate. Cook for 5–6 minutes, or until tender, turning once and brushing with the reserved marinade several times during cooking.

fish and cumin kebabs

kibbeh bil sanieh (layered lamb and burghul)

☀ ☀

Preparation time: 30 minutes
  + 30 minutes soaking time
Cooking time: 55 minutes
Serves 4–6

350 g (12 oz/2 cups) burghul (bulgur)
400 g (14 oz) minced (ground) lamb
1 large onion, finely chopped
1 tablespoon ground cumin
1 teaspoon ground allspice
olive oil, for brushing
Greek-style yoghurt, to serve

FILLING
1 tablespoon olive oil, plus extra,
    for brushing
1 onion, finely chopped
1 teaspoon ground cinnamon
1 tablespoon ground cumin
500 g (1 lb 2 oz) minced (ground)
    lamb
80 g (2¾ oz/½ cup) raisins
100 g (3½ oz) pine nuts, toasted

1 Soak the burghul in cold water for 30 minutes, then drain and squeeze out excess water. Put the lamb, onion, cumin, allspice and salt and pepper in a food processor, and process until combined. Add the burghul and process to a paste. Refrigerate until needed. Preheat the oven to 180°C (350°F/Gas 4). Lightly grease a 20 x 30 cm (8 x 12 inch) baking dish.
2 To make the filling, heat the oil in a large frying pan over medium heat and cook the onion for 5 minutes, or until softened. Add the cinnamon and cumin and stir for 1 minute, or until aromatic. Add the lamb, stirring to break up any lumps, and cook for 5 minutes, or until the meat is browned. Stir in the raisins and pine nuts and season, to taste.
3 Press half the burghul mixture into the base of the dish, smoothing it with wet hands. Spread the filling over the top, then cover with the remaining burghul.

kibbeh bil sanieh

silverbeet

Also known as Swiss chard or chard, silverbeet is a member of the beet family. It is often confused with spinach. Silverbeet has large, crinkled, deep-green leaves and silver stems, both of which are edible. The wilted leaves are used in salads, served as a vegetable and mixed with other ingredients like cheese to make a stuffing for savoury pastries and filled pasta. The stems are also delicious braised, boiled, steamed, dressed with olive oil and lemon juice, in béchamel sauce or served au gratin. Choose bunches with firm, inflexible stems and the smallest leaves, as they should be the youngest. Store silverbeet in plastic bags in the refrigerator, only washing immediately before use.

4 Score a diamond pattern in the top of the mixture with a knife and brush with olive oil. Bake for 40 minutes, or until the top is brown. Cool for 10 minutes, then cut into diamonds. Serve with yoghurt.

warm chickpea and silverbeet salad with sumac

✳ ✳

Preparation time: **30 minutes**
  + overnight soaking time
Cooking time: **2 hours**
Serves **4**

250 g (9 oz) dried chickpeas
125 ml (4 fl oz/½ cup) olive oil
1 onion, cut into thin wedges
2 tomatoes
1 teaspoon sugar
¼ teaspoon ground cinnamon
2 garlic cloves, chopped
1.5 kg (3 lb 5 oz) silverbeet (Swiss chard)
3 tablespoons chopped mint
2–3 tablespoons lemon juice
1½ tablespoons ground sumac

1 Put the chickpeas in a large bowl, cover with water and soak overnight. Drain and put in a large saucepan. Cover with water, bring to the boil and simmer for 1¾ hours or until tender. Drain thoroughly.

2 Heat the oil in a heavy-based frying pan, add the onion and cook over low heat for 5 minutes, or until softened and just starting to brown.

3 Cut the tomatoes in half, scoop out the seeds and dice the flesh. Add the tomato flesh to the pan with the sugar, cinnamon and garlic, and cook for 2–3 minutes, or until softened.

4 Thoroughly wash the silverbeet and pat dry with paper towels. Trim the stems and finely shred the leaves. Add to the tomato mixture with the chickpeas, stir to combine and cook for 3–4 minutes, or until the silverbeet wilts. Add the mint, lemon juice, to taste, and sumac. Season well, cook for 1 minute, then serve.

adas bis silq

1 To make the stock, put all the ingredients in a large saucepan, add 3 litres (105 fl oz/12 cups) water and bring to the boil. Skim off any scum from the surface. Reduce the heat and simmer for 2 hours. Strain the stock, discarding the chicken trimmings, onion and herbs. You will need 1 litre (35 fl oz/4 cups) of stock for the soup.

2 Skim any fat from the stock. Put the lentils in a large saucepan, then add the stock and 1 litre (35 fl oz/4 cups) water. Bring to the boil, then reduce the heat and simmer, covered, for 1 hour.

3 Meanwhile, remove the stems from the silverbeet and shred the leaves. Heat the oil in a saucepan over medium heat and cook the onion for 2–3 minutes, or until translucent. Add the garlic and cook for 1 minute. Add the silverbeet and toss for 2–3 minutes, or until wilted. Stir the mixture into the lentils. Add the coriander and lemon juice, season, and simmer, covered, for 15–20 minutes. Serve with the lemon wedges.

NOTE: You can freeze any leftover stock for up to 3 months.

kousa mihshi bi laban (stuffed zucchini with yoghurt sauce)

Preparation time: **20 minutes**
Cooking time: **1 hour 10 minutes**
Serves **4**

4 zucchini (courgettes)
375 ml (13 fl oz/1½ cups) chicken stock

FILLING
1 tablespoon olive oil
1 onion, finely chopped
1½ tablespoons pine nuts
125 g (4½ oz) minced (ground) lamb
55 g (2 oz/¼ cup) medium-grain white rice
1 ripe tomato, seeded and chopped
2 tablespoons chopped flat-leaf (Italian) parsley

adas bis silq (lentil and silverbeet soup)

Preparation time: **20 minutes**
Cooking time: **3 hours 30 minutes**
Serves **6**

280 g (10 oz/1½ cups) brown lentils, washed
850 g (1 lb 14 oz) silverbeet (Swiss chard)
60 ml (2 fl oz/¼ cup) olive oil

1 large onion, finely chopped
4 garlic cloves, crushed
35 g (1¼ oz) finely chopped coriander (cilantro) leaves
80 ml (2½ fl oz/⅓ cup) lemon juice
lemon wedges, to serve

CHICKEN STOCK
1 kg (2 lb 4 oz) chicken bones and trimmings (necks, ribs, wings), fat removed
1 small onion, roughly chopped
1 bay leaf
3–4 flat-leaf (Italian) parsley sprigs
1–2 oregano or thyme sprigs

½ teaspoon ground allspice
½ teaspoon ground cinnamon

YOGHURT SAUCE
250 g (9 oz/1 cup) Greek-style yoghurt
1 teaspoon cornflour (cornstarch)
1 garlic clove, crushed
1 teaspoon dried mint

1 Cut each zucchini in half lengthways. Scoop out the flesh from each piece, leaving a 3 mm (⅛ inch) border on each shell. This can be done with an apple corer, but be careful not to pierce the skins. Soak the zucchini in salted water for 10 minutes, then drain and pat dry.
2 For the filling, heat the oil in a frying pan, add the onion and cook over medium heat for 5 minutes, or until soft. Add the pine nuts and cook for 3–4 minutes, until golden. Cool slightly, then transfer to a large bowl. Add the remaining filling ingredients and combine well.
3 Spoon the filling into each zucchini half and carefully place in a wide, heavy-based saucepan or flameproof casserole dish. Cover with the stock, then invert a dinner plate over the top. Gently simmer over low heat for 1 hour.
4 About 15 minutes before the zucchini is ready, make the sauce by warming the yoghurt in a saucepan over medium heat. Stir the cornflour into 1 tablespoon water in a small bowl until smooth, then add to the yoghurt and stir well. Bring to the boil and add the garlic and mint. Season well, then reduce the heat and simmer for 8–10 minutes, stirring regularly.
5 Remove the zucchini from the casserole and serve the yoghurt sauce poured over the top. Serve hot with steamed rice.

carrot and coriander soup

Preparation time: **15 minutes**
Cooking time: **1 hour 15 minutes**
Serves **4**

2 tablespoons olive oil
1 onion, chopped
800 g (1 lb 12 oz) carrots, roughly chopped
1 bay leaf
1 teaspoon ground cumin
1 teaspoon cayenne pepper
1 teaspoon ground coriander
2 teaspoons paprika
1.25 litres (44 fl oz/5 cups) chicken or vegetable stock
250 g (9 oz/1 cup) Greek-style yoghurt
2 tablespoons chopped coriander (cilantro) leaves, plus extra leaves, to garnish

1 Heat the olive oil in a saucepan, add the onion and carrot and cook over low heat for 30 minutes. Add the bay leaf and spices and cook for a further 2 minutes. Add the stock, bring to the boil, then reduce the heat and simmer, uncovered, for 40 minutes, or until the carrot is tender. Allow to cool slightly before transferring to a food processor and blending, in batches, until smooth. Return to a clean saucepan and gently reheat. Season, to taste.
2 Combine the yoghurt and chopped coriander in a bowl. Pour the soup into bowls and serve with a dollop of the yoghurt mixture. Garnish with the extra coriander leaves.

carrot and coriander soup

spicy sephardi baked fish with vegetables

✳ ✳

Preparation time: 15 minutes
  + 30 minutes marinating time
Cooking time: 45 minutes
Serves 4–6

1 tablespoon cumin seeds
4 garlic cloves
1 small fresh red chilli, roughly chopped
60 g (2¼ oz) coriander (cilantro) leaves, stems and roots, chopped
1 tablespoon lemon juice
2 tablespoons olive oil
1.5 kg (3 lb 5 oz) whole fish (such as red snapper or coral trout), cleaned and scaled (ask your fishmonger to do this)
450 g (1 lb) new potatoes, sliced
2–3 roma (plum) tomatoes, halved lengthways, then cut into 1 cm (½ inch) thick pieces
100 g (3½ oz) green olives, pitted and halved
60 ml (2 fl oz/¼ cup) olive oil, extra

1 Dry-fry the cumin seeds in a frying pan over medium heat for 2–3 minutes, or until aromatic. Grind the seeds to a fine powder using a mortar and pestle or spice grinder. Put the ground cumin, garlic, chilli, coriander, lemon juice and 1 teaspoon salt in a food processor, and process to a smooth paste. With the motor running, gradually add the oil.
2 Using a sharp knife, make 3 diagonal incisions through the thickest part on both sides of the fish to ensure even cooking. Rub the spice mixture over the fish, cover with plastic wrap and leave to marinate in the refrigerator for 30 minutes.
3 Preheat the oven to 240°C (475°F/ Gas 8). Lay the fish in the centre of a large roasting tin and scatter the potato, tomato and olives around it. Pour 60 ml (2 fl oz/¼ cup) water and the extra olive oil over the fish and vegetables. Bake, basting often, for 40 minutes, or until the fish and vegetables are cooked through.

chicken with onions on flatbread

✳ ✳

Preparation time: 25 minutes
  + overnight marinating time
Cooking time: 1 hour 20 minutes
Serves 6–8

1.5 kg (3 lb 5 oz) whole chicken
1 teaspoon ground cinnamon
½ teaspoon ground white pepper
60 ml (2 fl oz/¼ cup) lemon juice
125 ml (4 fl oz/½ cup) olive oil
2 tablespoons sumac, plus extra, to garnish
½ teaspoon cardamom pods, lightly crushed
750 g (1 lb 10 oz) onions, thinly sliced
250 ml (9 fl oz/1 cup) chicken stock
2 large pitta breads, split open and separated
125 g (4½ oz) pine nuts, toasted

1 Cut the chicken into 8 even-sized pieces, removing the giblets and any excess fat, and place in a non-metallic dish. Combine the cinnamon, white

spicy sephardi baked fish with vegetables

pepper, lemon juice and 1 teaspoon salt and rub into the chicken pieces, then cover and refrigerate overnight.

2 Heat the oil in a large saucepan over medium heat, then add the sumac, cardamom pods, onion and stock and cook for 40 minutes, or until the onion is soft. Remove from the heat and discard the cardamom pods.

3 Preheat the oven to 200°C (400°F/ Gas 6). Place the onion mixture in the base of a ceramic baking dish, then top with a single layer of chicken pieces, skin side down, and cover tightly with foil. Bake for 20 minutes, then remove from the oven.

4 Tear the pitta breads into even-sized pieces about 8 cm (3¼ inches) across and place in a lightly oiled 25 x 30 cm (10 x 12 inch) ceramic baking dish. Lift the chicken from the onion and set aside, then distribute the onion and any juices evenly over the pitta bread. Top with the chicken pieces, skin side up, and bake for 20 minutes, or until the chicken skin is crisp and golden. Serve sprinkled with the toasted pine nuts and extra sumac.

psari tahina (baked fish with tahini sauce)

✳ ✳ ✳

Preparation time: 30 minutes
Cooking time: 30 minutes
Serves 4

1 kg (2 lb 4 oz) whole white-fleshed fish (such as snapper, bream or barramundi), scaled and cleaned
3 garlic cloves, crushed
2 teaspoons harissa
2 tablespoons olive oil
1 lemon, thinly sliced
1 onion, thinly sliced
2 large firm, ripe tomatoes, sliced
4 thyme sprigs

TAHINI SAUCE
2 teaspoons olive oil
1 garlic clove, crushed

psari tahina

3 tablespoons light tahini
2½ tablespoons lemon juice
1½ tablespoons chopped coriander (cilantro) leaves

1 Preheat the oven to 200°C (400°F/ Gas 6). Lightly grease a large baking dish. Make 3 diagonal cuts on each side of the fish through the thickest part of the flesh to ensure even cooking. Combine the garlic, harissa and olive oil in a small dish. Place 2 teaspoons in the fish cavity and spread the remainder over both sides of the fish, rubbing it into the slits. Place 2 lemon slices in the cavity of the fish.

2 Arrange the onion in a single layer on the baking dish. Top with the tomato, thyme and remaining lemon slices. Place the fish on top and bake, uncovered, for about 25–30 minutes, or until the flesh of the fish is opaque.

3 Meanwhile, to make the tahini sauce, heat the olive oil in a small saucepan over low heat. Add the garlic and cook over medium heat for 30 seconds, then add the tahini, lemon juice and 125 ml (4 fl oz/ ½ cup) water and stir until combined. Add more water, if necessary, to make a smooth, but fairly thick sauce. Cook for 2 minutes, then remove from the heat and stir in the coriander. Season.

4 Transfer the onion and tomato to serving dishes. Place the fish on top and season lightly with salt. Pour some of the sauce over and offer the rest in a serving dish on the side.

khoreshe fesenjan

khoreshe fesenjan (duck breast with walnut and pomegranate sauce)

Preparation time: **15 minutes**
Cooking time: **25 minutes**
Serves **4**

4 large duck breast fillets
1 onion, finely chopped
250 ml (9 fl oz/1 cup) fresh
   pomegranate juice
2 tablespoons lemon juice
2 tablespoons soft brown sugar
1 teaspoon ground cinnamon
185 g (6½ oz/1½ cups) chopped walnuts
pomegranate seeds, to garnish (optional)

1 Preheat the oven to 180°C (350°F/ Gas 4). Score each duck breast two or three times on the skin side. Cook in a non-stick frying pan over high heat, skin side down, for 6 minutes, or until crisp and most of the fat has been rendered. Put in an ovenproof dish.
2 Remove all but 1 tablespoon of fat from the pan. Add the onion to the pan and cook over medium heat for 2–3 minutes, or until golden. Add the pomegranate juice, lemon juice, sugar, cinnamon and 125 g (4½ oz/1 cup) of the walnuts and cook for 1 minute. Pour over the duck and bake for 15 minutes.
3 Rest the duck for 5 minutes. Skim any excess fat from the sauce. Slice the duck and serve with the sauce. Garnish with the remaining walnuts and the pomegranate seeds, if desired.

pitta bread

Preparation time: **20 minutes**
  + 40 minutes proving time
Cooking time: **5 minutes**
Makes **12**

2 teaspoons dried yeast
1 teaspoon caster (superfine) sugar
440 g (15½ oz/3½ cups) plain
   (all-purpose) flour
2 tablespoons olive oil

1 Put the yeast, sugar and 375 ml (13 fl oz/1½ cups) lukewarm water in a bowl and stir until dissolved. Leave in a warm, draught-free place for 10 minutes, or until frothy and slightly increased in volume. If your yeast doesn't foam, it is dead, so you will have to discard it and start again. Process the flour, yeast mixture and oil in a food processor for 30 seconds, or until it forms a ball.
2 Turn the dough onto a well-floured surface and knead until smooth and elastic. Place in an oiled bowl, cover with plastic wrap, then a tea towel (dish towel) and leave in a warm, draught-free place for 20 minutes, or until almost doubled in size. Punch down the dough and divide into 12 equal portions. Roll each into a 5 mm (¼ inch) thick round. Place on greased baking trays and brush well with water. Set aside to rise for 20 minutes.
3 Preheat the oven to 250°C (500°F/ Gas 9). If the dough has dried, brush again with water. Bake for 4–5 minutes. The pitta bread should be soft and pale, slightly swollen, and hollow inside.

flatbread with za'atar

✹ ✹

Preparation time: 35 minutes + 1 hour
    50 minutes proving time
Cooking time: 15 minutes
Makes 10

1 tablespoon dried yeast
1 teaspoon sugar
405 g (14¼ oz/3¼ cups) plain (all-purpose)
    flour
125 ml (4 fl oz/½ cup) olive oil, plus extra,
    for brushing
20 g (¾ oz/⅓ cup) za'atar (see Note)
1 tablespoon sea salt flakes

1 Put the yeast and sugar in a small bowl with 60 ml (2 fl oz/¼ cup) warm water and stir until dissolved. Leave in a warm, draught-free place for 10 minutes, or until bubbles appear on the surface. The mixture should be frothy and slightly increased in volume. If your yeast doesn't foam, it is dead, so you will have to discard it and start again.

2 Sift the flour and ½ teaspoon salt into a large bowl. Make a well in the centre and pour in the yeast mixture and 310 ml (10¾ fl oz/1¼ cups) warm water. Gradually combine to form a dough, then knead on a floured surface for 10–15 minutes until smooth and elastic, gradually adding 1 tablespoon olive oil at a time as you knead, until all of the oil has been incorporated. Cover and set aside in a warm, draught-free place for 1 hour, or until risen.

3 Punch down the dough with your fist and then knead again. Set aside in a warm place for 30 minutes to rise. Knead briefly and divide into 10 portions. Roll out each to a smooth circle about 5 mm (¼ inch) thick. Set aside, covered with a tea towel (dish towel), for 20 minutes.

4 Preheat the oven to 220°C (425°F/ Gas 7). Lightly grease two large baking trays. Place the rolls on the trays and gently press the surface with your fingers to create a dimpled effect. Brush with the extra oil and then sprinkle lightly with za'atar and sea salt flakes. Bake for 12–15 minutes. Serve warm.

NOTE: Za'atar is a Middle Eastern spice blend that is available from speciality food stores and delicatessens.

yeast

This single-celled organism causes food to ferment, converting it into alcohol and carbon dioxide. It is crucial for making leavened bread as it is the interaction of carbon dioxide, moisture, warmth and sugar that allows yeast to grow, enabling dough to rise. Active dried yeast is available in supermarkets and compressed fresh yeast is available in delicatessens. Fresh yeast is alive and moist and must be stored in the refrigerator. The dehydrated cells of dried yeast are also alive but are dormant until mixed with warm water. Dried yeast should be stored in a cool, dry place and can be frozen or refrigerated. Bring to room temperature before using.

kibbeh

✳ ✳

Preparation time: **45 minutes**
  + 2 hours chilling time
Cooking time: **25 minutes**
Makes **15**

235 g (8½ oz/1⅓ cups) fine burghul
  (bulgur)
150 g (5½ oz) lean lamb, chopped
1 onion, roughly grated
2 tablespoons plain (all-purpose) flour
1 teaspoon ground allspice
vegetable oil, for frying

FILLING
2 teaspoons olive oil
1 small onion, finely chopped
100 g (3½ oz) lean minced (ground) lamb
½ teaspoon ground allspice
½ teaspoon ground cinnamon
80 ml (2½ fl oz/⅓ cup) beef stock
2 tablespoons pine nuts
2 tablespoons chopped mint

1 Put the burghul in a large bowl, cover with boiling water and leave for 5 minutes. Drain in a colander, pressing well to remove the water. Spread on paper towels to absorb the remaining moisture.
2 Process the burghul, lamb, onion, flour and allspice until a fine paste forms. Season well, then refrigerate for 1 hour.
3 To make the filling, heat the oil in a frying pan, add the onion and cook over low heat for 3 minutes, or until soft. Add the lamb, allspice and cinnamon, and stir over high heat for 3 minutes. Add the stock and cook, partially covered, over low heat for 6 minutes, or until the lamb is cooked. Roughly chop the pine nuts and stir in with the mint. Season, then transfer to a bowl and allow to cool.
4 Shape 2 tablespoons of the burghul mixture into a sausage shape 6 cm (2½ inches) long. Dip your hands in cold water and, with your finger, make a long hole through the centre and gently work your finger around to make a shell. Fill with 2 teaspoons of the filling and seal, moulding it into a torpedo shape. Smooth

Shape 2 tablespoons of the burghul mixture into a sausage shape 6 cm (2½ inches) long.

Push your index finger through the middle of each sausage to form a cavity for the filling.

Spoon 2 teaspoons of the filling into each cavity and seal, moulding into torpedo shapes.

over any cracks with your fingers. Put on a foil-lined tray and repeat with the remaining ingredients to make 15 kibbeh. Refrigerate, uncovered, for 1 hour.

5 Fill a deep, heavy-based saucepan one-third full of oil and heat to 180°C (350°F), or until a cube of bread dropped into the oil turns golden brown in 15 seconds. Deep-fry the kibbeh in batches for 2–3 minutes, until well browned. Drain on paper towels.

pine nuts

These little nuts are expensive as the harvesting is labour intensive. Coming from several varieties of pine tree, the nuts are actually kernels found inside the pine cone, which must be heated for the nuts to be obtained. Pine nuts have a high fat content so they turn rancid quite quickly and it is best to buy them as you need them. They can be refrigerated in an airtight container for up to three months or frozen for up to nine months if necessary. Their flavour is greatly enhanced by dry-roasting in a frying pan or under a grill (broiler).

roast chicken stuffed with pine nuts and rice

☀

Preparation time: 30 minutes
Cooking time: 2 hours 30 minutes
Serves 4–6

1.6 kg (3 lb 8 oz) whole chicken
170 ml (5½ fl oz/⅔ cup) chicken stock

STUFFING
60 g (2¼ oz) clarified butter (see Note)
   or ghee, melted
1 onion, chopped
1 teaspoon ground allspice
60 g (2¼ oz/⅓ cup) basmati rice
30 g (1 oz/¼ cup) walnuts, chopped
50 g (1¾ oz/⅓ cup) pine nuts
55 g (2 oz/⅓ cup) sultanas (golden raisins)
125 ml (4 fl oz/½ cup) chicken stock

1 Preheat the oven to 180°C (350°F/ Gas 4). To make the stuffing, pour half the butter into a large frying pan, add the onion and cook over medium heat for 5 minutes. Stir in the allspice.
2 Add the rice and nuts to the pan and cook for 3–4 minutes over medium–high heat. Add the sultanas, stock and 60 ml (2 fl oz/¼ cup) water. Bring to the boil, cover, then reduce the heat and simmer gently for 8–10 minutes, until the water is absorbed. Allow to cool.
3 Rinse the cavity of the chicken with cold water and pat dry, inside and out, with paper towels.

4 When the stuffing is cool, spoon it into the chicken cavity. Truss the chicken, using kitchen string, then place in a deep baking dish and rub ½ teaspoon salt and ¼ teaspoon freshly ground black pepper over the skin using your fingertips.
5 Pour the rest of the butter over the chicken, then add the stock to the pan. Roast for 2 hours 10 minutes, basting every 20–25 minutes with juices from

the pan. Rest the chicken for 15 minutes before carving. Serve with the stuffing.

NOTE: To clarify butter, melt it in a saucepan over low heat, then remove from the heat and let the milk solids settle to the bottom. Only use the yellow liquid part of the butter on the top, which is called clarified butter. Discard the white milk solids at the base of the saucepan.

ricotta

Made from the whey that remains after the making of other cheeses, ricotta in Italian literally translates as 'recooked'. It can be made from cow's, sheep's and goat's milk and is strictly not a cheese, as cheeses are made from milk curd, not whey. Ricotta is most often used in cooked dishes, where its delicate flavour and creamy texture are complemented by savoury flavours like spinach or sweet flavours such as citrus. Use it within a few days of purchasing.

ataif mihshi (stuffed fried pancakes)

Preparation time: 20 minutes
  + 1 hour proving time
Cooking time: 1 hour 15 minutes
Makes about 16

vegetable oil, for brushing
peanut oil, for deep-frying

BATTER
1 teaspoon dried yeast
1 teaspoon sugar
185 g (6½ oz/1½ cups) plain (all-purpose)
  flour

SYRUP
500 g (1 lb 2 oz) sugar
2 teaspoons lemon juice
2 tablespoons rosewater

FILLING
250 g (9 oz/1 cup) fresh ricotta

1 To make the batter, stir the yeast and sugar into 60 ml (2 fl oz/¼ cup) warm water until dissolved. Leave in a warm, draught-free place for 10 minutes or until bubbles appear on the surface. The mixture should be frothy and slightly increased in volume.

2 Sift the flour into a large bowl, make a well in the centre and add the yeast mixture and 375 ml (13 fl oz/1½ cups) warm water. Using a wooden spoon, gradually stir in the flour and mix until smooth. Cover the bowl with a tea towel (dish towel) and leave in a warm, draught-free place for 1 hour, or until the batter has risen and the surface is bubbly.

3 Meanwhile, make the syrup. Heat the sugar and 310 ml (10¾ fl oz/1¼ cups) water in a heavy-based saucepan over medium heat, stirring occasionally, until the sugar has dissolved. Bring to the boil, add the lemon juice and simmer for 8–10 minutes, until the syrup is thick enough to coat the back of a spoon. It should be the consistency of thin honey.

6 Heat the peanut oil in a deep-fryer or heavy-based saucepan to 190°C (375°F), or until a cube of bread dropped into the oil browns in 10 seconds. Fry the stuffed pancakes 3 or 4 at a time for 2–3 minutes, until golden. Remove with a slotted spoon and drain on paper towels. Dip the hot pancakes in the cooled syrup and serve warm or cold stacked on a large plate.

ma'amoul b'jowz (walnut cakes)

✹ ✹

Preparation time: **15 minutes**
Cooking time: **20 minutes**
Makes **28**

200 g (7 oz) unsalted butter, softened
115 g (4 oz/½ cup) caster (superfine) sugar
2 tablespoons orange flower water
250 g (9 oz/2 cups) plain (all-purpose) flour, sifted

WALNUT FILLING
50 g (1¾ oz/½ cup) walnuts, chopped
55 g (2 oz/¼ cup) caster (superfine) sugar
1 teaspoon ground cinnamon

1 Preheat the oven to 160°C (315°F/ Gas 2–3). Lightly grease two baking trays and line with baking paper.
2 Cream the butter and sugar in a bowl using electric beaters until light and fluffy. Fold in the orange flower water and flour until combined. Press with your hands until the mixture comes together to make a stiff dough.
3 To make the walnut filling, combine all the ingredients in a bowl.
4 Roll heaped tablespoons of dough into balls. Press a hollow in the centre of each with your thumb. Place 1 teaspoon of filling into each hollow. Place on the trays and flatten slightly without folding the dough over the filling. Bake for 15–20 minutes, or until golden. Cool the cakes on a wire rack and then serve.

Add the rosewater and cook for another minute. Allow to cool completely.
4 To make the pancakes, lightly grease a heavy-based frying pan and place over medium heat. Stir 60 ml (2 fl oz/¼ cup) water into the batter. Pour 1½ tablespoons of batter into the pan, tilting it a little so that the batter spreads to about 10 cm (4 inches). If the batter is too thick, add a little extra water. Cook the pancakes for about 3 minutes, or until golden on the underside and bubbles appear on the surface. Remove them from the pan, stack them on a plate and allow to cool slightly.
5 Place 1 tablespoon of the ricotta on the unfried side of each pancake. Fold each in half and pinch the edges together to seal into a half-moon shape.

honey

The world's first sweetener, honey has been eaten in the Middle East since pre-Biblical times. In ancient Egypt, a form of fruit honey was extracted from dates and grapes, while Syrian bees were said to produce the best bees' honey. It is used to perfume and preserve Middle Eastern foods such as pastries and cakes, which were originally soaked in honey to prevent them drying out and to refresh them once stale. The aroma and flavour of honey depends on the flowers that the bees have fed on, not the bees themselves, as it is really processed flower nectar. This is why honey is generally classified by the name of the flower or tree from which it originates. The general rule is that the darker the colour, the stronger the flavour, so when a specific type is called for in a recipe, it can't necessarily be replaced by all other honeys. For all-purpose cooking and eating, use a pale, mild honey.

mahallabia (almond cream pudding)

Preparation time: 15 minutes
  + 1 hour chilling time
Cooking time: 40 minutes
Serves 4

500 ml (17 fl oz/2 cups) milk
75 g (2¾ oz) caster (superfine) sugar
2 tablespoons cornflour (cornstarch)
2 tablespoons rice flour
75 g (2½ oz) ground almonds
1 teaspoon rosewater
2 tablespoons flower blossom honey
2 tablespoons pistachio nuts, chopped

1 Place the milk and sugar in a saucepan and heat over medium heat, stirring until the sugar has dissolved.
2 Combine the cornflour and rice flour with 60 ml (2 fl oz/¼ cup) water and mix to a paste. Add to the milk and cook, stirring occasionally, over low heat for 20 minutes. Add the almonds and cook for a further 15 minutes, then add the rosewater. Spoon the mixture into shallow serving dishes and refrigerate for 1 hour. Serve drizzled with honey and sprinkled with the pistachios.

sufganiyot (israeli doughnuts)

✻ ✻ ✻

Preparation time: 40 minutes + overnight
and 30 minutes proving time
Cooking time: 20 minutes
Makes 14

185 ml (6 fl oz/¾ cup) lukewarm milk
1 tablespoon dried yeast
2 tablespoons caster (superfine) sugar
310 g (11 oz/2½ cups) plain (all-purpose)
    flour
2 teaspoons ground cinnamon
1 teaspoon finely grated lemon zest
2 eggs, separated
40 g (1½ oz) unsalted butter, softened
105 g (3½ oz/⅓ cup) plum, strawberry
    or apricot jam
vegetable oil, for deep-frying
caster (superfine) sugar, extra, for rolling

1 Put the milk in a small bowl and add the yeast and 1 tablespoon of the sugar. Leave in a warm, draught-free place for 10 minutes, or until the mixture is frothy and slightly increased in volume. If your yeast doesn't foam, it is dead and you will have to discard it and start again.

2 Sift the flour into a large bowl and add the cinnamon, lemon zest, egg yolks, yeast mixture, remaining sugar and a pinch of salt. Mix well, then transfer the dough to a lightly floured work surface and knead for 5 minutes. Work in the butter, a little at a time, continually kneading until the dough becomes elastic. This should take about 10 minutes. Place in a large bowl and cover with a clean, damp tea towel (dish towel). Leave to rise overnight in the refrigerator.

3 Place the dough on a lightly floured work surface and roll out to 3 mm (⅛ inch) thick. Using a 6 cm (2½ inch) pastry cutter, cut 28 rounds from the dough. Place 14 rounds on a lightly floured tray and place ¾ teaspoon of jam into the centre of each. Lightly beat the egg whites, then brush a little around the outside edges of the rounds, being careful not to touch the jam at all. Top with the remaining 14 rounds and press down firmly around the edges to seal. Cover with a clean tea towel and leave to rise for 30 minutes. Make sure the dough has not separated at the edges. Press any open edges firmly together.

4 Fill a deep-fryer or large heavy-based saucepan one-third full of oil and heat to 170°C (325°F), or until a cube of bread dropped in the oil browns in 20 seconds. Cook the doughnuts, in batches, for 1½ minutes on both sides, or until golden. Drain on paper towels and roll in the extra caster sugar. Serve immediately.

middle eastern yoghurt drink

Nearly every country in the Middle East has a version of this drink, often sold at cafés and street stalls. Beat 500 g (1 lb 2 oz/2 cups) Greek-style yoghurt in a bowl until smooth, then add 500 ml (17 fl oz/2 cups) icy cold water, beating until smooth. Add a pinch of salt and 1 tablespoon dried, crushed mint, or to taste. Serve chilled, with ice. Serves 4.

index

Page numbers in *italics* refer to
photographs. Page numbers in **bold**
refer to margin notes.